PAUL WELLER

Paul Weller
The Unauthorised Biography

Steve Malins

First published in Great Britain in 1997 by
Virgin Books
an imprint of Virgin Publishing Ltd
332 Ladbroke Grove
London W10 5AH

A catalogue record for this book is available from the British Library.

ISBN 0 7535 0087 6

Typeset by TW Typesetting, Plymouth, Devon.
Printed and bound by
Mackays of Chatham, Lordswood, Chatham, Kent.

For Brian Malins

Contents

Acknowledgements

Much-needed research information was provided by Fred Dellar, Pippa, Vic Smith, Chris Parry, Lucy O'Brien, James Anthony, Dennis Munday, John Harris, Jane Wilkes and Patrick Humphries. Thanks to the Radio One press office, Mal Peachey, Bernard MacMahon and Patricia Bush for their assistance.

Special thanks to Paul, John, Ann and Nikki for letting me get on with it.

Introduction

Paul Weller is a hyperactive mix of nervous, energetic contradictions. He's proud, dignified, yearning, dry, wistful,
graceless, neat, jerky, heroic, hungry, spoilt, brave, parochial,
severe and passionate. The fact that he's grown up in public means
that the black and white definitions that the media have tried to
label him with are outdated through regular changes of tone, style
and approach. The man who was once obsessed with the world-
changing, fanatical drive of youth as the lead singer in The Jam has
ironically come into his own in his mid 30s, with his most personal
and biggest-selling music of a twenty-year career. His career has
already gone through three distinct eras, spread across four decades
(the 60s are as relevant to this artist as any decade in which he's
released records). In the early 80s he switched from airborne,
pent-up emotion in The Jam to the loafered, slicked-back manner-
isms of The Style Council, and left everyone guessing his next
move. In the 90s he overturned his values again by returning to the
guitar and flashing hard with pure, stomping British R&B. Yet for
all this radicalism and musical diversity, there is also an unbending
earnestness and blinkered arrogance in Weller which invites criticism. The finality of The Jam's end left a sour taste in the mouths
of several associates, particularly Bruce Foxton and Rick Buckler.
It's understandable that an artist needs to sever the past in order
to move on, but Weller's tunnel vision makes him a somewhat
insensitive character at times.

Furthermore, The Style Council enabled him to open the
floodgates to an incredibly eclectic range of influences, but he was
out of his depth as a parodic 80s ironist because ultimately he still
wanted to be judged as a credible, authentic and serious voice in

Paul Weller

the music scene. By the end of 1989 the band had been dropped by their record label and Weller was left out in the wilderness for two years. So how has he made such a successful return, with *Stanley Road* selling over a million copies in the UK?

Weller's solo career stripped away the confusion of the 'Council'. He dumped the baggage of horn sections and backing singers in order to return to his own writing and R&B-influenced guitar playing. There was more focus. Weller's recent solo albums are humanistic, raw, direct and personal. They strike a chord, especially through the voice, with those who deserted him in the 80s as well as with a new, younger audience. The latter is partly down to 90s Britpop culture which came at the perfect time for Weller. As the only lasting credible icon – Madness, Mozza and Macca had all blown it – he has taken his place in the UK as the unchallenged 'Modfather'. Overseas, however, he remains almost unknown – possibly the biggest contradiction of his career.

While Weller's sussed, Mod outlook is rooted in the need for change and determination to be constantly on the ball, this is also a man who has been managed by his father throughout the whole of his career. These solid foundations have enabled him to move on to the next phase of his work with the back-up of a close-knit support group. Former Polydor International employee Sara Silver, who worked closely with The Style Council, argues: 'Paul has a protection system for his own sanity. Emotionally he's had a few ups and downs in his life – his first girlfriend was supposed to be for ever and ever and wasn't. But the guy never cracked up and went into some alcoholic haze, got heavily into drugs or developed a superhuman ego. He's still loose about life, still kind of shy. He's stayed the same person. He'll still ride the bus. He's still out and about. I think it has a lot to do with the security that his dad provides for him as his manager. They've also built up a regular crew of people around themselves who are completely loyal to Paul and look out for him.'

However, anyone who falls out with the singer by breaking unwritten rules will find themselves outside the inner circle for good. While it has many good points, the set-up also breeds suspicion and wariness, contributing to Weller's reputation as a severe, unapproachable figure.

At various stages of his career he's tried to shrug this off, especially in The Style Council when he attempted 'humour' for the first time. At the end of the day, however, Weller's dry wit is often as sparky as his self-doubting mood changes. His wife Dee C Lee once summed him up as 'the most miserable person I've ever met, not very hairy, can't hold his drink, but is none the less a lovely old bastard.' Noel Gallagher has also joked, 'People think Weller's some deep god, but he's a moany old bastard like Victor Meldrew with a sun tan.'

Yet Weller is also far from the awkward, grumpy, dogmatic character who has often turned up for interviews. He's too lively and forward thinking to be labelled with such a dour image. This book is an unauthorised glance into the contradictory world of Paul Weller. It's about the inspirations and tensions at the core of his career which have made him a figure who is either loved or loathed in the UK (there's never been much middle ground) and yet is treated with indifference overseas; a man of principles, codes and ethics who constantly changes his mind; a shy, sarcy humorist who attempted to be one half of the Marx Brothers with the equally unfunny Mick Talbot; and the best songwriter of his generation, give or take the odd cod-jazz instrumental . . .

1 Keep it in the Family, 1958–73

David Bowie: 'I was talking with a friend of mine not so long ago who also comes from suburbia. And you're given the impression that nothing culturally belongs to you, that you're in this wasteland. I think there's a passion for most people who have an iota of curiosity about them, to escape and get out and try to find who one is and find some kind of roots. Both of us got out for the same reasons – a desperation, an exhaustion with the blandness of where we grew up.'

Paul Weller: 'I've never really been happy wherever I am.'

'Our family was always tight-knit,' explains Paul Weller. 'My mum and dad both had funny childhoods – they never got on with their parents – so they put a lot of time into me and Nikki. We were a very insular family. Just us against the world.'

The singer's close relationship with his parents has been the basis for the extended family around him throughout his life. His career revolves around the passionate, hard enthusiasm of his father, a man who Weller idolises, respects and loves deeply. John Weller is a stockily built figure described by his son as a man of 'incredible energy' – 'one of my heroes.'

John Weller didn't move to Woking, where he's lived for most of his adult life, until 1957. He was born in Brighton on 28 November 1931, and raised in Lewisham, one of south London's tough, working-class districts. At the time of Paul's birth on 25 May 1958, John was working as a taxi driver. Over the following few years he had a series of jobs, as his son later described: 'He knocked off lead in the winter of '63. Bad weather called off the building trade so he found other means of survival. He was an all-round athlete, a trainee journalist after leaving school, a man who boxed for England, who won the ABA, to hod carrier, to cabby . . .' Reportedly he was featured in the credits to *Grandstand* for a while and to this day he makes a bee-line for boxing clubs and bars around the world whenever he's on tour, and occasionally drags his son and tour manager Kenny Wheeler off to Vegas for a big showbiz fight.

Paul Weller

In his mid-twenties, John Weller met a teenage girl, Ann Crad-dock, whom he would wed within a year. Wellingborough-born Ann spent her early years in Chingford, Essex. After marrying they moved to Walton Road, Woking (a place whose only claims to fame are Brookwood Cemetery, which is the biggest in Western Europe, and the 'sandpits' of Horsell Common where the Martians landed in H. G. Wells's *War of the Worlds*), and eleven months later they had their first child, John William Weller. There was an early alarm when Ann contracted polio of the throat shortly after the birth, but fortunately its only effect on the family was confusion over their son's name, which Ann apparently blurted out from her sick-bed. When everyone recovered and settled into a routine of sleepless domesticity, their first child was renamed Paul.

Ann worked as a part-time cleaner to supplement her husband's income. Her son's fine, straight hair (which still frustrates him whenever he tries to grow it long) and sinewy, thin physique are passed on from her side of the family rather than the squat, bulldog strength of John Weller. According to rock photographer Pennie Smith, who has spent the last twenty years focusing her camera lens on Paul Weller, 'I think he gets his physique from his mum who's also quite wiry. He's tall and moves quickly, which is quite unusual compared to most people. He's got a fast metabolism which you can see in his physique and he never sits still.

'He's got a presence in a room because he carries himself very well and he's very upright. You're aware of his height because of that. His dad is obviously a very direct, self-contained, determined person which you can see in Paul.'

Weller himself has said that he's inherited a determination to see things 'out till the end, impatience and stubbornness' from his dad.

John Weller, who was once described by Boy George as a man 'who could bite the head off a chicken just as easily as Ozzy Osbourne,' declares, 'Paul did always want to be someone. I don't think he got that from me and his talent certainly didn't come from me. But I did give him a "let's do it" attitude – nothing ventured, nothing gained.'

Weller's long-term schoolfriend, Steve Brookes, confesses he's still a bit bemused about the origins of his old mate's complex and often contradictory personality. 'I don't think he's like either of his parents really,' he chuckles. 'His dad's very single-minded and

Paul's obviously got that but other than that I can't really see that much similarity. I suppose physically he looks more like his mum than his dad but I wouldn't say his nature is any more like one than the other. I think he's a one-off which is probably just as well. The world doesn't need two,' he jokes, referring to Weller's mix of edginess and energetic stubbornness.

Weller has never tried to disguise a temperament which see-saws between engaging open-mindedness and abrasive self-doubt. On days like the latter the shutters are down and lines are clearly marked which shouldn't be crossed. It's this which has given Weller a reputation for being awkward and intimidating, but the roots of this changeability are hard to explain. 'I'm a very moody person and people get pissed off with that around me,' he confesses. 'They get fed up with me being moody.

'I get these insecurities or a sense of failure, or the idea that I'm not living up to what I want to get to ... I don't know how often, 'cos there's no pattern to it but often enough to notice. They can last for two or three weeks and then I come out of it. It's part of my personality, just like other people like having cornflakes for breakfast.'

Not that he has a manic personality. He doesn't swing madly between extroverted, thigh-slapping tomfoolery and pallid intro-spection. There's a hard edge to him and a sense of self-awareness and control even when he's relaxed.

'I don't think he is very humorous, or at least his humour is very, very dry,' opines Pennie Smith. 'I wouldn't call him grumpy but he's not the sort of person you'd see laughing uproariously. I think he works by gut instincts. He's good at giving off vibes. You can tell from his face if that's one photo too many.'

John Weller says it all when he concludes, with deadpan humour, 'He's about the most moodiest person I've ever met in my life.'

His childhood was happy and normal. Although the discovery of a rat in Paul's cot convinced the Wellers it was time to move from their first home, the singer has always played down the image of a family living on the breadline in post-war England. His family made do, relocating to a Victorian terrace house, 8 Stanley Road, within view of Woking train station. There was no bathroom, no hot water and an outside toilet. When young Paul needed a wash Ann would boil a kettle and fill a plastic bowl. Like all kids, he often needed an urgent clean-up. Weller's earliest memory is of his dad taking him to work on his shoulders: 'I used to wear these tartan trousers (or Rupert trousers as my mum called them) and on this particular occasion I wet myself (literally) whilst on his shoulders and it left a tartan stain around his neck! I think I must have been a messy child.

'My mum used to work at the mosque in Woking as a cleaner and one day when I went to see her there I fell into a pond they had in the grounds and shit myself (literally). I ran back up to the mosque to tell her of my calamity and loads of little jobbies came rolling out of the bottom of my trousers.'

The mosque where Ann worked was the first to be built in England, attracting a further influx of Asian immigrants who form a significant part of a very cosmopolitan local community.

The Wellers lived in Stanley Road for fifteen years, during which time Paul got to know 'every bump in the wall, every crack in the floor,' giving him the roots which he would later draw on for inspiration in the 90s. The terrace houses on the Wellers' street were built in the 1880s for the working-class community, many of whom worked for the wealthy residents of the local villages. This class division was still in place when Weller was growing up. Poor council estates and working-class terraces were in stark contrast to the affluent areas of Hockering and Hook Heath, with their surrounding golf courses. Weller sometimes noticed 'differences' when he went to friends' houses in the richer areas, but his parents weren't particularly interested in politics. 'My family weren't at all political ... I don't think they see any solutions in politics and sometimes I'm inclined to agree with them,' he said. 'I suppose I educated myself. I had no idea about politics, never thought about politics – my family weren't at all political.'

They didn't see any answers in religion either. Weller: 'I come from a family of atheists. With my dad, it's just you're born, you live and then you die.' In 1962 the Weller family routine was changed by three events – the arrival of a baby girl, Nicola, their son's morning trips to Maybury County First School, which was just around the corner from their home, and Paul's new interest in pop music, which the young parents indulged and encouraged at every opportunity. On one memorable occasion, Elvis Presley's quiffed-up looks, lopsided grin and cool rebel posing held the four year old entranced in the aisles of the Woking Odeon cinema, where he danced and strummed a blue Beatles plastic guitar (with the faces of the Fab Four and printed signatures) in imitation of his celluloid idol. Fifties pop and rockabilly were popular in the Weller household, where the toddler strutted around with his toy guitar, copying artists like Chuck Berry, Little Richard and, of course, Elvis.

For a few years he restricted his pop ambitions to watching himself run through his pop-star moves in the mirror, until one day, 'Me and my friend sang "Fire Brigade" by The Move,' he recalls. 'This must be 1968-ish with me on a plastic guitar and him playing "drums" on a biscuit tin! But from that early age [10] I wanted to be in a group, I think.'

Weller remembers seeing The Beatles on TV for the first time, playing their Royal Command Performance in '64 or so. Ann was also a fan. 'My mum was young – she had me when she was eighteen – so she'd be buying singles. But it was The Beatles for me, especially from about '67: "Strawberry Fields", "Penny Lane", the *Mystery Tour*.'

Although some old school friends claim that Paul's father was just as mad about music as his mum, John claims ignorance of the new pop styles which were filling the living room: 'His mother was into sixties music. I wouldn't know one from the other, to tell you the truth.'

An early step towards maturity appears to be the moment when Weller held a mini jumble sale in his bedroom to raise money to buy the 1967 *Sgt Pepper* album out of his own pocket. 'I put away my toys after that – well, I sold them – and I gave up on the idea of being a footballer. I was obsessed with music.' Weller's football ambitions had been encouraged by his father, who for a short time organised a football team with the intention of finding a place for Paul, then a Chelsea fan, to play in. However, his son's abilities didn't match those of team mates, and the idea soon fizzled out.

When Ann found some *Beatles Monthlies* at a jumble sale, Paul started cutting them into scrapbooks. He pored over the interviews and fact files, looking for similarities between himself and his idols – Paul McCartney in particular. Although in later years Weller claimed that John Lennon was his favourite Beatle because of his attitudes and principles, as a kid he was obsessed with McCartney.

Paul Weller

He was excited to discover that both himself and The Beatles' bassist were Geminis and 'he's got a chipped front tooth like me. He did it in 1966 falling off a moped. When I was a kid I took it as a sign, the both of us being Geminis and the tooth. I know it sounds strange but I did.' Weller chipped his tooth when a tin drum rolled down a hill and hit him in the mouth, 'probably playing Batman or something like that.'

He had thirteen or fourteen of these scrapbooks by the time The Beatles broke up. 'I remember I was in the newsagents the day they split up, April 1970. I was just devastated.

'Even up to '73, '74 – a good few years after they'd split – I'd still buy their solo albums religiously. Even Ringo's. Even *Sentimental Journey*, for fuck's sake. That's how dedicated I was.'

One day Weller went into the back garden and burnt all his Beatles scrapbooks.

John: 'I tried to stop him but kids are like that. Probably regrets that now.'

At the end of the 60s, Paul was strumming an unplugged electric guitar his dad had bought him for Christmas. Neither Paul nor his parents realised you needed an amp to go with it at the time, although this hardly mattered as he didn't make any serious attempt to learn to play it.

He was still listening to music religiously, however. As well as The Beatles, he was a fan of The Kinks and other English pop groups like Amen Corner, The Herd, Love Affair, Spooky Tooth and The Zombies. 'I had pin-ups on my wall from this magazine called *Fab 208* of bands like The Herd and I really wanted to look like them. I couldn't though because I wasn't allowed to grow my hair. I used to have one of those horrible crappy cuts that all kids have.'

By this time he was nearing the end of an unremarkable, contented stint at Maybury Primary School. 'I don't really remember anything about primary school,' he says, 'until the last year when I used to read Greek mythology and worry about the thought of going to Sheerwater Secondary the following year. Sheerwater had a really bad reputation. There were loads of stories about what they used to do to the new kids.'

Weller's fears about a bullied initiation into the new school proved unfounded. A typical eleven year old, he was worried about the strange new environment. Sheerwater had a large influx of kids from parents born in London who had recently moved to the satellite town, as well as a varied ethnic mix, so it was quite an unusual place. Pupils were drawn from a wide area and Weller's friends from primary school were scattered among the different classes, leaving mostly strangers who shared Weller's south London accent sitting in the desks opposite his own. The capital's presence must have hovered heavily over the place – a bright, aggressive culture far removed from Woking's suburban atmosphere. 'It [London] was where it was happening,' recalls Weller. 'London was a special day out.'

The young music fan started to make his own trips to London, fired by his new interest in clothes. 'I remember when I started to get into clothes, seeing something like a Ben Sherman shirt in the window of a shop, saving up every day and going back from day to day to stare at it.' He got his first Crombie when he was twelve, paid for with money he used to make from a morning paper round and an *Evening News* one. He used to save up and go to London's Petticoat Lane on a Sunday to buy loafers, DMs and Sta-Prest trousers as part of a new suedehead look which had evolved out of the shaven skinhead culture. According to Steve Brookes, Weller's interest in the cropped hair, DMs and sportswear of the cult fashion didn't make him stand out from the crowd. 'Everyone had a similar sort of angle on it,' he says. 'The smoothie look with the Sta-Prest trousers. I think he wore pretty much what everybody else wore. He was quite well into shoes; he had a lot of different pairs of shoes.'

Richard Allen's pulp fact and fiction novels, *Skinhead* and *Suedehead*, were cult favourites among streetwise kids in the 70s, despite the fact that their author was an experienced, prolific hack trying to make a living rather than the rodent-faced, razor-sharp hero of classroom folklore. Weller loved the mix of smart, classic clothes and working men's gear which accompanied the suede-head's short hair, and it was also easy to adapt elements of it into his school uniform, creating touches of individuality and rebellion. He was ahead of his peers, however, in sussing out the music of the cult. 'I was a suedehead first time around. About 1970. I missed the skinhead thing but that was the first time I listened to black music in a big way. At the dance on Thursdays it was reggae or Motown; Chairman Of The Board, Sex Machine.'

Ska and soul music, the roots of suedehead culture, were played at local clubs like The Atlanta, Woking Football Club and Knaphill Disco, which Weller was the first in his crowd to investigate. His parents' indulgence of his fanaticism for music also meant that they helped him rapidly build up an enviable collection of seven-inch singles of reggae and Motown singles which gave him an edge over his contemporaries. He also started to play his guitar, but his dreams of forming a pop band were thwarted by the lack of a Lennon to his McCartney.

Steve Brookes, who was born the day after Weller, arrived at Sheerwater from south London in Christmas '71. He'd had an unsettled childhood and by this time had already been to six different schools. One of Steve's friends, Roger Pilling, introduced him to Weller. 'Pilling dragged me across the playground to meet Paul [who] sort of looked me up and down and wandered off,' remembers Brookes. 'It improved from there, really!'

The two swiftly formed a special bond, as Weller explains. 'We really did love each other then – not homosexually – but the kind of pure love you very rarely get with the opposite sex. We just thought exactly alike. We wouldn't even have to speak sometimes – we just knew what the other was thinking. *Paradise Lost*, you know.'

Steve Brookes, whose parents had split up, often slept over at the Weller house, in a sleeping bag on the floor. 'Paul's bedroom was upstairs at the front of the house. He had a double bed which I thought was a bit unusual but it was probably an old one that used to belong to his parents. At night it used to get freezing cold in there and he'd have a huge pile of blankets on his bed. He'd be buried underneath it all. Even his head never used to come out. He just used to have his mouth poking out somewhere to breathe. He'd acclimatised to it and knew how cold it was.

'He only stirred when his mum brought up tea and biscuits and he managed to consume these with minimal exposure to the cold. Waking up was always a very gradual process from Paul's point of view and I spent many mornings willing him to wake up so we could get the day underway.'

Alongside the double bed was a wardrobe, electric heater, amplifier, little Dansette record player, electric guitar and a chest of drawers – home to all his records.

Weller's closest friends are still almost all male, as former *Vox* and *Guardian* journalist Lisa Verrico noted when she went on tour with him in 1994: 'The way that middle-class people have girlfriends is that they're really good friends. Their friends could be male or female. I don't think Weller has that. I don't think as a female you'd get into the sort of friendships Paul has with men.

'The first time I saw him do a proper gig we all went back to the hotel afterwards and got really pissed. The next day in the morning Paul's sitting there with his sunglasses on with all these other hungover blokes and they were like a little group of boys. They all kept sneaking off to the toilet to have a spliff and they were coming back laughing, 'Guess what we've just done.' I was thinking, I can't believe them, they're like a bunch of twelve year olds with little secrets and special passwords. They've all got girls they fancy and they talk in code about them. I think he definitely fits into that nineties lad thing, which is why he really liked Oasis. But he's not a lad in a really arrogant way. He just really likes to hang out with boys.'

Brookes: 'You can't have the same sort of friendship with a woman that you can with a man. I also think that Paul is probably prone to have one friend at a time. He doesn't have a big circle of close friends. I don't think he's changed in that respect. He's always been that way.'

This friendship between men especially applied to Paul's special bond with his father: 'I suppose we've always had quite a unique relationship when I compare it to what other people have said about their parents – quite a lot of people have felt detached from their parents whereas I've always been the opposite and we've always been friends. We always used to go out drinking when I was younger.'

John Weller: 'I wish I'd had more of a relationship with my old man.'

Weller wrote his first song in '71 or '72. 'I was about fourteen,' he says vaguely. 'I can't remember the actual title of it but it was after I'd learnt about three or four chords on the guitar. I expect it was something like 'I Love You Baby' and it was shit. At least I tried though. It was a bit Bob Dylan-ish I think [Weller had been turned on to Bob Dylan by his schoolfriend Dave Waller], like 'Blowing In The Wind' or something. I'd only just got a harmonica and I made a stand for it out of a coathanger. I thought it was pretty radical at the time.'

Steve Brookes gives another affable chuckle as he remembers, 'Me and Paul used to buy lots of harmonicas because we thought you had to get a different one for every key you played in.'

He and Brookes also started taking guitar lessons together. 'We only did a few,' says Brookes. 'We'd sit together in this guy's front room and he'd try to teach us American dance band stuff.'

In the summer of '72, Weller and Brookes played their first gig in the music room of Sheerwater School after their music teacher John Avery encouraged them to put the show together. They played covers of 'Blue Suede Shoes' and 'Johnny B Goode' and a couple of their own songs like 'Crossroads'. Brookes recalls in his book, *Keeping the Flame*: 'About halfway through we dared to look up only to find that seventy per cent of the audience was female.' The duo didn't have a name at the time. 'We were probably known as the Wankers From Woking or something,' he says with a grin.

Ann Weller 'couldn't believe it' when her 'shy' and 'reserved' son started performing in front of people. 'My mum was always very surprised when I said I wanted to get into a band and I wanted to go out and play live because when I was younger especially I was very shy and very quiet, so she was freaked out and quite amazed that I'd get on-stage in front of people and make a fool of myself. There's a real extrovert side of me as well as being very moody and introverted. Playing live brings that out.'

Brookes: 'He's a powerful presence on-stage which he isn't in real life. He's quite a reticent person. He was always shy. Even now if you talk to him, especially on the telephone, he's got quite a diffident manner.'

Weller: 'Maybe it's my complexes but I get the impression that most people dislike me anyway, so I always start the conversation from that point of view. It can only get better.'

Pennie Smith observes, 'He's a very functional sort of person, very much what he presents. He's very self-contained and private.

'It's funny. I've had long conversations with him but afterwards

I've forgotten what we said together. It's like even when he's quite chatty he's still a bit removed. He's a difficult person to remember in a strange way. He's a bit abstract and I don't even know quite why. I think the only way to get to know him is through his lyrics. He doesn't have a lot on the outside.'

Weller's first on-stage performance was actually several years earlier as a crown-carrying page boy at a beauty queen competition during a family holiday at Butlins. 'That was also my first erotic memory, the Miss Butlins contest. I was backstage watching all the girls getting changed. It was very exciting.' After developing a crush on Stella Stevens at primary school, Weller's first kiss was 'a chicklet called Denise. I was a young sperm of seven or something.

'I think I had my first girlfriend when I was around thirteen. All lovey-dovey and cuddling. Then, when I was fourteen I went steady with a girl for eight months (she's my cousin now). My mum and dad thought I was ill because I spent all my time with her and didn't go out playing football with the lads. My parents were dead against it. I didn't get on with them for ages around that time.'

He discovered masturbation – 'a new toy!' – and lost his virginity at fourteen. 'The girl, who was far more experienced in these matters, was thirteen.

'I remember the first time I had sex with a girl I couldn't get it up and I blamed it on the girl, telling her that there was something wrong with her rather than me, which I think was a terrible thing to do now and I really regret having said it.

'My only problems – apart from spots – when I was younger concerned birds. I was always too shy and I could never think of anything to say. So I'd get more and more frustrated and ended up insulting them.'

Steve Brookes, who, before they spoke, first spotted the young Weller snogging a girlfriend at a bus stop, remembers, 'Paul used to pull them apart and tell 'em how dreadful their hair was and then they'd walk off, all in the line of fun. But some of them didn't walk off. He wasn't shy with girls because he used to get plenty of birds. We used to walk around with guitars all the time because we sussed out that it was a good way of pulling birds.'

Weller: 'When I was younger, I just fell into the same mentality that you should try and lay as many girls as possible – and treat them badly. I used to be a right sexist prat. After a while I found I wasn't very popular with the girls.'

He continued to hark back to these early encounters when he was in his mid-to-late twenties. 'Sex is always on my mind, I suppose, but I've got quite a warped view of it, I guess. I still yearn for the way sex was when I was fifteen or sixteen; the innocence of that time.

'I think it's important in that I feel a real strength from it. It's like when you're younger and you go to a party and see someone you're attracted to and they're attracted to you. It's like a really powerful arrogance . . . I don't know if it's the same with girls . . . But I like that powerful feeling. It makes you aware of yourself, your body.'

'If he likes a girl he flirts with her. He's definitely a flirt,' says Lisa Verrico.

Verrico spent a lot of time with Oasis and Paul Weller when their friendship first started in 1994. She sees a lot of parallels between them in their attitudes towards women. 'In the same way as Oasis are really working class and are polite to women – you can read what you like about Liam but I know he is polite to women and Noel is definitely – they have this thing that all women are like their mothers. Paul has that too.'

When Weller revealed to *19* magazine what he regarded as the most important feminine qualities, they certainly reflected the warm but pragmatic strength of his mum, Ann: 'Women are all the things that men aren't. Men generally are selfish, arrogant, insecure and childish. Women are seldom any of these things. Men and women tolerate each other because they are so lonely. I like women for their inner strength and ability to adapt to most situations. Also their practicality.'

He didn't always recognise these qualities in girlfriends or the other female in the family, his sister Nicola, as his mother explained in Paolo Hewitt's book on The Jam, *Beat Concerto*: 'What's a five year old got to do with a baby? When he was fifteen and she was ten, he didn't want to know. They didn't quarrel or fight, they just didn't speak. Just "hello" and that was their lot.'

This age gap wasn't the only problem for Nikki as she grew up in the shadow of a brother who, unusually for his age, was already fixed in his ambition. John Weller's close relationship with his son was based on a male togetherness which the ex-boxer had dreamt about before Paul's birth.

John Weller: 'To tell you the truth, having a boy ... was something I always wanted. People get married and say they don't care if it's a boy or a girl. Well, I always wanted a boy, even before I met my missus.'

2 This is the Modern World, 1974–76

Paul Weller: 'When I was fourteen or fifteen, all I wanted to do was just be in a pop group and be liked and I don't think there's anything wrong with that.'

Paul Weller: 'To me [being a Mod] is like a religion. It's like being a Catholic – it's like my code. It gives something to my life. I'm still a Mod, I'll always be a Mod, you can bury me a Mod.'

When Paul Weller was fourteen his musical interests began to widen rapidly. In 1972 he and Steve Brookes saw their first gig – Status Quo at the Guildford Civic Hall.

Weller: 'I sat in the back row and was still deafened. It was the confirmation I needed.'

That summer the two friends went through a short-lived hippy phase, flashing back to the Californian philosophies and West Coast psychedelia of the late 60s. They grew their hair long, and bought loon pants, T-shirts with billowing arms and afghan coats from a shop in Woking called Squire, and listened to Bob Dylan, Jimi Hendrix and *Sgt Pepper*. Brookes: 'In about '72 we went through quite a hippy period where we had longish hair and loon pants. When you look back you can't remember whether we looked like that for three months, six months or a year. Our flower-power period thing was a short-term thing. We got into dope around the same time. Our mate Dave Waller was fairly heavily into anything that was drug influenced.'

Waller was a fellow outsider at Sheerwater whose main interests were blues, cannabis and politics. His maturing, adolescent tastes had a big impact on Weller. Together with Waller and Brookes, the aspiring pop star wrote 'psychedelic poems', dropped acid at a Windsor Free Festival, walked barefoot through the streets of Woking and fantasised about fame. 'When I was younger, I wanted all the usual trappings of fame – girls, money, glamour, flash cars. You either grow out of that or you don't.'

Although they had dope-y fantasies of padding barefoot through mansions filled with marijuana smoke, in reality their experiences with drugs were schoolboy pranks, such as smearing shoe conditioner inside their cuffs at school. 'It was this clear liquid, Lady Esquire shoe conditioner,' says Brookes, 'and it used to get you out of your brains . . . that and a couple of light bitters was a good night out in those days.'

The Jam's name evolved out of this bluesy, stoned time when Brookes and Weller transformed their primitive riffs into jams which would last for half an hour. Brookes: 'We used to go round this bloke's house and smoke all day long and listen to Led Zeppelin when his mum and dad were out. When Dave Waller was in the band we were more into that hairy phase. I was listening to The Groundhogs, Deep Purple, all sorts. It was a follow on from the sixties John Mayall's Bluesbreakers thing where all these supergroups like Humble Pie were heavily influenced by the blues boom of the sixties and had moved on. We were also into Led Zeppelin and we would have these endless jam sessions where we'd play the same song for half an hour.'

It's ironic that to most fans the name is synonymous with three-minute, abrasive pop songs. 'I think Paul's sister, Nikki, thought it was a good name later,' said Brookes. 'She said there was Marmalade and Bread, and now there was Jam. It turned into The Jam a bit later.'

Weller's relationship with his mother grew a little frosty during this period. 'Although adolescence had its good moments I didn't get on too well with my mum for a few years. I think it was because when I went out pissing it up with my mates she suspected we were taking drugs.

'I gave up taking drugs at sixteen, even though I never abused them. There's no answer in drugs. It's bollocks that it can help you write better.' Despite saying this, Weller still enjoyed the odd recreational binge.

It wasn't a significant bust-up with his mother, though, and the growing pains swiftly passed. By the time Weller was eighteen he already had a lot of premature pressure and responsibility to deal with, and it was Ann he leant on for security and support.

Still only fourteen at this point, however, it was through his parents' membership of the local Woking Working Men's Club, that Weller and Brookes played gigs there on midweek nights from November 1972 onward. Their acoustic six-song debut set featured covers of songs by Tom Jones, Chuck Berry and Donovan, along with some original lyrics by the pair and their own songs 'Loving By Letters', 'One Hundred Ways To Love You' and 'More And More'. The pair had played about 'six or seven' gigs together when Dave Waller joined them on guitar and Weller switched to a Hofner bass, exactly like the one Paul McCartney used to play in The Beatles, which Ann had bought for £75 from a shop in Kingston.

Weller's on-stage appearance was hardly that of a fledgling style guru. He and Brookes dressed up in orange loon pants, black and white shirts and blue and white plimsolls. John Weller reasoned that if the band looked 'respectable' they would appeal to the old-fashioned publicans who were booking the band at this stage. John retained this attitude when The Jam made their first appearances on *Top of the Pops*. He chased around after the band, collecting cups off the dressing-room floor and folding their ties. 'They may not have us back,' he argued, 'and we need them more than they need us.'

In the winter of '72, Steve Brookes went to a boarding school on the south coast and his family moved back to Colindale, north London. He spent as many weekend evenings as he could at the Wellers' and, despite the move away from Woking, he and Paul grew closer. Weller: 'He more or less lived round our house and he used to share my room . . . Every experience, all the new things we experienced, we were doing together.'

The year ended with their first paid professional gig at the Ball and Wicket at Upper Hale near Farnham on New Year's Eve. But 1973 brought yet more upheaval for Brookes, as he moved to Borehamwood in Hertfordshire. When he saw his old school mates, 'I noticed a real change in Paul and Dave. They had become much more rebellious and scornful of authority.' School had brought out an openly rebellious side in Paul, who had become a troubled individualist. 'For the first two years at Sheerwater I really tried to get stuck in,' he says. 'I really tried to work hard. But I gave up by the third year. I couldn't be fucking bothered. Oh . . . it was all right doing my homework when I was twelve and thirteen, but by the time I was fourteen I started discovering sex, music and drinking, and there was no way I was gonna stay in and do some poxy maths homework.

'School is where I decided I would show the bastards like that that I didn't need their rules or their education ... I hated all my teachers passionately. They were all bastards and bitches talking to me as if I was nothing.'

The only subject he was interested in was English, and he showed an early flair for writing essays, stories and poems, which he used to scribble with a sly enthusiasm. He also read George Orwell's novels on the quiet, half-grasping some of the socialist philosophies. The author's detailed, journalistic style and humanistic approach to left-wing politics would prove to be an important influence on Weller in the future. However, this self-educated, out-of-hours enthusiasm failed to feed back into his schoolwork. In his last year at Sheerwater, he was skipping off lessons more than he was actually there, aided by his teachers who used to send him home for petty acts of rebellion such as smoking and swearing.

Although there were arguments, John Weller didn't push his son during his final months at school. 'They turned a blind eye to it really,' says Brookes. 'They'd realised what sort of direction he was heading in.' John accepted Paul was unlikely to get many qualifications and had only one aim – to enter the pop scene in some way. 'I was mostly miserable,' says Weller. 'I was so shy and just completely obsessive – I gave up friends, girlfriends, everything, for the band. I was just twenty-four hours a day music. I lived it, ate it, slept it with my guitar. Not screwed it, not quite, but slept with it. I was a maniac.'

At fourteen, Paul made himself a promise: 'If I hadn't made it by the time I was twenty I'd give it up and go and do something else ... You see, I've always had this thing about youth; this thing about ageing.'

Weller later revealed a contempt for less ambitious or arrogant classmates. He saw them as passively accepting their lot and growing old before their time. 'Some of the kids who went to school with me are like little old men already, like Toby jugs,' he stated with obvious frustration in the early days of The Jam, when he was still a teenager.

Weller was fortunate, however, to have a father who gave him

Paul Weller

100 per cent support by booking gigs and setting up their gear at the working men's clubs. John Weller states in *Beat Concerto*: 'I'm not really an educated person. I couldn't put a lot of stock in education because I've never had it. I figured that Paul wasn't a brains trust anyway, none of us were, but I knew he was good at what he was doing . . . I didn't have a thousand pounds to put into them but I had a thousand hours, so that's what I did.'

His parents would also avoid paying bills in order to spare some money for their son's constant need for amps and guitars.

Dogmatic attitudes in school also applied to music. Weller only hung out with like-minded kids who were into 60s pop and soul. 'When I was at school there were battle lines – either you had long hair and an army greatcoat and carried a copy of *Dark Side of the Moon* under your arm or you were a skin – or suedehead – and you listened to strictly soul or rocksteady . . . It's a way of thinking that's particular to Britain and there are problems with it but it's also what has made music in this country special and has done for the last thirty years.' Weller's tendency to see music in black and white terms only to contradict himself later is rooted in the kid in the playground bonding with his mates over a favourite album and dismissing everyone else's tastes.

In early '73 a local drummer, Neil 'Bomber' Harris, joined the band. Harris had grown up in Woking's Maybury Estate, where he'd been giving the neighbours an ear bashing since his parents had bought him a drum kit as a Christmas present when he was six. His enthusiasm was irrepressible and his parents forked out for drum lessons a few years later. At Sheerwater Comprehensive, John Avery gave him further encouragement and for a short time he played drums in a cover band with a mate, Bruce Foxton. It was clear at the first practice in Weller's bedroom that Harris was a much better player than anyone else. Oddly, the noise generated by this fledgling band on guitar, bass, drums and a 'rinky dink' piano situated under the stairs in the hallway, didn't seem to upset the neighbours. John Weller recounts: 'You could stand down in the shopping centre . . . and hear them good and proper. Downstairs we couldn't hear a bloody thing we were saying and it must have driven the neighbours crazy but we never had one complaint from any of them. I can remember Teds dancing on the pavement across the way.'

The group's first success together was when they won a cup for the best local group in spring '73 at the Sheerwater Community Association talent contest, beating the local rivals Rock Island Line who had appeared in the David Essex movie, *That'll Be the Day*. Their performance was typically flamboyant, full of the rock 'n' roll leaps which they slipped into their shows at local venues.

Engraved on the trophy is an early indication of Weller's ambitious, cocky assertion that he was the band's main driving force – it read, to the slight irritation of the others, Paul Weller and The Jam. In particular, Steve Brookes had a right to complain because he sang over half the songs and also co-wrote most of the originals in the set. 'I didn't blame Paul,' says the affable Brookes, who gives him the benefit of the doubt over the 'error'. 'I don't think it was intentional, it was just a mistake. John had probably mentioned Paul's name and it all got a bit confused. You see, it was a bit like when your school team wins a football competition. There was a big cup and then we all got these little cups with individual names on it. That's probably what caused the confusion.'

At the time the band's songwriting was based on a sly flick through The Beatles songbook for some quick inspiration. Songs like 'Forever And Always', which they wrote in this period, were blatant rip-offs of the Fab Four. Not only that but Brookes and Weller's vision of how to make it in the music business was based on The Beatles' career. They set out to write great pop hooks into their songs, planning more experimental work once they'd broken through into the charts. The early Jam even tried to pay homage to The Beatles by playing a gig on Weller's roof. However, as it was sloping they had to make do with setting up their instruments in the back garden.

Not long after their cup-winning triumph, Neil Harris missed a youth club gig by taking a holiday and when he returned he discovered he'd been replaced by Rick Buckler. Weller: 'Rick was the only drummer around at school. There were only about three drummers of our age group in the whole of Woking.'

Born on 6 December 1955, Paul Richard Buckler arrived five minutes before his twin brother Peter. His father, who worked for the post office, was a regular churchgoer, and Buckler went to Sunday school and became a member of the Boys' Brigade. He attended Goldsmith Primary before Sheerwater Comprehensive,

Paul Weller

where he was on the other side of the musical battle lines as a long-haired fan of Black Sabbath. He'd already played in a rock band, Impulse, and had gone through numerous part-time jobs at a fish shop, motorbike warehouse, and a drawing office, to name but three.

That summer Weller and Brookes also tried their hand at some part-time work, when they joined John Weller on his building site. John taught a traditional method of throwing bricks up – three at a time – to a workmate standing on the scaffolding. However, his son failed to get the hang of this, and usually had to dive for cover as the bricks fell back to the ground. Fed up with their own clueless slapstick attempts at the building trade, the pair sat around on piles of sand, smoking cigarettes and topping up their sun tans.

Weller also had a go at window cleaning. 'That was useless. The other bloke had a bit of form, he'd been in borstal, and we didn't have a car so every time we went out with the ladder we'd get stopped by the police.' According to Brookes his mate was going through dramatic changes in his dress sense at the time: 'We were more rockers really than Mods at that time. He had long hair, a leather jacket which his dad had got from a building site and these blue suede zip-up boots and jeans.'

Weller's fashion sense wasn't the only disaster area at this time. The new line-up started off by staggering around drunk on-stage at the Sheerwater Youth Club, and their last gig with Dave Waller was at Chobham Youth Club just outside Woking. 'He wasn't a good guitarist,' says Brookes. 'In the end we had to ask him to leave. He wasn't bothered about it, which was part of the problem really.'

The slimmed-down band attempted their first session at a studio in Kingston. This was swiftly followed by a recording of 'Takin' My Love' (later released on the B-side to 'In The City') and 'Blueberry Rock' in a studio near Swiss Cottage, London.

In January 1974 The Jam became the resident Friday night band at Michael's Club at the top of Goldsworth Road, playing sets which included 'Little Queenie', 'Twist And Shout', 'Roll Over Beethoven' and 'Johnny B Goode'. Weller's long-time friend, Paolo Hewitt, recalls Michael's as an 'after-hours drinking club which attracted some of Woking's livelier characters.'

As their repertoire showed, Weller was listening to a lot of Stax and Motown records at the time. Brookes: 'We got into the

Motown thing – a bit of Marvin Gaye. Paul got into Smokey
Robinson in a big way. We'd listen to R&B stuff like John Lee
Hooker's "Dimples" and Humble Pie at the time as well. We had
their *Smokin'* album, which was a really bluesy album, but they did
a version of "Roadrunner" on it. That led us back because we
wanted to hear the original and that takes you on to different
things.'

Weller wrote a song called 'She Made Me Shimmy', which had
an early Motown feel to it. At sixteen, Weller thought he 'sounded
like Otis Redding'. The trio also recorded 'Loving By Letters' and
'More And More' at Bob Potter's studio in Mytchett, near Cam-
berley in Surrey. 'Paul and I were dominating a bit I suppose,' says
Brookes. 'Rick just sort of went along with what we were doing,
until occasionally he'd get pissed off. It must have been difficult for
him because we were in one camp and he was kind of on his own.'

The balance wasn't right. In the summer they auditioned a new
guitarist, Bruce Foxton, by playing The Beatles song 'This Boy'.
Foxton decided to stay with his heavy rock band, Rita. However,
a few months later Rita found themselves in a musical dead end –
they hadn't played any gigs during that period – and he decided to
join The Jam.

Born on 1 September 1955, Foxton had been a pupil at Sheerwater Junior and Comprehensive Schools, where he enjoyed
football and technical drawing. His father had worked as a painter
and decorator, and a football pools collector on the local estates.
Foxton had two elder brothers; Ray who was working as a bus
driver and Derek, a nine-to-fiver in the print trade. When Foxton
left school in '71 he also became an apprentice compositor in the
print business. Although he listened to his older brothers' Motown
records he was also a rock fan. His dubious tastes for the likes of
Bad Company led him into joining Rita.

There were problems in rehearsals as the new line-up tried to find
the right balance. The band realised that Foxton's rhythm guitar
playing wasn't as good as Weller's, so the new recruit was asked to
play a new instrument – Weller's beloved Hofner violin bass. Bruce
had a tantrum. Brookes: 'Being the youngest one in his family had
made him a bit precious and he was prone to stamp his feet a bit
when he couldn't get his own way.

Paul Weller

'I didn't have a problem with Bruce. We used to go out for beers and stuff, but there was a lot of piss-taking going on and as the new boy he took the brunt of it at first. He was prone to moan a bit. It was probably his way of asserting himself.'

As Foxton wasn't familiar with the bass, he used to dash on stage halfway through the band's sets to play the songs he'd had time to work on. He did this at The Jam's unlikely support slot to Thin Lizzy (John Weller pulling strings again) at the Greyhound, Croydon, and got a cheer from the crowd who thought he'd arrived late.

Meanwhile, after his long bouts of truancy, Weller left school in 1974 at the age of fifteen, with two CSEs in English and technical drawing and a passion for the left-wing writer George Orwell. 'I read *1984* for my English CSE and they let me write a poem for it rather than an essay. It was called "Room 101". Oh, and they put one of my paintings in the school hall.'

In spite of his interest in Orwell, Weller knew little about politics. 'I left school with no idea what was going on in society, even down to how to fill in a form.' He went on the dole, resolving to avoid getting a job until he'd tried to put his dreams into action. 'I didn't want to work. I didn't want to become Mr Normal.'

Steve Brookes moved to Woking in September and initially spent time drawing dole money and writing songs with Weller. However, Brookes had to start work to help support his mother and he also became seriously involved with a new girlfriend, Jenny, leaving his mate to brood resentfully in his room. Weller confesses, 'He met this bird and was really involved with her. I used to get really jealous of that. It was like she took him away so that really split us up.'

By the autumn Foxton was a full-time member playing whole sets, although there were still doubts about how serious he was. At Michael's he ran out in the middle of a performance to catch up with his girlfriend after they'd had an argument. Given that Weller was irritated by the presence of Jenny, which he felt was affecting Steve's commitment to the band, Foxton's action looked like instant dismissal. Yet Weller soon calmed down and rapidly shrugged off the incident, while continuing to take the odd dig at Brookes. Nevertheless, on 23 March 1975, at the Woking Liberal Club in Walton Road, the out-of-favour guitarist had one of his greatest moments when he played a solo on a battered piano while being chased around by the club owner. This slapstick had followed a set which was pulled mid-song just before midnight, a move which understandably angered the band. Weller thought Brookes's response was hilarious but he was less pleased that it had totally eclipsed his own.

In 1975 the band entered a talent contest at the ABC Cinema in Woking. Contestants appeared during the interval of a film called *That's Entertainment* but a disgruntled Jam were soundly beaten. They were now advertising themselves as The Jam: Maximum R&B, and playing gigs at the Fulham Greyhound in London, thanks to John Weller's old boxing contact with the venue's owner. There were also bizarre one-off appearances at Chelsea Football Club, HM Prison Codingly and a police ball. Their sets were now dominated by soul cover versions as Weller refined his tastes into a tighter, sharper R&B vision. Brookes recalls, 'By this time we started getting into the short-haired bands rather than the long-haired ones.'

At the turn of '74/'75 Weller had become obsessive about Canvey Island pub rock band, Dr Feelgood, particularly their guitarist Wilko Johnson. *'Down by the Jetty* [released in January '75] is a great English R&B album. I used to love Wilko, he was like the English Chuck Berry. I went to see 'em in the Guildford Civic. He came out, did this huge lick with his legs out and they were off. Yeah! It's like that Lennon quote when he went to see a rock 'n' roll movie and he thought, Now that's a good job, I'd like to do that.'

Brookes was also impressed by the Feelgood's raw, R&B-based sound and Johnson's tight, stuttering guitar which mixed rhythm and lead playing. They began to speed up their live material, with Weller imitating the edgy sound of his new hero's style. This transition opened him up to the next major change in The Jam's sound and philosophy. After hearing The Who's 'My Generation' on a tacky compilation album, Weller saw a vision for his own band. The Who's hard, tight sound and the exuberant, nervy youth anthems 'My Generation', 'I Can't Explain' and 'Anyway, Anyhow, Anywhere' acted like a speed-injected buzz on Weller – but this wasn't a rootless transition. The 60s Mod band had started off as The Detours, playing a mix of R&B and Motown covers which shared common ground with Weller's already-formulated tastes. Songs by James Brown, Marvin Gaye, Martha and the Vandellas and Chuck Berry belonged to the repertoire of both acts.

The Who's fabricated Mod image, which had been manufactured by their fast-talking publicist/manager Pete Meaden, inspired Weller to turn back the clock by turning himself into a Mod, a fashion which had died out five or six years before. The first Mods were middle-class boys from rich Italian families in London who had money to spend on smart, cool, casual clothes. This elitism was more powerful in the minds and threads of working-class kids who started to define a sense of flamboyant pride in themselves through their clothes. Details were all-important and fashions mutated overnight, as the early faces competed with each other to constantly find new definitions of 'cool'.

The term 'Mod' was rooted in the Modern American jazz of the 50s, where an adventurous, competitive edge also existed between pioneers Charlie Parker, John Coltrane, Miles Davis and Charlie Mingus. Bebop and the Blue Note label were 'cool'. Trad jazz and Ella Fitzgerald certainly were not.

Eugene Manzi, who works as a press officer at London Records, has been a close friend of Weller's from the mid 80s onward. He was one of numerous original Mods that the eager-to-learn artist hooked up with. 'I used to go down Carnaby Street in the early 60s before it became what it became. There were about three shops down there and we sort of discovered this street. We couldn't believe they were showing underpants in the window. You didn't see it in those days, mainly because they were gay shops. It was near the London Palladium and all the dancers from there would come out and buy briefs. We thought they were like knickers because we were used to Y-fronts. They were in different colours too, which was unheard of. So we used to go down there and I got my suits made by John Stephens in Carnaby Street. It was special to me too because it was kind of Italian style,' says Manzi, who is of Italian descent.

John Stephens's shop, His Clothes, in Carnaby Street, became a Mod mecca by selling garments of different colours, styles and fabrics. His clothes were also relatively cheap and well made. Mod culture fitted Weller's personality as tightly as his now legendary mohair trousers. He was vain and loved clothes. In its purest form, Mod had expressed the attitudes of adolescents like Weller in the early 60s. 'They were not a group, just a scattering of daring and determined individual stylists,' wrote Richard Barnes in his seminal book, *Mods!* 'They were incredibly vain, a bit snobbish and totally narcissistic.'

The look was smart, casual and cool, a style reflected in Weller's off-the-wall comment, 'Cleanliness is next to godliness which is next to modliness.' He was also elitist in his soul and R&B tastes in music, demonstrating a knowledge and eclecticism well beyond most of his peers who just bought the glam, pop or prog rock records of the day. Kevin Pearce, author of the Mod book, *Something Beginning With 'O'*, argued, 'Naturally the best Mods had the best wardrobes, the best record collections, the best bookshelves, the best minds ... Mods were snobs in that great, proud, self-educated way.' Weller's earlier enthusiasm for suede-head fashion meant that he'd already been part of the Mod lineage. The two youth cultures had defined themselves in subtly different ways through black music, dancing, Sta-Prest trousers and Ivy League shops.

Mod was a London scene which had acted as a magnet for dreamers in the dreary Essex and Surrey satellite towns of the 60s, as Barnes described: 'The ticket living in some dreary suburb, sitting in the Wimpy trying to make his cheeseburger last all night, staring out at the rain, was still part of the Mod myth. He was going to get a chromed scooter and five suits in Tonik or ice-blue mohair, and have some basket-weave shoes hand made, and get his hair styled in Wardour Street and go dancing in the West End clubs every night. He was a Mod. He had his stake in the myth.' Weller also identified with this aspect of Mod culture. He was stuck in the suburbs planning an escape route. 'I couldn't wait to get out of Woking. I didn't want to stay in this little town for the rest of my life.'

Weller absorbed the culture and spent his gig money on the classic Mod trinity – clothes, records and a scooter. The parka-clad scooter boys of the 60s were a Mod sub-group, although the later mass invasions of Brighton in the second half defined the scooter in the minds of the public as an essential Mod accessory. 'My first scooter was a GP 150,' reminisced Weller later. 'I saved up for it [he bought it for £70] and my dad gave me some money. I was seventeen. Its original colour was turquoise but I got it sprayed black with yellow stripes down the side [with Motown written along one side] and I had my fly-screen with WOKING across it and PAUL. And I had my mirrors in an X-shape and a big rip aerial and my mum had an old coat, not an afghan, but an old fur coat, and she cut it up and made it into some seat covers for me . . . I loved that scooter.' As he later admitted, 'I think people thought I was a bit eccentric. It must have been weird to see me driving around on a scooter with a parka on in 1975.'

Beat Concerto author Paolo Hewitt was a Woking local who first met the lean young Mod at the town's Curtis Shoes where he had a Saturday job in 1974: 'Weller looked like an anachronism – in contrast to the prevailing soulboy look he came in as if he had just stepped out of a world that had vanished five years previously.'

At the height of glam Weller walked the suburban streets in loafers, white socks, Ben Sherman shirt, Harrington jacket, green fishtail parka and Levi Sta-Prest trousers. It was a streetwise, working-class, sharp style.

Despite its initial middle-class, Jewish origins, Mod was imbued with working-class ethics. On the sleeve of The Who's *Quadrophenia* album, Pete Meaden defined Mod as 'an aphorism for clean living in difficult circumstances'.

Weller: 'I can always spot a Mod, even the ones in their fifties. Not 'cos they walk funny but because they still care about it. It's vain and narcissistic but it's very working class as well. Taking pride in yourself because there's nothing else.'

'Paul wouldn't talk to me so much about the sixties, as ask me about it,' laughs Eugene Manzi. 'What was it like in the sixties? What sort of clothes did they wear in the sixties? I just tell him what a great time it was in the sixties. For a start it was full employment so you could literally leave school, be a plumber one day and five years later be the managing director of an advertising agency because people were judged on talent, not exam results. Being working class is dear to Paul. I think he identifies with that period in the sixties when working-class people like Michael Caine could suddenly get into films and working-class photographers like David Bailey came through. It was a time of social change in England. You didn't have to speak with a certain accent to get a job.

Working classes weren't just working in factories, there was a chance to better yourself without having to change or pretend you were always middle class.'

Weller also drew inspiration from a more authentic British Mod band from the sixties, namely the Small Faces. Led by Steve Marriott on guitar and vocals, with bassist Ronnie Lane, drummer Kenney Jones and keyboard player Ian McLagan, the Small Faces were at their peak from 1965–68. They were heavily influenced by black R&B and Motown records, scoring their first Top Twenty hit with 'Watcha Gonna Do' in 1965. They also had a number one hit with the single 'All Or Nothing'. They were later at the forefront of a cultural collision when Mod turned psychedelic, a short-lived time which also influenced Weller's later solo work. The hit 'Itchycoo Park' and Weller's own favourite, 'Tin Soldier', captured this shift in style. Linguistic comic Stanley Unwin linked tracks on the whimsical, lavish pop of *Ogden's Nut Gone Flake*, an album which had a bigger influence on Blur than Weller, who has mixed feelings about the record, although its circular Pop Art cover had an effect on him.

By the time they released *The Autumn Stone* album in 1968, contractual disputes and a frustration with being constantly tagged as a pop band ruptured the Small Faces. They weren't able to make the leap to rock credibility until 30 years later, when Blur talked about them as a reference point at the height of their success in the mid 90s. Marriott left to form Humble Pie, while Lane, Jones and Rod Stewart formed a new band, Faces. A later reformation in the late 70s is best forgotten.

Weller claims he was hooked on the band 'from the first time I saw them on TV in '67/'68 doing "Tin Soldier" with P. P. Arnold.' He describes them as 'the ultimate group, the sort of group you could only dream of being in.

'They didn't give a fuck but weren't above taking the piss out of themselves as well as everyone else and the whole music biz charade. They were even the same height! They were destined to be in a band together.'

However, Steve Brookes remembers the Small Faces becoming a big influence only after Weller's discovery of The Who: 'He played *Ogden's Nut Gone Flake* a fair bit around about '74/'75 and we were both aware of the singles "Itchycoo Park" and stuff, but I don't think they became an influence until he got more into The Who, which was around '75. We used to listen to the Small Faces' album quite a bit but when we were together we were still doing the Beatley stuff and a lot of the things that the Small Faces were doing were really beyond us, to play.'

These days Weller enthuses about the Small Faces' material on the Immediate label, launched by ex-Rolling Stones manager, Andrew Loog-Oldham. 'All their stuff in '67 was great,' says Weller, naming 'I'm Only Dreaming', 'I Feel Much Better', 'Talk To You' and 'Here Comes The Nice' – 'the ultimate Mod/pill song' – as career highlights.

'Tin Soldier' is his favourite song of all time, his most treasured possession is a collection of Small Faces picture sleeve EPs and singles, and he's also declared that he would have 'Rollin' Over' played at his funeral. Weller has remained fanatical about the band's style. 'Steve's haircut around "Itchycoo Park" [summer '67] was for me his best look,' he told Paolo Hewitt in the 90s. 'You have to have a small tugboat to pull this one off; petite but tough.'

Such is his detailed interest in the look of the Small Faces, he reeled off the following list of fashion triumphs for *Mojo* magazine: ' "Itchycoo Park", on *Beat Club*, for the Paisley jackets and checked pants. "All Or Nothing" on Swedish TV for the coats. Ian McLagan in Quant-style PVC, Ronnie Lane in black fur-collared car coat. "I Can't Make It" from *Beat Club* appearance, pre-psychedelic gear. Just hip. Stills from a French TV outdoor show. Steve's wearing a red, white and blue hooped sweater, Kenney is in white Levis and blue suede shoes, Mac is suited with brown and banana yellow weave shoes and Plonk is in some serious desert boots.'

Meanwhile, tensions were building inside The Jam as they streamlined their music into a harder, more direct, youthful sound. Weller thought Buckler was 'really fucking awkward'. In fact, he didn't have much of a relationship with either the drummer or Foxton: 'I would try to avoid speaking to them. I just really hated them.' Brookes got on OK with Foxton but the pair never became close friends. His relationship with Weller rarely flashed back to the warmth of the old days and was often tainted by the singer's moodiness and Brookes's determination to avoid becoming, as he saw it, a Wilko Johnson clone. John Weller was effectively holding the group together. He was also taking the brunt of the disappointments as he took the band's tapes (recorded at TW Studios in Fulham) around to 'Decca, Pye . . . you name it' in his old Austin.

Buckler: 'John was like the backbone of the thing from the word go.'

Brookes played a handful of gigs in '75, the last at Woking Football Club in the September. 'Paul had showed me a picture of The Who, I think it was, in their black suits,' says Brookes. 'He wanted us all to have these suits and his dad was ready to put some money down to have them made. He'd recruited the other two to his way of thinking so I was outnumbered. I loved our satin bomber jackets and white shoes, so I wasn't happy about it. I just didn't want him to order up a suit for me and then waste the thirty or forty quid because I wasn't happy about wearing it. So I left. They didn't actually wear the suits straight away. They'd probably ordered them in instalments as they got the money together, so they forked out for a jacket, then half a trouser leg, then a sleeve,' he laughs.

He moved back up to north London and lost touch with Weller for a while, although The Jam did turn up for the opening of Brookes's guitar shop in spring '79. Over the next decade they occasionally bumped into each other but Brookes wasn't impressed by these encounters until a recent reunion which appears to have sealed their friendship again.

For a while, The Jam considered finding an organ player in the style of the Small Faces' Ian McLagan to replace the departed original member, but this idea was dropped when they couldn't find anyone who was good, reliable *and* committed.

Tensions remained inside the band, however. There was a brief split when Foxton and Buckler felt they'd been ripped off by John Weller on the takings from a gig. It was resolved after a few days apart. A few months later, Weller, who had recently moved with his family to a two-up, two-down terrace house in Balmoral Drive on Maybury Estate (home to Foxton's family as well) ended up scrapping with the bass player after an argument at a Hope and Anchor gig. Foxton walked away with a black eye.

The tunnel-visioned Weller couldn't understand why his Hope and Anchor opponent was not only holding on to his printer's job but he was also reluctant to change his style by cutting his hair and getting rid of his flares.

Weller in 1982: 'I think he's insecure. Like something would worry him and he'd just keep on and on about it. It would get everyone down a little bit, so arguments started that way. He'd panic and really go on about it.'

Even so, Weller remembers the days of travelling between Surrey (where they didn't have much of a local following) and London with rose-tinted nostalgia. 'In terms of fun the early days were the best, travelling up the A3 in a borrowed Transit. There was no pressure because in our youthful arrogance we thought we were gonna make it anyway, so we didn't give a fuck.'

Steve Brookes believes that Foxton began to become more committed to the band after he left. 'I think I left a bit of a vacuum. I don't think he believed in the band as much as me and Paul to begin with, but after I'd gone he sort of grew into the role. He filled that gap.'

3 Woking-Class Hero, 1977–80

Sara Silver, ex-Polydor International: 'He's a humble person but has an ego of steel. He has anger and it gets to the surface very quickly.'

Steve Marriott: 'I've only seen The Jam once on a video and I thought it reminded me of me in the old days. So for me to say that, sure I like me. They looked exactly like we did and they played very similarly. At the same time I admire their taste.'

Ed Pillar (founder of Acid Jazz Records): My mother did the Small Faces fan club in the sixties . . . [one day] she commented on the fact that Steve Marriott was on the telly. "Come and have a look," [she said] and in fact it was Paul Weller but he was wearing exactly the same outfit as Steve Marriott that we had in some of the photos at home.'

Paul Weller: 'Rock is supposed to be fun, something to unwind to at the end of the day.'

The Jam's roots in working men's clubs, their Mod suits and R&B sound would have linked them into the growing pub rock scene of the mid 70s if it wasn't for the first energised, youthful, working-class musical movement since the 60s – punk. 'The really important thing about punk for us was that it connected us into a contemporary scene for the first time,' says Weller. 'Before that we didn't play to people of our own age.' The band's posters, which were plastered all over London in 1976, advertised 'rock 'n' roll, maximum rhythm 'n' blues'. Punk's fierce, abrasive communication with youth had some Mod influences. The Sex Pistols, who used to play the Small Faces' 'Watcha Gonna Do About It' in their early sets, blasted through two-and-a-half minute songs with the stoked-up ferocity of early Who. The Clash also had Mod roots, as Jon Savage explained in his book on punk, *England's Dreaming*: 'The Clash began as a classic Mod group; angry, smart pop. They speeded up the heavily chorded, stuttering sound of The

Paul Weller

Who and The Kinks.' There were also parallels in the choice of drug – speed. Jane Suck's description of punk in *England's Dreaming* has strong echoes of Mod's dandy, androgynous culture: '[I started] taking speed: once I started injecting I didn't have to worry about my sexuality. I became asexual – I think many people were – it was an incredibly asexual movement.'

Weller connected instantly with punk's raw, modern approach: 'The Pistols and The Clash were the two groups for me; the first contemporary groups that I'd ever liked ... And the details – they had short hair, straight trousers, they didn't have beards. It made a difference to me because I was a Mod by this time and they used to play covers like 'Substitute' and Troggs tracks.

'I feel that the Mod scene was very close to the punk thing; wholly youth, like going out with green hair. It changed you, made you something. It's something that every kid goes through. You just wanted to be noticed. To be recognised.'

He also gave up all his Otis Redding affectations: 'It was only when I started listening to The Clash that I thought I should sing as naturally as I talked and that The Jam should be a very English-sounding band.'

The Pistols, led by a rodent-faced north Londoner calling himself Johnny Rotten, also had a youthful edge to them which attracted Weller. 'In the summer of '76 I read a review in the *NME*,' he said, 'and it sounded just what I was looking for, really: a young band who had loads of attitude.'

The Sex Pistols gig at the Lyceum in London, which he watched with a speed-and-lager-fuelled sense of euphoria, proved to be a significant turning point for Weller: 'I came up to see the Pistols at the 100 Club, that two-day festival with The Clash and then the Lyceum all-nighter ... They were the last band on – six in the morning or something – and we were all speeding out of our heads.

'That was it for me: I've got to be part of this. It was happening, after a hick town like Woking. People have a chance to be themselves in London. In Woking, if you had the wrong cut trousers you'd get your head kicked in.

'I'm glad I was down the 100 Club in 1976. I don't think there can be a more exciting time than that.'

On 21 October 1976, at Queensway Hall, Dunstable, The Jam supported the Pistols in front of a small crowd, which was the first time Foxton and Buckler saw the group which was influencing The Jam's vision. Although it wasn't a life-changing moment for the pair as it had been for Paul, for the first time the band were all pulling in the same direction.

At the end of '76 Weller wrote a new song, 'In The City There's A Thousand Things I Want To Say To You' as a homage to London's punk scene. 'I wanna say, I wanna tell you/about the young idea/and if it don't work at least we tried,' he sang with youthful passion. It captured the charged atmosphere of the London punk scene at its height and at one point Weller was so pleased with it, The Jam would open, close and encore with the song. Weller even made himself a badge with the original title of the song printed on it.

However, for all his initial enthusiasm, the easily alienated Weller soon felt like an outsider. 'The scene was quite art school and we were sort of ostracised,' he said with a mix of chip-shouldered sensitivity and razor-sharp instinct. 'It was quite cliquey and elitist, in a London way. They were really hip and we weren't. We were just three green kids from Woking, from a little hick town, and I guess our attitudes were like that as well.'

The Jam's suburban roots did make them different, later inspiring some of their young fans to move to the metropolis. Just as the 'tickets' belonged to the Mod myth, so too did the young punk travelling up to London's underground clubs on a Friday night. 'Julie Burchill said that she was part of the suburban army who used to sleep with underground maps under their pillows,' says one old fan. 'Paul Weller tapped into that quite well because he was the same and he influenced me in that I also moved to London.'

In contrast to the cheap, affordable clothes of His Clothes in the 60s, Weller complained about the money-led exclusivity of Malcolm McLaren and Vivienne Westwood's Chelsea punk mecca, Sex. 'I liked the attitude of punk but I also thought a lot of it was fake. We all saved up about twenty quid to go down to McLaren's shop on the Kings Road – was it called Sex at the time? – and we went in to buy some mohair jumpers and found we couldn't afford anything. We thought, this is bullshit. At the same time what I got from those bands as a punter was good because it inspired me.'

Weller's enthusiasm for high street shops Mr Byrite, C&A and Marks & Spencer certainly provided a humorous contrast with the rhetoric which began to take route at the World's End curve of

Paul Weller

Chelsea's Kings Road. McLaren's price tag on the mohair jumpers probably did Weller a favour. He became a leader in the punk movement without taking a spray-can to his clothes, a safety pin to his skin or even a Sex mohair jumper – at least publicly. The story of Weller's trips to Sex in Chelsea hints at some experimentation with punk fashion, which included the odd painted stripe and safety pin. However, none of these youthful experiments crept into The Jam's on-stage image.

Even The Clash's street-graffiti style only edged into the background of The Jam's photographs, through the band's aerosol-painted lettering and the monochromatic shot of The Clash's territory – Notting Hill's Westway – on the cover of their second album, *This is the Modern World*. That apart, The Jam made no concessions to 'punk' fashion, sticking rigidly to their Mod roots.

John Weller initially had doubts about the band's smart, conservative image: 'The Jam used to dress in black suits and white shirts and black ties, and I thought, Christ, is that gonna work out? Oh well, we'll give it a try, and it just so happened that it did. It made them stand out a bit more as well. So everybody used to come with whatever they had – if they had a black coat or a black suit they wore it, or a white shirt, black tie, and it was great.'

These style gurus were doing it on the cheap too, as they didn't exactly have a big wardrobe of freshly dry-cleaned suits. As Pennie Smith recalls, 'Weller's clothes looked as if they'd stand up at night without him.'

When the singer sang to crowds dressed in bondage trousers and ripped, garish T-shirts, he dismissed punk's rebel chic as arty, glammy and middle class: 'The Roxy myth is a load of bollocks. It was never a working-class street club. It was full of bourgeois idiots dressed up in Nazi gear.'

Weller wasn't the only punk embracing Mod fashion. Subway Sect wore Sta-Prest trousers, Fred Perrys and Gabicci cardigans which the Duffer Of St George shop would later replicate in the 80s. Their bluesy, experimental sound also demonstrated some of the sussed eclecticism of Mod and the band's singer Vic Godard knew his French literature and political theory a lot more deeply than Weller. As a solo artist he moved away from punk into a northern soul and cabaret jazz, pre-dating Weller's appropriation of both by several years.

The Jam's ties and suits were later adopted by more mainstream new wave acts, The Knack and The Cars, the conformist appearance fitting the music a little too snugly. However, no one could doubt the animated passion of The Jam, and Weller's image not only set them apart in '77 – it also didn't date as fast as the off-the-peg punk look. The clothes conveyed a diffident, elitist, yet resolutely working-class dandyism which was at the heart of Weller's Mod philosophy. Nevertheless, their uniformity clashed with the original technicolour individualism of punk. The Jam failed to embrace any of the fetishist, gender reversals of punk's first design pioneers, Malcolm McLaren and Vivienne Westwood, who mixed 50s Teddy boy flash with S&M imagery to create menacing, camp and theatrical styles for both sexes. As Mods they were old-fashioned Carnaby Street rather than futurist *Clockwork Orange* clones. It was accessible and cheap but also unimaginative compared to both The Sex Pistols and The Clash, who were mixing cultures and ideas through their clothes. It was also a fair reflection of their blunt, street-inspired, working-class songs.

In October '76, The Jam first came to the music press's attention when they played an impromptu gig in Soho Market on a Saturday morning in October, sponsored by Rock On Records. John Weller had, as usual, done a little bit of wheeling and dealing to get The Jam plugged into the punk scene and Soho's power supply. 'I got to know this stallholder and asked him if we could use his electricity. We plugged in a three-pin and played off the back of a lorry.' Mark P. of *Sniffin' Glue*, Richard Ingham, who wrote a paragraph about the gig in *Sounds*, and The Clash were down there (The Jam first came across Joe Strummer when he was still playing in the 101ers), but this first press encounter infuriated Weller when he read Caroline Coon's review in the *Melody Maker*, which accused The Jam of being 'retro'. When Weller next appeared on-stage he stuck the review on to a piece of cardboard with his own response, 'How can I be a fucking revivalist when I'm only 18?', handwritten underneath. Mark P.'s review in *Sniffin' Glue* also expressed reservations. 'They're a restricted band 'cos they play sixties R&B, but within the structure they're great. This sixties revival thing's all right for a start but what we need now is more serious bands who have got something to sing about. The Jam are good but they've got a lot to think about (and change) before they break into the London scene with any credibility.'

Meanwhile, the band came face to face with their increasing popularity while they were playing a residency at the Red Cow in Hammersmith in 1977. Weller: 'The time I thought we'd really made it was when we did a four-week residency at this pub . . . The first week there were fifty people there, the second week a hundred people; by the fourth week it was queues around the block. The management came up to our dressing room and chucked in a free crate of lager. I thought, We're taking off.'

Sounds journalist Chas de Whalley, who had been closely associated with the London pub rock scene and admits to wearing flared jeans at the height of punk, was the first journalist to write a full review of The Jam in the weekly music papers. 'I first saw The Jam very early in 1977 at the Nashville after I had spent eighteen months writing first for the *NME* and then for *Sounds* about artists like Nick Lowe, Elvis Costello, Stranglers and Rockpile. I got this call from one of the guys at the Nashville saying, "You've got to come down, the main band has pulled out but the support are playing two sets and we think they're fantastic." I was absolutely blown away because there was the whole sixties image which really honed in on the non-political side of what punk was supposed to be about. Secondly there was lots of melody which a lot of the punk bands didn't have. There was also this energy factor.

'Two or three weeks later I saw them again at the Roxy club in Needle Street. They were uneasy there. They weren't actually very well accepted by the Roxy crowd. The thing I was impressed by was that they came straight to the back with John Weller and started moshing the crowd, effectively creating their own encore.'

Clive Banks, who would later take the role of The Jam's media plugger, recalls, 'The Roxy had piss all over the floor, the stage was six inches high and in the corner, and you could hardly see the band at all. It was completely the wrong sort of venue for The Jam. They were a cleaner looking thing, but also much more vibrant than most of these punk things.

'The Jam played the pub rock venues, the Red Bull, the Nashville. They did tend to single out places which were slightly off the beaten track and out of town so their crowd would have to travel.

It would then become very much their event rather than something they were joining. You want to have your own fans; Weller wanted a smarter audience.'

The band's sets at the Roxy were still filled with soul numbers – Arthur Conley's 'Sweet Soul Music', Lee Dorsey's 'Ride Your Pony' and Martha & The Vandellas' 'Heat Wave' – which was a very different approach to the thrash and burn of their punk rivals. One ex-punk, Gary Blackburn, who now works with Weller as a plugger for his solo material, recalls, 'When I saw The Jam I walked out after three numbers because it wasn't what I thought punk was supposed to be. My experience of punk up until then had been The Damned at the 100 Club, that kind of thing where it was so menacing and frightening. It was nothing about the music really, just a mad atmosphere and all these crazy people who followed them around. The Jam seemed like an ordinary group; too neat in their Mod suits. We were all there in bondage trousers, looking for a fight basically, and The Jam looked a bit squeaky clean.'

Not that Weller wasn't drawn to a touch of aggro. He went at Sid Vicious with a broken bottle after an argument at London's Speakeasy club and cut the young punk before making a quick exit. A year later he went for a man who knocked over his drink at the bar of the Leeds Hilton. It turned out to be the manager of the Australian rugby team. Once again Weller disappeared immediately but Foxton was less fortunate. He ended up being kicked in the ribs by several of the rugby players. The manager pressed charges and Weller was taken to court where he was fined and bound over to keep the peace. He also gave Bruce Foxton a shiner after the latter sat on Weller's Hofner bass, breaking the neck in two. Wiry, macho and with an ugly temper which could erupt almost instantly, this son of an ex-boxer would lash out on the spur of the moment, especially when he'd had a few drinks.

On 15 February 1977, The Jam were signed to Polydor by Chris Parry for a one-single deal with the option of an album: 'In January '77 I was in A&R at Polydor. I'd tried and failed to sign The Clash and Pistols and then Shane [MacGowan] from The Nips said to come down to the Marquee and see this great band, The Jam.' An initial demo session was cancelled when the IRA bombed Oxford Street on 29 January. According to Parry, a few days later, 'We did

Paul Weller

an eight-track tape at Anemone Studios and it convinced me. I went into Polydor and told them, "You've fucked me around on The Pistols and The Clash – don't do it to me again." And they agreed.'

Weller faked indifference to the news of the band's deal, telling a friend he was more excited about finding an old Who badge in the back of a drawer.

Parry had a contract ready by the following week. 'I asked John if he wanted to take it away to check the small print but he said, "No, if you say it's OK, it's OK."

'It was a very lightweight deal with four annual options and a £6000 advance. No one could knock it and, with renegotiations, it remains one of the few in-house deals at Polydor which is successful.'

John Weller: 'Sure, I trusted the guy. But also we were skint. Six quid let alone six thousand would have been handy.'

John Pearson, who would become The Jam's product manager at Polydor, opines: 'I don't know whether they felt shamed by the deal or not but it was a deal. Where do you start? Who gives a fuck about the size of the deal? So what if The Clash got £100,000 and The Pistols £40,000, it's only a loan. Polydor was committed to that band and they broke them. Two or three hits in you can renegotiate and the record company will only be too pleased to renegotiate. An advance is a loan. Someone's got to pay it back. John Weller didn't sell them short.'

Weller had rejected an earlier deal from Chiswick which was even smaller – £500 and the free use of a PA. He wasn't simply taking the first wad of cash on offer. The option for an album was taken up before the band released their first single and the contract was renegotiated for a bigger sum of money, an increase in royalty rate from six per cent to thirteen, and the guarantee of international promotion three months after the initial signing. Although John Weller was learning quickly, there were some foibles in his dealings with Polydor. In particular, none of the Wellers had a bank account or a telephone, so Parry had to put the original advance through his own to 'give them the readies'.

Nigel Sweeney, who worked with Clive Banks as a plugger for The Jam and The Style Council, experienced the same cash-in-hand approach of the Weller set-up. 'They all used to be cash people.

42

They were all paid in cash. John was Mr Cash; I don't remember anyone having a credit card. Paul was absolutely a cash person as well.' The Weller camp's money-in-the-pocket approach was certainly part of their manager's direct, straight-talking philosophy: 'I'm Johnny Blunt. I tell people what I think. Getting into showbiz didn't frighten me at all. We'd spent three and a half years together doing working men's clubs, football clubs and wedding parties, and when we got an offer we weren't exactly unready to accept it. I started picking a lot of brains: take six opinions, apply your own intuition and then hope for the best was my method.

'I knew some of the record business people thought I was a pushover. I saw the faxes that got sent behind my back.

'When I think about it the only chance I took was with Paul's life, not mine, because I never had nothing going for me anyway.

'I'd spent my whole life in debt and hassles and I said to myself there was no way I was going to drop a group of eighteen year olds in the shit. Gradually my ideas developed. The artistic side is left to the band because I haven't got a clue; the politics we talk about between us and the finances are left to me. They know if The Jam has four bob we get a shilling each.'

The Jam instantly reached a Top 40 audience when they released their debut single, 'In The City', on 29 April 1977. It was produced by Chris Parry and one of Polydor's in-house engineers, Vic Coppersmith-Heaven. 'I'd been a producer already back in the late sixties,' says Vic Smith, as he later shortened his name to. 'I'd had a lot of freedom but became less and less impressed by what I'd been doing. That bit of self-criticism was the best thing that ever happened to me. I went back to engineering and worked on all sorts of things from the Stones' "Honky Tonk Woman" and Joe Cocker's "With A Little Help From My Friends" to Black Sabbath and a sixty-piece orchestra ... Chris popped up out of the blue, played me some tapes and took me to see The Jam at the Half Moon and the Red Cow.'

The B-side was a fresh version of 'Takin' My Love', a Weller co-write with Steve Brookes, although the latter wasn't credited and has never received any royalties. 'I've never been bothered about that,' says Brookes. 'It's not an issue. Fifteen pence a copy over twenty years still adds up to almost nothing. The song was shit

Paul Weller

anyway so I'm glad I didn't have my name on it,' he laughs. 'Besides, the version on the record is about four times faster than the one we used to play together and it's got a different riff on it.'

As for Weller, he wasn't completely satisfied with the recorded version of 'In The City' – 'I don't think the recorded version ever caught it; it was always different live' – but it touched a chord among a young following. DJ, journalist and record company A&R man Gary Crowley recalls the impact of that first single. 'My taste in music pre-punk I guess was quite similar to what Paul was into. Not so much Motown music but more The Beatles and sixties culture. I was fourteen and at school in central London. Any school project that we were given I would invariably bring it round to the sixties. I vividly remember seeing them on *Top of the Pops* when they did "In The City" and it just all connected. I thought, This is the band I've been waiting for. They were of a similar age and obviously I could see the sixties thing straight away with the suits and everything. Also their songs, compared to a lot of punk bands at the time, were melodically a lot easier on the ear.

'Then we saw them play at Battersea town hall. It was 75p to get in and Boys were supporting. Six or seven of us went from school in our uniforms, and we got there so early the doors weren't even open. We had cotton wool in our ears because none of us had been to a concert before and we stayed down the front through the whole gig.

'I just remember being impressed by the look of the band; you know, the black suits, which in hindsight probably weren't as sharp as they could have been – maybe they were a bit too straight in the leg for my liking. All the red and white gleaming Rickenbackers which Paul and Bruce played. I was really into the energy and the scissor kicks.'

Weller had absorbed The Clash's political, confrontational edge into new songs, notably 'Bricks & Mortar'. He'd developed a rudimentary knowledge of political theory through a combination of Joe Strummer's call to arms, an enthusiasm for George Orwell and one-sided discussions with his more informed friend Dave Waller, who'd become a Marxist beat poet with an escalating drug habit. 'Some of those early Jam songs were awful – my attempts at being socially aware,' said Weller a few years later. 'But that was just me apeing The Clash after reading interviews with Joe Strummer and Mick Jones, saying people should be writing about what's happening today. I'd never even thought of it before. I was busy re-writing "My Generation".'

Not surprisingly for an eighteen year old, his social conscience was only half-formed and often contradictory. It was built around an idealistic and romantic vision for the country which included a sense of patriotism and nostalgia for the vibrant optimism of the sixties. He wanted to instil some pride and passion in working-class youth. 'They might have been stupid and have naive expectations because, you know, I was a lot younger than the others. Strummer was twenty-six or twenty-seven when all that happened. So although people like him were a lot smarter than me in terms of being mature intellectually, I had a different sort of feeling for it. I thought it was going to lead somewhere else.' Beyond that, he just wanted to be in a great pop band.

However, the unease Weller had felt as a suburban-born outcast in the punk scene was now fixed in his mind. This irritated him above everything, and he shrugged off the punk scene as insular, self serving, cosy and middle class. Not surprisingly for an eighteen year old, he thought in absolute black and white terms about almost everything, and not for the last time in his career revealed an ability to blank out or simply misunderstand the contradictions of his opinions. In the band's first *NME* interview, published on 7 May 1977, he announced that he was a supporter of the royal family: 'The queen's the best diplomat we've got. She works harder than what you or I do for the rest of the country.' He also declared, 'I don't see the point in going against your own country. All this "change the world" thing is becoming a bit too trendy. I realise that we're not going to change anything unless it's on a nationwide scale.' He told a punk fanzine the same week, 'We'll be voting Conservative at the next election.'

Buckler made it worse by grumbling, 'It's the unions who run the country.'

'It made us a lot of enemies which we wanted to, I wanted to, anyway,' says Weller, who defended his statement as a two-fingered retort against the radical chic of The Clash and anarchistic, anti-monarchy sloganeering of the Pistols.

Although the contradictory Weller has circulated a story about hatching the idea of voting Tory with Polydor's press office as a way of 'hyping' the band, he was probably being more honest when he explained: 'I dunno, maybe I meant it at the time. It was prior to The Clash tour and things were getting very cosy, you know – they wanted us to fit into their little niche and be nice and political – left wing and all this shit, right? And we made a lot of enemies on that tour – all the other groups hated us – and I enjoyed that. They were on about complacency and they all fitted into that anyway!

'I think at the time I was completely ignorant, not only politically, just generally. When I think now how thick I was it's quite amazing that I ever got anywhere. All I was really good at was playing guitar . . . I was a stupid person, an ignorant person.'

The Clash sent a sarcastic telegram in response. 'Maggie will be proud of you. See you in South Africa for gun practice.' The Jam's experiences on The Clash's White Riot tour the same month further alienated them, as an argument grew between John Weller and the headliners' manager Bernard Rhodes, who wanted the Woking band to help him subsidise the unsigned acts on the bill – Buzzcocks, Slits and Subway Sect. However, as The Jam had already had to pay for the use of The Clash's PA and 'buy' their way on to the tour, John Weller decided there was too much money coming out of their £100-a-night payments. They left the tour after only a few dates when they alleged that the support band's PA was being tampered with in favour of the headliners at the Rainbow in London. Such petty squabbles left a sour taste in the mouth for those who'd hoped that punk was going to be a vital, unifying and radical force, but Weller argued, 'The sense of unity in punk went the minute the bands all got signed up. Once that happened we were all competing against each other. When it stops being a minority thing, there's immediately competition and it's not always friendly competition.'

The band followed their White Riot debacle with their Jubilee shows: three gigs in Chelsea, Tower Hamlets and Battersea, which were intended to fly in the face of the Pistols' 'God Save The Queen'. They also released their debut album, *In the City*, which peaked at number twenty in the UK charts. Recorded in eleven days in a sixteen-track studio at Stratford Place a few weeks earlier, it had taken 100 hours of recording and mixing and was produced by Chris Parry and Vic Coppersmith-Heaven, who recalls, 'The

46

band were very much into things happening quickly and not getting too involved in the production side . . . In fact, I took more time on the mixing than The Jam had on putting down the tracks.'

Parry recorded some of Weller and Foxton's vocals in the lift down the corridor and it sounds like it too. Vic Smith still enthuses about the record as his 'favourite' Jam album. However, Weller was 'dissatisfied' with the final results. 'It didn't sound particularly authentic either way. I think it was because I was caught between this Mod thing and the punk thing.

'I was trying to copy Townshend. I fucking idolised him – I like the way he moves on-stage and therefore it was quite natural I should want to be like that.'

Even so, Weller was less enthusiastic about The Who's state of disrepair in 1977: 'Instead of Keith Moon going round smashing up cars, use that money instead of wasting it. That's what really pisses me off. This is the old order and they're all wasting their bread. Paul McCartney brings his cats up on a plane and all this sort of shit.'

As for the songs on The Jam's debut album, 'Sounds From The Street' signalled their distance from other punk bands: 'I know I come from Woking/And you say I'm a fraud/But my heart's on the street where it belongs.' He also adds, 'I try to be true . . . at least I'm doing something.' The worst line is a surf-inspired image, 'The USA's got the sea, yeah, but the British kid's got the streets.' Weller was attempting to inject a garage-y, surf feel into some of the material and this works best on 'Away From The Numbers', which turns into a great pop song after its clattering, Who-like intro. ' "Away" was supposed to be a surfing type song,' he says, 'a bit Beach Boys, hence the chorus "ooos" and "ahhhs". It's a very "Mod" song, if you see what I mean. I wrote this over Christmas when I stopped going out and stayed in feeling sorry for myself. It also took me months, about six, to finish it. "Sounds From The Street" was also meant to be a surf song but we didn't have the vocals to bring it off.' The pop art-spirited, surf riffage of the *Batman* theme was an indirect homage to The Who, who had played the tune on their 1966 EP, 'Ready Steady Who'.

There were touches of introspection on 'I Got By In Time' in the line, 'I don't mean to fail anyone/but you know it's something that I do.' The early Stones R&B flash of 'Non-Stop Dancing' expressed

Paul Weller

Weller's view of music as a release, paying tribute to the northern soul all-nighters through references such as, 'The kids are screaming for the James Brown style.' Their cover of Larry Williams' 'Slow Down' (via The Beatles' version of the song) chugged with rockabilly quiffability in a style similar to early Clash, while 'Time For Truth' stuttered with an instantly catchy 60s pop sensibility.

The politically simplistic 'Bricks & Mortar' was less successful, announcing 'while hundreds are homeless/they're constructing a parking place'. Although it wasn't very articulate, it did capture the mix of rage, resentment and confusion which Weller was taking into the band's shows at the time. 'We're not into drugs. We don't need it. We don't need that to go on-stage with.'

Crammed full of hooks and ten-second guitar solos, 'In The City' was a breathlessly energetic pillage of 60s pop and punk attitude, with early hints of Weller's songwriting talent. The music papers were supportive – with reservations. Chas de Whalley argued in *Sounds*, 'Messrs Paul Weller, Rick Buckler and Bruce Foxton certainly operate close to the speed of light . . . yet this album creates grave misgivings . . . Paul Weller's songs are invariably built around great hooks but are too often padded out with pretty dubious non-melodies.'

Barry Cain in the *Record Mirror* recognised the importance of the band to their young audience when he wrote, 'It's been a long time since albums actually reflected pre-twenty delusions and this one does.'

Tony Fletcher, who would later run the band's Jamming! label, was a schoolboy fan: 'All the songs on that first album made sense if you were thirteen. I always got the feeling that older people looked down their noses at The Jam and I can see why because in retrospect most of their records were quite uncouth, unsubtle records but they spoke to the people they were written for and you can't really argue with that.

'On a musical level they didn't let me down, on a personal level they didn't let me down. At my school we were all absolutely mad on them. They were a schoolboys' band. In the early days subtlety wasn't their strong point but they did speak for us. I think they did embody youth.'

Gary Crowley: 'His age was important. His background as well. There were these other bands around like The Stranglers who were these old men in black. The fact that he was only a couple of years older than his fans was very important. It made him more tangible.

'He was always uncomfortable with the idea of being a spokesperson of the generation. But I suppose he was somebody who played a very important role in my life and a lot of other people's lives as well. There were people like Jimmy Pursey and Bob Geldof who were always very ready to take that mantle. Paul was more reluctant and maybe that's what was appealing. That mystique.'

Paul Weller: 'People like Geldof, setting themselves up for the kids, make me spew.'

John Weller shared his son's enthusiasm, drive and empathy with youth. 'I've always loved the kids. I used to run football teams, thirty of us on the top of a bus going off to matches. I've spent that much time with youngsters that when I meet anyone in their forties I look on them as old farts. Now when normally my kids might have gone away I'm seeing Paul whenever I want to and working with him. It's great.'

This connection with youth inspired a sudden rush of Jam fanzines over the next few months. Gary Crowley: 'At my school Dave Dorrell [manager of Bush, journalist and DJ] turned our school magazine into a punk magazine. That seemed to be the order of the day really. Either you had a band or you had a fanzine. I couldn't be bothered to learn an instrument. We had this phonebox outside the school which became my office at lunchtime which I would commandeer for that hour and ring up record companies and blag records. I remember reading this fact file thing on The Jam in the *Melody Maker* and there was a number on it and I rang it and Paul answered. I've been told I speak quite quickly anyway but this is going back years so I must have been almost unintelligible then. Anyway, we'd named our fanzine *The Modern World*, so he said, "Well, look, why don't you come and see me at Polydor tomorrow?" I took a friend who brought a camera. He was deemed to be the photographer and we spent a couple of hours with him.'

Tony Fletcher: 'I started a fanzine after the copy of *Sounds* came out which had Mark Perry's quote about anyone can do it. I did one with a heavy metal fan at school which was highly embarrassing for a few issues, but then we were both thirteen years old. He'd write about Rush, I'd write about The Jam.

Paul Weller

'With The Jam everybody knew that the fan club address was the Weller address, so I wrote to him. Within a week I had a letter back from Paul which was absolutely astounding and he said, "Yeah, come up to the studio and we'll do the interview next week." So I went up and met him and he was very good to me as a little kid. It's a very odd position to be in when you're fourteen years old and you meet your heroes and they're actually very friendly to you. I guess we became penpals. I'd send Paul a new copy of the fanzine and he'd send me back an autographed copy of their album. So there were these very kind touches. I did sort of feel what a cool big brother he would be to have but there were certain levels of protection. In all the years I knew him I never actually had his home phone number.'

The Jam set off on their first full tour on 4 June 1977. They originally had a stamina-sapping 42 dates booked. By mid July they'd played 36 times and they cancelled the rest due to exhaustion. John Weller left scams and media games to other managers, but he was over-compensating by working the band too hard in the area he could understand – the face-to-face promotional power of live shows. Chas de Whalley believes the schedule was not only insane, it was premature: 'They did a nationwide club tour before the nation was ready for them and before they were ready to play it. Their sound used to be a panic more than anything else. They couldn't actually hear themselves, so it was a bit of a mess to be honest.'

Chris Parry: 'It sounded good but the level on-stage was so phenomenally loud I couldn't understand how they could enjoy it.

'TV people weren't prepared to have that much noise,' he adds, which explains why the band started blowing out some television appearances at this point. 'The soundchecks were unnecessarily pressured because everyone was so loud they were all saying, "Turn this up" and "I can't hear that!" ' recalls Parry. 'It spun off on the support bands. In my opinion they didn't get a fair shake. The Jam weren't trying to screw anyone up but they took so long to set up, the other bands got very limited facilities. It's all very well to be Jam, Jam, Jam but you owe something to the industry that feeds you.'

John Weller also admits, 'At first our soundchecks were dynamite fucking murder because our equipment was no good.' In

Foxton and Buckler's book, *The Jam*, the bassist accuses the band's manager of wasting £1500 of the band's small advance on a useless PA system.

The tinderbox situation of the band and John Weller stuck together in a red Ford Cortina, driving all over England, inevitably sparked into arguments and moody silences. John Weller was still learning the ropes and didn't feel secure as a manager, leading to several flashpoints between the four. 'The worst thing I went through was feeling left out – no, "inadequate" is the word – when we were discussing longer term plans ... The only side of the business I really like is being on the road where things are happening. The rest is tinsel to me.'

Chas de Whalley: 'There were people involved in management who felt John Weller was making big mistakes already at that early point in their career. And I thought they were being brought on too quickly. But there again perhaps by following your own nose and not knowing how everybody else does things you can carve through a lot quicker. My reading of it is that Paul was actually in charge. John was the guy you had to go to to get decisions and approvals but ultimately what Paul says goes. Another concern early in their career was that Paul wasn't being ordered around by his management as much as Elvis Costello was by Jake Rivera, for instance.'

On the inside, Chris Parry sometimes clashed with John over his hands-on, basic, straightforward approach which didn't always pay attention to the 'tinsel' of media coverage for the new band: 'I was eternally frustrated at the way they operated. On the road John would always be in the launderette cleaning the suits when the band were supposed to be doing interviews.' Parry had the option of taking up a more managerial position with the band. 'I'd worked pretty hard on the band for six months and I even had a management contract with them . . . though I never took it up.' However, the tense, overworked atmosphere around the band was already testing some of his patience and enthusiasm. 'Fancy owning fifteen per cent of The Jam! But it was starting to get too hot, too much tension. I wasn't enjoying it. It's not that I didn't like them as people. I was just piggy in the middle.'

Although The Jam took on a schedule which bordered on the self-destructive, their fans certainly came out winners as the band burnt through their energy reserves in sweaty, raw shows, which inspired many of those who saw them. This was a major factor in establishing the band's following for the next few years. John Weller was also building up a cornerstone of solid, loyal roadies and crew members which would give the band stability and maintain a sense of jobbing normality throughout Weller's career. 'We've always surrounded ourselves with steady people. Even the roadies stay with us for ages. But then I've threatened them with getting their arms broken if they leave!'

Over the next few years John Weller began to build this extended family around a giant, bearded and intimidating-looking man, Kenny Wheeler, who originally looked after the merchandise when John's daughter Nikki and wife Ann started getting hassled by skinheads. He's been an essential figure in the Weller camp ever since.

Nigel Sweeney: 'Kenny protects him like crazy. Kenny's life has been Paul Weller. He's probably around Paul more than his wife and kids at certain times. They've had a fantastic life, all of them. Kenny is an incredibly loyal person towards the Wellers and Paul's stuck by him as well because I'm sure there have been times when Paul wasn't touring and things weren't going that well where they might have broken up the relationship.'

In fact, the Wellers have held on to their roadies for years. In 1995, Lisa Verrico encountered some of the same tub-bellied hirsute characters that had shifted gear with The Jam: 'I think because Paul's dad is his manager and the crew are old and they were all crew for sixties bands who he was really into, it's kept him really down to earth. His crew are really bizarre.'

By the end of the 1977 tour The Jam had got rid of the Union Jack backdrop due to the rise of the National Front violence and the ugly jingoism of the Jubilee year. Weller said he just liked the colours, although naturally he was once again drawing on the heritage of The Who and their use of the red, white and blue in the 60s.

The band then drew fresh criticism for playing a sell-out show at the cavernous Hammersmith Odeon in London which lacked the intimacy of their other dates. John Weller took the decision because he felt that punk had to break out of the clubs. 'The first Odeon gig, nobody wanted to do that but it worked. That was the first big one that we did. Had we not done that we would have still been fucking playing in the Red Cows of this world. Simple as that.'

They played at the same venue again at Christmas. Tony Fletcher: 'The Hammersmith thing in retrospect was dreadful and everything that punk shouldn't have been. A gig at the Marquee a few months later [part of February '78's London Blitz tour] was everything I ever wanted, everything I'd waited fourteen years for.'

On 8 July 1977 the band released a new single, 'All Around The World', which set out Weller's rejection of The Sex Pistols' nihilism: 'What's the point in saying destroy? We want a new life for everyone.' They played the song on Marc Bolan's TV show, despite Weller's hatred of 70s glam. At the time Bolan was more credible than he had been for years as many of the punk bands acknowledged him as an influence. The Jam, however, had nothing in common with the gender-playing fashion streak in punk which shared an obvious affinity with T-Rex. Nevertheless, Bolan's early band, John's Children, were a cult Mod act and as fifteen-year-old Marc Feld from Stamford Hill, he was the first Mod to be interviewed by the English press, namely *Town* magazine. His Mod sympathies failed to help register The Jam in his short-term memory. He had to glance at The Jam's badges to remind himself of the name of this new band on his show.

In August The Jam reconvened in a country studio and attempted to rehearse new material. They usually ended up down the pub. They eventually recorded at Island's Notting Hill studio where Weller, in the flush of a new relationship with a girl called Gill who he'd met in Dunstable during the band's first full UK tour, kept disappearing.

Vic Coppersmith-Heaven, who was once again sharing production duties with Chris Parry, recalls the tension at the London sessions. 'Paul was constantly fifteen feet in the air. I remember looking up from the desk in a sudden silence to see a Rickenbacker flying across the studio. It was totally wrecked.'

Parry was exasperated by The Jam singer's pig-headedness: 'Paul's insistence on using Rickenbackers,' he sighs. 'They won't stay in tune! We must have wasted two or three days just tuning.'

The mood darkened further over the next few weeks. He'd fallen heavily for his new girlfriend Gill and he was unhappy about spending time away from her as the band packed for their first American shows in October. To make matters worse, the young frontman was terrified of flying and got drunk on the plane, arriving with nerves shot to pieces and a bad hangover. The vibe around the band remained frosty and resentful as they ploughed through two sets a night in 'crappy clubs', totalling sixteen American shows in their twelve days in the country. Weller was also under pressure to write new songs for a quick follow-up to their debut album, and spare moments were further eaten up.

Problems with the PA led to the cancellation of their gig at San Francisco's Old Wardoff, a decision which infuriated Parry. 'They couldn't get the rigs to take that volume. When it happened in San Francisco John said they wouldn't do the show. That killed me, I couldn't take that attitude.'

The Jam played several nights at the Whisky-A-Go-Go in Los Angeles, winding Weller up further as it was a place he particularly hated. They went down better during an eventful gig at New York's punk club CBGB's, where Weller encouraged the audience to trash the place and announced that the band were splitting up.

Chris Parry describes the tour as 'a nightmare'. Weller was homesick all the time he was out there, and Joe Strummer claims that he took a postcard of Woking with him to stare at on the tour bus. 'Well, that's almost right,' said Weller. 'From the first moment I was disappointed. The only thing I like about it is that the clothes are really cheap.' Weller's cynicism towards America was typical of Britain's island mentality, but it was strange, given the influence of Detroit's Motown sound and the southern Stax style on him as an adolescent. The Americanisation of Britain in the 1950s was also at the root of Mod's sharp, cool confidence, as Richard Barnes explains in his *Mods!* bible: 'Local family grocers were being replaced by supermarkets. "Frothy" coffee bars and Wimpy bars appeared. Twenty-four-hour launderettes took over from laundries, bagwash and municipal wash-houses. It was all part of an Americanisation that was taking place. Modernists identified with all these new "convenient" innovations. They thought England still too fuddy-duddy and conservative. They were the generation of the soft sell. The advertising industry had been Americanised too since the introduction of commercial television.'

Weller's criticisms of the American music industry were well founded but it took a particularly robust, blinkered attitude in a nineteen year old to blot out any curiosity towards a culture which had been integral in forming his philosophy and musical tastes.

This infuriating ability to deny what is in front of his nose has remained with Weller through most of his career, much to the amusement and irritation of his critics.

No one was too sure about what The Jam actually achieved through their first American experience. They were playing to an older audience in the States, undermining Weller's determination to reach out to people close to his own age. At nineteen he was himself below the legal drinking age and there were restrictive licensing laws which prevented a lot of younger music fans from going to the gigs at all. Those people who did see The Jam were mostly media and fans of the New York underground scene from the mid seventies (Patti Smith, New York Dolls) and earlier, stretching back to the eras of Iggy Pop and Lou Reed. 'People in CBGB's were like a throwback from an era past,' complained Buckler. There was also confusion stirred up over Weller's right wing and anti-punk comments earlier in the year. The American branch of Polydor promoted The Jam as the new English band you could take home and introduce to your mother as an attempt to disassociate them from the violence of the English scene. They were pro-monarchy, played gigs supporting the queen – always a good angle for the American market – had made anti-punk statements in the media, 'voted' Conservative and were a more melodic alternative to their homegrown rivals. TV shows were told it was OK to put them on because they wouldn't try to beat anyone up or swear at the interviewer. Their debut album was also sold with a sticker warning DJs that ' "Art School" and "Time For Truth" contain language that segments of your audience might find offensive.'

Of course, when the real thing arrived, Paul Weller's surly refusal to glad-hand either the record company or the media, his attempt to start a riot at CBGB's, the abrasive power of the band's live shows and willingness to tell the press conferences to 'fuck off' while he did a couple of fanzine interviews, inspired some – college radio and alternative magazines like *Trouser Press* – and intimidated others. He was candid about his distrust of politics which contrasted with The Clash's rebel rousing leftism. 'We've got absolutely nothing to do with any political party,' he told *Rolling Stone*. 'We don't lean left or right; couldn't give a fuck about any of it. It's just that I don't like using the word "politics" because in Britain it's a really trendy word. We don't believe in anarchy. It's fairly obvious it doesn't work. It's a noble idea but it's really like suppressing human emotions.'

He made no attempt to disguise the fact that he didn't like Americans, didn't want to be there and had no commercial ambition – at least as far as the States was concerned. 'Britain's very creative. There's nowhere that can match Britain artistically – in all arts,' he declared with patriotic arrogance.

When Weller returned he moved into a flat in Baker Street, London, with the small, dark-haired Gill Price. Although arguments constantly ignited the relationship, they settled down into domesticity which gave Weller a new independence from his parents – at least in his home life. He grounded himself in everyday chores and withdrew from the music industry. 'We share everything because my girlfriend just wouldn't do it on her own,' he later said of the relationship. 'When I hear about women "accepting" their roles – they go home and cook food for their husbands – it makes me sick. Washing socks for their men, other quaint little clichés – it makes me puke. I think it's an insult to both sexes. And I couldn't bear anyone doing those things for me anyway. I can do most things – I can cook, I can iron. I've got a washing machine which helps. I'd hate to be reliant on someone else in that sense.'

As Gill and Paul cut themselves off by spending most of their time at home watching TV, a sense of distance between the singer and his Woking friends grew almost overnight. 'I never went out with other people,' said Weller. 'I never mixed. I never spoke to other people at all, even within the band.'

Foxton confirms that the bond between the trio was also stretched by this change of circumstances: 'I think out of the three of us I was probably closer to Paul ... but then once he met Gill it started to drift apart for obvious reasons.'

After an exhausting and tense few months, Weller had started losing interest in The Jam. 'I think meeting Gill ... fucked me up quite a lot. It really tore me between carrying on or not.'

Their next single, 'The Modern World', came out on 21 October 1977 with the line 'I don't give two fucks about your review' which was included on the forthcoming album version, replaced by 'damn' for the radio version. This concession showed their determination – indicated earlier by their Hammersmith Odeon gigs – to be a forward-looking pop group, rather than stand on the eroding punk principles. However, the song itself was full of brash, anti-retro fighting talk from Weller as he drew inspiration from the arrogance of his adolescence, declaring, 'Even at school I felt quite sure/that one day I would be on top/And look down upon the map/of teachers who said I'd be nothing.'

The album, *This is the Modern World*, came out the following month (only six months after their debut), stalling at 22. Weller wore a Who badge on the cover and the band were framed by the tower blocks of London's Westway – The Clash's stomping ground. Tension betwen their sixties influences and punk sensibility were still unresolved by *This is the Modern World*.

Paul Weller had a vague concept behind the album, a half-formed, tentative idea which centred around an 'authority voice' culled straight out of George Orwell, whose *1984* establishment victim, Winston Smith, gets a namecheck on the album. The central track to this half-hearted, Orwellian nightmare was 'Standards' (a musical variant on 'I Can't Explain'), which replicated the authorities' recent response to The Sex Pistols in the lines: 'We'll outlaw your voices, do anything we want/We've nothing to fear from the nation.' 'Here Comes The Weekend' was also intended to express the establishment's position when Weller sang, 'Don't hang around and be foolish/Do something constructive with your weekend.' However, a lot of critics misinterpreted the song as an attempt to give some clumsy advice to the kids. 'The Combine' (in *One Flew Over the Cuckoo's Nest* one of the characters uses the expression 'the combine' to describe the system) dealt with the pressure to conform in the crowd, a fresh twist to the urgent need for escape portrayed in 'Away From The Numbers'. However, the song's ugly, awkward title summed up the album's rushed, poorly edited lyrical ideas. 'In The Street Today', which was a collaborative lyric effort between Weller and Dave Waller, descended into parodic punk clichés summed up by the statement: 'The kids want some action and who can fucking blame them?'

Musically too, *The Modern World* often sounded confused, scratchy, one dimensional and above all, lumpy. In particular, Foxton's 'London Traffic' and 'Don't Tell Them You're Sane' were lifeless, but Weller doesn't deserve much credit either for the tracks 'London Girl', 'In The Street Today', 'The Combine' and 'Standards'. On these songs the hoarse vocals and slashing Rickenbacker riffs lacked any of the trashy, garage appeal of The Jam's flawed but energetic debut.

Nevertheless, *This is the Modern World* doesn't deserve to be completely dismissed. There were some good songs which matched the best moments on their debut album, notably the wide-eyed optimistic mood of 'Life From A Window', the Gill-inspired ballad 'I Need You (For Someone)' and the gentle, subtle harmonies of 'Tonight At Noon', which was influenced by poet Adrian Henri, a member of the Liverpool poetry group, which also included Roger McGough. They also threw in a lively, staccato version of Wilson Pickett's 'In The Midnight Hour'.

In spite of its flaws, *This is the Modern World* still has its admirers. Tony Fletcher: 'I thought the second album was brilliant. You've got to knock the Bruce tracks off but 'I Need You (For Someone)' was one of Weller's best ever love songs. I had that song played at my wedding. There's a cult of Jam fans – you bump into them in different parts of the world – a cult of solidarity when you find someone else who loves *This is the Modern World*. You find yourself sitting down and singing the whole album. The tower block front cover was the worst cliché but the inner sleeve had some great drawings which really helped to capture the teenage angst of that album.'

Melody Maker's Chris Brazier was the most accurate in his summary: 'Paul Weller should mature into one of our best song-writers, provided he keeps his mind open . . . this album only hints at what The Jam are capable of.'

This is the Modern World soon slipped out of the charts, leaving the band stranded at the end of '77 with a smaller audience and a lack of direction. The problem for Weller was that the punk scene was dying. Inspired by the energy of the London scene, Weller had rapidly transformed The Jam from slightly old-fashioned, Woking-based loners into a band that really mattered to their fans. However, the colourless insecurity of their second album revealed that he didn't know where to take them next. He felt there was no fresh music to draw inspiration from, or for that matter, vent his fury against: 'The Clash became just like any other rock band. All those pictures of them in biker jackets with their hands in their pockets, like we might be holding a gun or a fucking water pistol. And the Pistols' records just got worse and worse; all that multi-layered guitar. Years later they sound like real mainstream rock, don't they? It's only the vocals that make it sound like something else.'

He only respected Joe Strummer for his 'professionalism . . . only 'cause he's been playing for years and he's a real pro. That's what I like about him. Same as me. I've been playing for like six years, so I'm obviously a pro, ain't I? Quite obviously.'

After feeling embarrassed at the start of the year about the band's ability to play, Weller was now retreating into the rhetoric of a world-weary, jobbing, professional musician. Over the next year his knee-jerk reaction to the new, forward-looking bands Magazine and the American new wavers, Devo – 'I think it's elitist music dealing with something the average kid knows nothing about anyway. I had to go to look "devolution" up in the dictionary' – was to dismiss them as arty and distant. By doing this he left himself, for the moment at least, in a dead end which was no more musically adventurous than lesser punk bands such as The Adverts, 999, Chelsea et al.

March 1978 proved to be another low point as the band played to hostile audiences as a support band for the Blue Oyster Cult in 20,000 seat stadiums, another early managerial mistake which further entrenched Weller's attitudes towards America. The Stateside critics were as luke warm about *This is the Modern World* as their English counterparts. *Rolling Stone* declared, 'Paul Weller no longer has the single-minded ferocity punk rock requires, but he has yet to learn how to play anything else – which leaves him somewhat stranded for the moment, like Quadrophenia's Jimmy on that forsaken rock.'

At the same time the band released their worst single, the Foxton-penned 'News Of The World'. It was a step backward and only reached 27 in the UK charts. If the lyrics of the A-side were embarrassingly weak, a quick listen to Weller's disastrous 'Aunties & Uncles' on the flipside confirmed that he was struggling to come up with fresh ideas. However, the echoing slogans, 'Punk rock! Power pop!' caught the mood of the times. The Jam were credited with starting a new movement of 'power pop' bands, which unfortunately summed up acts who took new wave to an earnest, unimaginative nadir.

Paul Weller

Things were rapidly going from bad to worse. When Chris Parry heard their next sessions, he told the band their songs were 'shit' and they scrapped them. Weller: 'We were at the demo stage. Only "Billy Hunt" and " 'A' Bomb" were reshaped and used and we just took the best parts of the other stuff, a few riffs and bits and pieces.'

This is confirmed by Dennis Munday, who started working with the band as their A&R man at this point. 'There was never a lost third album. There were just lots of half ideas.'

Some of these musical morsels included Bruce Foxton's song 'The Night', which was later released as the B-side to 'Down In The Tube Station' and 'I Want To Paint', described by Weller as 'more of a poem than a song'. The title came from another poem by Adrian Henri. Weller's relationship with Gill proved the inspiration for a lot of the new material. Most of these 'silly love songs', as he later described them, were scrapped, although 'English Rose' (which he'd written when he was away in America) was salvaged, albeit uncredited, for their next album.

Although Weller accepted Parry was right in rejecting the new songs, relations between the band and the record company were strained. 'I walked into a difficult situation,' says Munday, who had been working on Polydor's jazz roster until that point. 'There was this huge row going on where they delivered tracks which were rejected and it took me a long time to build up a relationship with Paul. When I first started working with them I was known as the record company's spy. There was a lot of suspicion and some paranoia. There was definitely a split between the group and the company at that point.'

Dennis Munday adopted a supportive, easy-going approach to his new charge, which gradually earned the band's trust: 'I very rarely go over the top. My attitude was if you don't have to make a decision then why make a decision? So I would tend to not make any decisions and take a very passive view of everything – when listening to demos.

'He was never one to ask for things that cost a lot of money. He always delivered his records on time. He's very on the case, much more than a lot of artists I've worked with.'

Weller commented in 1978: 'The British branch of Polydor are really nice to us now but as I remember, nobody spoke to us for two years. And I've got a long memory. I don't forget things like that. It's something young bands should remember too. They're constantly trying to pump your ego all the time so you've got to avoid that. There may be one or two of them who feel for you but that's about it.'

John Pearson, who was working as a rep for Polydor in the early Jam days, viewed the Jam/Polydor relationship a little differently. 'Paul was always "Fuck the record company this, fuck the record company that." We loved the band and were working really hard for them. We couldn't understand why they had that attitude. But Paul was very young. He saw everything in black and white in those days.'

Clive Banks also encountered Weller's sense of frustration with the record business, which the young artist didn't believe was giving him the credit, support or money he deserved. 'I've never heard Paul talk about money but I think him and his dad would talk about it between them and be very, very focused on it,' he argues, 'much more than he would admit to. He's an angry bloke on these things. I think he always felt that people weren't giving him enough and he was doing a load. You know, "I'm doing the gigs, I'm doing the record, you fuckers are doing nothing. What are they doing in France? Why aren't they selling my records? I'll go over there when they're selling my records." Well, it's all pretty naive really. Everything an artist does in the UK they have to do in every territory in the world. There is no difference. There is no universal radio. You need to get into those territories and break the barriers down.'

The summer of '78 proved to be a testing time for the band. According to Foxton, 'We were near to committing suicide then.' They were burnt out, short on ideas and uncertain about whether they had a future after punk.

A half-drunk Bruce Foxton gabbled to a journalist, 'I'd really like to open up a guest house or a small hotel. I've seen all these people open one up one year with just four or five rooms, the next year it's seven or eight, then the next year they're having an extension built. You can't go wrong . . . when it all falls through – which could be tomorrow, who knows – that's what I think I'll do.'

Weller talked about opening up a value-for-money Mod clothes shop, as if he was also ready to leave The Jam for a quieter life.

Meanwhile, for the first time in his life, he had to deal with a sizeable amount of money when the royalties on the band's debut album arrived at his accountant's office. For a twenty year old who didn't even have a cheque book, it was a new pressure and he was completely unprepared. 'We had a meeting with our accountants and lawyers and I said I really wanted to give my cheque away,' he revealed in *Beat Concerto*. 'I didn't even want it in my possession. The publisher would write it out and I'd just hand it over, give it to fucking charity or something. They said, "Well even if you do that you've still got to pay tax", so I thought I'd fucking keep it then.'

Eugene Manzi: 'A lot of working-class people who come from ordinary backgrounds and then make a lot of money do feel guilty about it – I certainly would. He shouldn't do because he's not your normal flash geezer; anybody can dress like him. He buys second-hand records and clothes. It's got nothing to do with money, it's got to do with soul really.'

Paul went back to Woking to live with his parents for a while because he and Gill had been forced to move out of their flat, and he started to write new songs. On 11 August The Jam released a Kinks cover, 'David Watts' (taken from 1967's *Something Else From The Kinks*), backed by ' "A" Bomb In Wardour Street'. 'We had a David Watts at my school . . . in fact he was called Mark Watts. He was really infuriating. While I was out smoking in the toilets or bunking off, he would sweep the field both academically and on the sports field. Last time I heard he was a copper.'

They chose the single, which peaked at 25, after a word of encouragement from producer Mickie Most, who was consulted by John Weller and Chris Parry after the band appeared on his TV show, *Revolver*.

' "A" Bomb In Wardour Street' was also impressive: 'It was a feeling I got when I went down the Vortex one night,' stated Weller. 'It was very heavy and everyone was there for the violence, kicking each other in. I just thought how the scene had changed. They used to be there for a purpose – to see new bands and talk about new things.'

Tony Fletcher: 'It was such a big thing for a band like The Jam to have a hit single. It was kind of like a victory for the kids. Now that you get Menswear going straight into the top ten it's like, well, what were we getting worked up about? But in the years straight after punk there was no way that battle was automatically won. It was a steady hammering at the doors. The Jam were lucky to clear 150,000 albums at their peak.'

Meanwhile Chris Parry was dropped from the sessions for the new album which were taking place at Mickie Most's RAK studios in St John's Wood, leaving Vic Coppersmith-Heaven to produce the album. 'In the first stages of *All Mod Cons* Chris, who was heavily involved in the administrative side with Polydor, was popping in and out of the sessions, trying to do two jobs really. He'd appear after we'd been working for a while and tell us we should be doing things differently. It came to a point where I said quite openly that it had to be either Chris or myself.'

Parry: 'John Weller came into the office and said, "Have you fallen out with Vic Smith? I think you'd better get down to the studio because they're all saying they don't want you to produce any more." Driving over I thought it all out. Fiction and The Cure were coming up . . . When I got to RAK I asked each of them individually whether they wanted me to go. Rick and Bruce said yes. Paul said he liked what I'd done but as Vic controlled the desk he agreed with the others that I wasn't essential. So I went down the pub with Vic and did a deal for the work I'd already done on *All Mod Cons* and that was the end of it.'

Dennis Munday: 'At that stage it was also put to me that we should get rid of Vic because he didn't tell the record company what was going on. Chris only did four or five tracks on *All Mod Cons* and then there was a split up between The Jam and him. It was quite a triangle. It was put to me that it was in my interests to get rid of Vic. Martin Rushent was openly talked about. I knew Martin and he was completely the wrong personality. They would have been at each other's throats.'

On 6 October they followed up the success of 'David Watts' in the strongest way possible, with 'Down In The Tube Station At Midnight'. Weller described the song as a short TV play in a three-minute pop song: 'A geezer on his way back from work and he's going home with his take-away meal and he gets beaten up by some thugs on the platform. He assesses his life as it flashes across his eyes and his last thought is that the take-away curry is getting cold on the floor.' Not that he wanted to be seen as a victim: 'I'll write a song like "Tube Station" and the next minute I'll get in a fight.'

Paul Weller

Weller himself wasn't sure about the song when he first wrote it. According to Parry: 'I don't think Paul's always right in his decisions about scrapping songs. He's very impatient in the studio, The Jam being so much a live band. For instance, at one stage he wanted to dump "Down In The Tube Station At Midnight". It wasn't working and he said it was rubbish. But when I read the lyrics I was totally knocked out and told him he had to be joking.'

Vic spent fifteen hours mixing it. They recorded the B-side, 'So Sad About Us', as a tribute to Keith Moon who had just died. He was also featured on the back sleeve.

All Mod Cons was released the same month and instantly signalled that The Jam had found their own voice. The critics were almost unanimous in their praise, with Philip Hall in the *Record Mirror* enthusing, 'Forget the crash, bang, wallop revivalist style of their early days. The Jam have come of age.' Charles Shaar Murray wrote in the *NME*, 'It's not only several light years ahead of anything they've ever done before but also . . . one of the handful of truly essential rock albums over the last few years.'

Now twenty, Weller was moving into Ray Davies-inspired song-writing, detailing his observations about working-class life rather than trying to write rallying calls to the British youth. 'To me, teen anthems belong to teenagers and they end at twenty years old.' He was trying to pass this mantle on to a younger generation. 'What I'd really like to see is fourteen-year-old groups coming out on *Top of the Pops* playing great music, serious music.'

The catchy 'Billy Hunt', which had been talked about as the album's first single, was shot full of comic book imagery and a sense of humour ('I'll spy like James Bond and die like King Kong'). Like a lot of The Jam's best work it describes one of life's misfits who fantasises about having his revenge on people who put him down – the bullies, teachers, the foreman at work: 'No one pushes Billy Hunt around/Well, they do, but not for long,' sings Weller, with the worm-turning fantasist dreaming of being an unstoppable force. ' 'Cause when I get fit and grow bionic arms/The whole world's gonna wish it weren't born.'

Weller described the character in the song as 'the type of person who wishes he was David Watts but is, in fact, Billy Hunt. There's a bit of him in everyone really. He's the person who's always put down and can only take so much before he breaks out. He dreams of being Superman and has Clark Kent posters on his wall or Farrah Fawcett-Majors. There's a bit of me in it . . . I have David Soul instead!'

The songwriter summed up the more caustic 'Mr Clean' as 'about a certain type of person . . . I was in a hotel with my girlfriend and he was just like one of those lecherous businessmen who have weekends away from their darling wives and I thought, I wonder if your wife knows you're out doing this . . .

'It's just the straight image, the pin-stripe suits and moral attitude. I just think they should be more honest. They're the sort of people who kick their televisions after seeing The Sex Pistols.'

Although Weller was guilty of class stereotyping, musically 'Mr Clean's restrained, softly sung approach was more stinging than the vein-bulging, two-minute dramas of their previous albums. Vic Coppersmith-Heaven's slow, painstaking work in the studio created a simple, clean sound which Weller filled in with more sophisticated arrangements and ideas, such as the imaginative guitar fade-out of 'In The Crowd'. This track explored the pressure of following the pack expressed in 'The Combine' (from *This is the Modern World*) and exaggerated it into a paranoid vision which echoed the work of George Orwell and Aldous Huxley's *Brave New World*: 'When I'm in the crowd, I can't remember my name/and my only link is pots of Wall's ice cream/When I'm in the crowd, I don't see anything.' Weller: 'It's the feeling that I used to get when I used to go shopping. You're in a supermarket with a trolley and you walk around with that synthetic music in the background – suddenly you become dehumanised, like a robot.' There was also a flashback to the individualism of 'Away From The Numbers', which Weller sings at the end of the song.

'English Rose', with its lapping wave sound effects and gently picked acoustics, was overtly romantic. 'Fly' also opened with a lilting, unplugged first verse and then built up into a dreamily introspective song, achieved with a subtlety that went far beyond the anthemic ambitions of *In the City* and *This is the Modern World*. On 'The Place I Love' Weller pulled away from the surface sociability of the music business, retreating into more solitary images of overgrown gardens, moss and walls, which obviously referred to his home town.

'To Be Someone (Didn't We Have A Nice Time)' focused this

Paul Weller

disgust with fame more directly, with Weller lashing out at the shallow, glamour-obsessed side of pop stardom: 'Getting drugged up with my trendy friends/They really dig me and I dig them/And the bread I spend is like my fame/It's quickly diminished.'

After the success of 'David Watts' and 'Down In The Tube Station At Midnight', Weller's position as a figurehead and spokesperson was elevated above that of just another band on the punk soapbox. He was now a fully fledged hero to his fans. 'I liked it at first,' he confessed, 'because that was part of the fantasy when I was a kid, to be whatever the Beatles were. But it was frightening, the hysteria when The Jam were at their peak ... The Jam would try and stay behind after gigs to meet people and break down this barrier but it never worked that way. People still see you differently. I'd see people come into the dressing rooms, shaking.'

Bruce Foxton didn't contribute any songs to the new album. 'Why I don't have any songs on the album is because none of the ones I wrote were good enough,' he owned up. 'I just carry on writing and trying to keep up to a high standard. Obviously the third album was very important for us and all the tracks had to be really good. So I just keep writing until I come up with something that everyone is really pleased with.'

They promoted the album with The Apocalypse Tour, closing each set with a crash of thunder and Weller's scream of 'apocalypse' at the end of ' "A" Bomb In Wardour Street'. It was one of The Jam's most effective gimmicks and showed a willingness to experiment a little more with the live format. The pent-up energy of their live shows had always overcome their unimaginative presentations but Weller knew he had to keep adding new variants to keep them from becoming stale.

In March '79, The Jam returned with a new single, 'Strange Town', which twisted around a Motown beat with an alert, rhythmic guitar line. They spent four or five thousand pounds on it on two versions which Vic Smith and the group still weren't very happy with. They finally spent another two days mixing it. The record company saw this as a chance to remove Smith but Weller was having none of it and he gave the producer his full support. Polydor backed down.

Vic Coppersmith-Heaven: 'Paul was fantastic. I couldn't have had a better friend. He stood by me totally and although I don't think Polydor understood at all, they had to go along with him.'

The new single dealt with the alienation created by the British class system but thankfully it took an off-beat angle on a serious issue, giving it a depth, wit and weirdness that The Jam's early material lacked. Paul Weller: ' "Strange Town" is a free form poem and it combines a lot of ideas. Like there's the UFO theme – "I'm really a spaceman from those UFOs" – and there's lines like "You're betrayed by your accent and manners". I used to think class war was a myth but you do find the way you talk and the way you are marks you out.' The B-side was even better. 'The Butterfly Collector' dealt with the egotism of the music industry and its groupies and hangers-on. Some of the lines were written about Weller's own encounter with punk groupie, Sue Catwoman – a cartoonish fetishist who used to hang out with The Sex Pistols. It was a twisted but lovely track which was covered in a somewhat bizarre fashion in '95 by Garbage. The band's singer, Shirley Manson, recalls: 'I wanted us to do it because I fell in love to that song.'

In April 1979 The Jam went on another American tour. By now they had a big following in the cosmopolitan cities, Los Angeles and New York. DJ Mark Simone from New York's Radio WPIX held a competition on air for 50 tickets for a Jam gig in the city. He announced that he would stand at a crossroads in Manhattan and the first 50 people who recognised him would get a free ticket. Hundreds of fans turned up and the police had to whisk him away in a squad car. The fans actually followed them through the traffic as far as the police station where they were eventually dispersed.

Despite this, Weller still felt frustrated and unhappy in the States, where they'd gained a brattish, sulky reputation. Even in New York Weller announced on-stage, 'I have to say in all honesty this place ain't really us.' In the rest of the country he was as remote as an alien visitor. Mainstream American radio was still pumping out slick, FM-friendly rock acts like Boston and REO Speedwagon.

Dennis Munday: 'In the early days The Jam would have had to completely change their sound to make it in America. It's only in the last few years that America is really listening to that style of music. In the late seventies and early eighties Americans were into that refined, over-produced super-sound production and The Jam wasn't that. But they were huge on the college circuit.

'I only ever went on one American tour and I remember they did a press conference and there were loads of the press in there – it was quite a heavyweight affair – and Paul just turned round and said, "We're going to do an interview with a couple of fanzines and the rest of you can fuck off." It's only now that recession has hit white America that they now have got real attitude over there, as opposed to a designer rebel attitude.'

A review in *Rolling Stone* of the band's gig at The Palladium, New York, indicated that the American critics weren't impressed by Weller's fuck-off attitude. 'The Jam's energetic music is enjoyable enough; too bad their extra-musical behavior is so embarrassingly immature.'

Clive Banks: 'Paul was seen as immature because he was compared at the time with groups like Journey. These were real tired, rehearsed old hacks who would know the telephone numbers of the journalists and had that forced warmth. That never would be for him at all. His inroads through the British and European media were through very young journalists. It would be through the young radio guy, or the young researcher who worked for the producer at the radio station, who would slip the record in. He had a young circle. Gary Crowley was connected to this, Paolo Hewitt was connected to that. The whole thing was webbed out like that and there was a point, when it reached the coast, where his career stopped. The records sounded very small in their sound and very aggressive because of what was being played on the radio at the time.

'The other problem was that Polydor was absolutely crap overseas at that time. They were OK in Europe but in America it just didn't exist.'

Weller was irritated further by record company suggestions that he should get in George Martin to produce the next album, 'in order to get the American market'. This only made him dig his heels in, as he turned his back on the States and returned to England for The Jam Pact Spring Tour.

On 17 August The Jam's next single, 'When You're Young', charted at number seventeen. At first glance the lyrics celebrate youth: 'Life is timeless, dreams are long, when you're young/you used to fall in love with everyone/Life is a drink and you get drunk when you're young.' However, it contorts into a cynical swipe at bottled-up, frustrated dreams as reality takes over: 'But then you find out life isn't like that/. . . the world is your oyster/but your future's a clam.' There's a sense of urgency, nostalgia and bitterness to the song which touched a chord with fans who were having their first taste of adulthood through sex, exams, the dole and jobs.

Tony Fletcher: 'I still think "When You're Young" just summed up life at that point when you're going in to do your O-Levels. If he did get elevated as a spokesman for a generation that's probably because he deserved it.' The B-side, 'Smithers-Jones', was one of Bruce Foxton's best songs and was later re-recorded for their next album, *Setting Sons*.

Although the single did OK, Polydor were more excited about another one of their acts, Sham 69, whose 'Hersham Boys' had gone into the Top Ten the same month. Dennis Munday admits with a wry smile, 'At the time there were many people at the label who felt that Sham 69 had a bigger future than The Jam. Sham 69 were selling twice as many copies of their singles. I tried to tell people that every generation there are one or two major artists thrown up who will be important for years. I wrote a letter telling the managing director that Paul Weller was one of these guys, but no one really believed me. Of course, even Sham 69 thought they weren't receiving enough backing from the record company. In one afternoon I had the managers of Sham 69, The Jam and Siouxsie And The Banshees all coming into my office to complain that I was giving the other bands more attention. John Weller complained about Sham 69 and vice versa. I had a cup of coffee and shut up shop for the afternoon. But that's how bands are. They've always bitched about each other and they always will.'

Tony Fletcher also observed Weller's irritated competitiveness with the other punk acts: 'You couldn't like The Clash around Paul Weller. You either liked The Jam or The Clash; it was very obvious that there was this rivalry going on. I think they did fight for that mantle as the best punk band. When The Police and The Boom-town Rats started having hit singles, you could put this down to jealousy – I remember saying I liked "Roxanne" and I was almost kicked out of the studio. There was no solidarity with anyone else who came out of punk. Towards the end of The Jam's career, Dexy's were coming along. Everyone like Gary Crowley and Paolo Hewitt was into them but Weller just didn't want to know. He didn't want to know about anything that was in his domain.'

Paul Weller

Clive Banks noted The Jam's sense of isolation as their records failed to break into a wider market and support from radio and TV continued to be sporadically partisan. 'All that seemed to happen to Jam records was they'd go in the chart and then fall down,' he says. 'Radio was really sparse. I think for him it was a struggle because he was always fighting the things around him like the radio and the telly. There were always so many people who didn't play his records or who didn't support him. I think he felt the band was moving forward in a vacuum. They were making space for themselves and getting bigger, rather than joining in the existing space, which does make you feel rather lonely. I worked on the early Boomtown records but Bob Geldof did everything that Paul wouldn't do. He'd do any television that moved, any interview that he could. He'd spend twenty-four hours a day manipulating the media whereas Paul would always shy away from it. He didn't want to talk to journalists and answer endless nonsensical questions from people who wouldn't write anything particularly good anyway, born out of the fact that he wasn't a particularly good interview. I think, also, he was a big fan of The Clash and they were just so credible. I'm sure that must have pissed him off. They didn't appear to be doing any of the pop stuff and yet they were having tremendous success.'

Nevertheless, in the summer of '79, a risible Mod revival was in full flow, following in the wake of *All Mod Cons* and The Who's *Quadrophenia* movie. 'I would have been in it [*Quadrophenia*] if they'd asked me to star in it – if they'd asked me to be the lead actor in it,' said Weller. Most of the new Mod bands were laughable and one-dimensional. They stole heavily from The Jam and The Who but ignored the codes and philosophies of the original Mods. Secret Affair, who built their Prisoner look around dark, tight suits and shades, rivalled Mick Talbot's Merton Parkas as the worst Mod band of all time. 'Looking good's the answer/ And living by night,' they declared in their mirth-inducing Mod anthem, 'Time For Action'.

Only the slightly hipper Chords and Purple Hearts (named after the 60s speed pills, favoured by Mods who wanted to stay up all night at the clubs) made this revival remotely worthwhile. There were also some fans who worked their way from Mod to Two Tone in a matter of weeks, checking out new records by The Specials and

Madness, then working their way back to Prince Buster and original Jamaican ska. This revival spilled out from The Jam's gigs, which had already changed three times – from working men nursing their pints in Woking through to punk audiences, and now a growing number of parka-clad Mods were dominating the crowd. *Something Beginning with O* author, Kevin Pearce, described their audiences as an 'ugly sea of green . . . [of] uniform parkas, patches, Shelly's shoes and blind devotion.'

At the end of the summer Weller didn't have enough material for a new album but his self-imposed deadline was already coming up fast. John Weller booked some studio time at the Townhouse in London's Shepherd's Bush and his son started to write and record in long daylight sessions which were often invaded by the band's fans.

Tony Fletcher: 'When they started recording down at the Townhouse the whole cult of The Jam and the way they were so available meant that five hundred people would turn up for soundchecks and thirty people a day would find their way into the studio. I'd call Paul and say, "Is it all right if me and my mate come down this afternoon because we're gonna bunk off games?" and he'd say, "Well, yeah, but there's twenty-five people in the control room right now." And there would be. Half the Mods in London would be down there.'

Vic Coppersmith-Heaven: 'I'd often turn round to see a crowd of Mods behind me.'

On 26 October The Jam had their first Top Five hit with 'Eton Rifles', which reached number three. The prolific Weller had written the satire on public school 'revolutionary' politics while on holiday in his family's caravan at Selsey Bill, near Portsmouth.

Clive Banks: ' "Eton Rifles" was the first time they got airplay and carried on up the charts. We had quite a struggle at the time to get people on the radio to play them with any rotation. I think that's why Polydor brought us in because radio seemed to elude them completely. We had The Who, quite a hefty roster. Gary Crowley also started working in the office. When I met Gary he was fifteen and he came in the office as a messenger boy. He was very important to me in my relationship with The Jam. He was the link between us really. He used to take the barriers down. I think there's always been someone like that in all Paul's relationships in the music business, whether it's with the record company, their international people or the promotions side. As a young journalist Paolo Hewitt also gave Paul a direct relationship with the music press.'

The Jam released their next album, *Setting Sons*, in October, which followed up on the success of 'Eton Rifles' by becoming their first Top Five album. In spite of Weller's support for Vic Coppersmith-Heaven, he had doubts about the album's production. 'I was really unhappy with *Setting Sons*. To me it was a real let down. It could have been another group. The sound was really horribly professional, on the verge of being slick. I was never particularly pleased with it.'

Weller originally had the idea of writing an album about the lives of three boys who grow up together and then change in their attitudes when they become adults. One becomes a Wolfie Smith type of character on the far left, another turns into a hardnosed businessman and the third is Weller himself, who can see both points of view. The songs 'Burning Sky', 'Wasteland' and 'Thick As Thieves' trace this theme, with Weller probing lost idealism, class barriers, the break up of local communities and the hardening of dogmatic attitudes with age. 'Burning Sky' was written as a letter by a character who has lost all his vital, youthful optimism under the strain of paying the rent, filling in forms for the tax man and getting ahead by being a 'realist'. In 'Wasteland', the character who is left behind now rots in his home town, which has transformed from his childhood playground into a wasteland. This song possesses a nostalgic, melancholy haziness which contrasts sharply with the brittle, direct mood of 'Burning Sky'. Weller didn't have time to follow through this story but most of the songs on the album do relate to each other. The suburban townies of 'Saturdays Kids' with their 'bingo accents' and 'fur-trimmed dashboards', the public schoolboys in 'Eton Rifles', the stressed housewife in 'Private Hell', working-class cannon fodder of 'Little Boy Soldiers' and nine-to-five Surrey commuter 'Smithers-Jones', spill together into a class-conscious, imaginatively detailed vision of a local community in a London satellite town.

'Little Boy Soldiers', which boasted a musically adventurous, complex structure, possessed a humanistic attack on imperialist ambitions fed by the lives of young soldiers. 'Smithers-Jones' is also at the mercy of the job market which makes him dispensable and at the mercy of the boss. Foxton's lyric is a more sympathetic variation on the hypocritical 'chap' portrayed in 'Mr Clean', with Weller adding the last lines: 'Work and work and work till you die/There's plenty more fish in the sea to fry.' However, the speed of recording meant that there are two throwaway tracks which pointlessly top and tail the album – 'Girl On The Phone' and a cover of 'Heatwave', which was a live favourite.

Musically, Weller acknowledged a fresh source of inspiration, which demonstrated he'd changed his mind about some of the 'arty' new wave bands of the era. 'I borrow from everything,' he said. 'Like "Private Hell". After I saw Joy Division on that TV show we did with them I sort of worked out this bass and drum bit – they've got one song which starts off with bass and drum, so I sort of nicked that a bit. But after it goes through loads of different stages it becomes ours, you know . . . And also there's a bit in "Strange Town", the vocal part, which is nicked off the Buzzcocks' "What Do I Get?" ' 'Private Hell's description of a housewife under stress also echoes Siouxsie And The Banshees' 'Suburban Relapse' in the lines, 'Alone at six o'clock you drop a cup/You see it smash/Inside you crack/You can't go on but you sweep it up.'

Weller's storytelling approach failed to deflect attention away from himself as a 'spokesman'. Every word he said in the press was analysed by journalists who put their own dour, po-faced interpretations on this 21 year old's views. Not surprisingly he drew back, becoming increasingly vague and evasive when he was faced with a tape recorder: 'We're not supplying answers,' he declared, 'we're not even questioning things. I'm just stating what I feel at the time. I'm not coming out with my theories on world politics because I don't think it's very important. It's not up to me to say. I'm not a spokesperson or anything like that.

'I'm sitting there in front of the TV moaning on about world politics saying, "Look at these bastards" and Gill just says, "Yeah, shall we start tea then?" And she's quite right. Maybe I'm only an armchair radical but every night I watch the news and I get so frustrated. I write it all down, then in the morning throw it away because it's rubbish, just paranoid rantings and ravings. Still, after six or seven pints I do start to cheer up. That's basic philosophy for you. Yeah, I think lager should be on the National Health.

Paul Weller

'It's a lazy attitude, but in another sense it's a realistic one. There's all this stuff going on in the world – Cuba and nuclear threats – but as long as I've got enough for a pint I can tolerate it.'

Paul Morley was exasperated by Weller's humdrum comments and vague analogies when he interviewed him for the *NME* in November 1979. 'Paul Weller is very skilful at ducking and weaving,' he wrote. 'Not self-conscious or embarrassed but very careful. He doesn't want to assume responsibility – although accepting that to some extent he already has an amount – or pretend importance. He seems to want to appear correct and orderly with little to say for or against anybody, and little to say about himself . . . Feelings come in spurts and dribbles, somewhere amongst the pauses, shrugs, "I dunnos", "yeahs" and "in a sense". Time goes by slow.'

Chas de Whalley: 'I think the problem was in those days that journalists didn't have a sense of humour. It was all part of a political movement.'

'I'm portrayed as humourless because people associate me with politics,' the singer complained, 'and politics are dull. Also, you should hear the questions I get asked in interviews. They're so serious and one-dimensional, even though I'm willing to answer everything from my social life to what colour socks I wear.'

Weller was terrified about losing his sense of perspective in the wake of this media-feeding frenzy. Stevie Wonder's 'Uptight' was one of his favourite songs of the year because of 'the line that says "No one knows better than I, but I know I'm just an average guy." '

Weller: 'That really sums it up as far as I'm concerned. It's a question of saying we're just the same as everyone else but we have our pride and self-respect and we know we're good. As far as I'm concerned, we're the best . . . but anyone can do it.'

Weller's escalating reputation was reflected in the reviews of *Setting Sons*. In particular, the *NME*'s Tony Stewart touched a nerve within the band when he concluded, 'More than ever, it's a one-man band . . . *Setting Sons* is Weller's personal statement . . . the success of this album doesn't rely on familiarity and identification, but on his talent alone. It's Paul's best album yet; almost his first solo album too.'

Such comments hit Foxton the hardest, as many of his songs had been filtered out and left unused since Chris Parry rejected the sessions following *This is the Modern World*. Obviously hurt, he hit back in the press: 'It's much more all three of us. Nothing has really changed in that respect. But recently the press have been picking up on *Setting Sons* as being a Paul Weller solo album. Why weren't the others solo albums as well then? There's always been the same amount of effort going into it from everyone.'

Weller's growing stature as a songwriter increased the gulf between them dramatically, leaving Foxton to pick at his own deficiencies with the paranoia of a full-blown inferiority complex. Clive Banks observed the other two at close hand. 'I always saw them as petrified of Paul. Sure it was the three blokes but it was a hundred per cent Paul really and never anything else. They must have gone to bed every night and thought, Fucking hell, what if he doesn't want to do it any more? I never heard them express any opinions. You'd get the odd outburst from Bruce. He'd get a bit uppity. He always seemed to be massively stressed. The whole thing seemed to be stress from start to finish with him. Even on-stage he appeared to be always looking over his shoulder to see whether it was all right with Paul. I think the process was totally uncomfortable for him. He certainly looked that way. You got the feeling that he didn't assert himself in the beginning and it just got worse for him.'

Meanwhile, the maturing Weller was now contextualising his work rather than summing up The Jam with mouthy, rallying calls to youth. He drew comparisons between punk and the British version of the 60s pop art movement which he'd discovered through The Who's target T-shirts and Mod-appropriated Union Jacks, and via the Small Faces artwork: 'I've read a few books on pop art,' he stated, 'and I think it had a lot in common with the punk thing. Before the pop artists came along there were the expressionists who were just dealing with their own self-indulgent art, but the pop artists brought into art everyday images that ordinary people could relate to which is why it really interests me. I see The Jam along those lines; using things that everybody knows are there but presenting them in a different art form.'

Weller made a bizarre stab at pop art-cum-humdrum surrealism through a Jam publicity shot which pictured the suited trio gathered around everyday objects in unusual locations – a fridge containing a pair of shoes is set in the middle of the shot, while the singer's left knee is bent over a saw and Foxton is pretending to dig the photographer's studio with a spade. He wrote an experimental track, 'Pop Art Poem', the following year, which echoed Roy Lichtenstein's cartoonish approach in the 'Zap!, Power!' refrain.

Weller's interest in pop art wasn't his only diversion from music. At the turn of the year he set up his own publishing company, with his old friend Dave Waller as co-director. His girlfriend, Gill, also helped with the day-to-day running. Riot Stories was intended to give an outlet to other writers and poets who he felt had as much, if not more, to say about Britain in 1979 as he did. It followed through his principles which he'd laid down a year before: 'I'm bursting with fucking ideas but it all takes money. It's a vicious circle. I can't do nothing until I've got money. I'd love to have a publishing company so that I could publish young poets, people like Dave Waller.

'No one gives a crap about people like him. All they want to do is read Shelley and Keats, people like that. I'd love to have a record company to help young bands. But it all takes bread and right now I haven't got that sort of bread. But if I don't do that when I have got bread then I'm the biggest cunt out.' Now he had cash in the bank, he set about doing something positive with it by publishing Dave Waller's *Notes from Hostile Street*, which became available on mail order.

He also published *Swing and Go* by Aidan Cant, and *Mixed Up Shook Up*, a magazine which was crammed full of poetry by young writers. It also included some of his own poems: 'Most of them were quite bleak . . . I thought at the time poetry could get quite popular like, say, music is.' Although the magazine only ran for three issues and most of the work in it was amateurish and cliché-ridden, Weller had shown that he wasn't a hypocrite and that he really was determined to follow through his ideas. That was more important to him than the actual quality of the work itself, although he was undoubtedly passionate about poetry which he thought had a chance of becoming an important underground art form, potentially rivalling music as a source of innovation in the 80s. This conviction stayed with him throughout the next two years. He took a break from The Jam in November 1981 to read some of his own work at the Poetry Olympics in London's Young Vic, a bill which also included Henri's Liverpudlian contemporary

Roger McGough (whose son, Nathan, later became manager of The Happy Mondays). In 1981 he also published *Jambo* by David Ward, but Riot Stories lost its momentum after the death of Dave Waller from a heroin overdose in Woking's Wheatsheaf Hotel in August 1982. A trickle continued – *Spongers*, The Jam biography *Beat Concerto*, Terry Rawlings' Small Faces biography *All Our Yesterdays* and The Style Council book, written by two Italian journalists, entitled *Internationalists*.

In November 1979, The Jam played a UK tour, featuring Mick Talbot as the anonymous keyboard player at the back. They were supported by The Vapors, who had been spotted by Foxton who co-managed them with John Weller for a while. The band wrote one masturbatory anthem, Turning Japanese, and then broke up as the follow-ups flopped and egos swelled out of control. Weller's insistence that his father choose between The Jam and The Vapors as soon as the latter band had a sniff of success didn't help matters. There could only be one decision and it hints again at the competitive streak inside the singer which seemed to demand all or nothing from everyone around him.

When they visited America again in February 1980, the band's status was once again raised a notch or two when they sold out the 3,000 capacity New York Palladium. However, their international position was completely eclipsed in March 1980 when The Jam became the biggest band in their home country. Their double A-sided single 'Going Underground'/'Dreams Of Children' went straight in at number one, the first time this had happened since Slade's 'Merry Xmas Everybody' rushed to the top in 1973. The anti-nuclear message of the single was coupled with a desire to retreat, which became all the more understandable in the wake of their biggest success. The other A-side, 'Dreams Of Children', was also one of Weller's best songs, but was largely ignored by the radio. Its psychedelic feel reflected Weller's interest in British artists such as Pink Floyd's Syd Barrett and of course The Beatles, rather than Californian, LSD-fuelled mysticism.

The single capitalised on the band's fan base through a deliberate week-long delay on the release date, which meant a build up of pre-release orders, followed by a full week's sales as opposed to the three days usually granted to new releases at the time.

The band were on tour in America when they first got the news that the single was likely to top the charts. John Pearson was the man who spoke to John Weller, as the manager sat in his hotel room at the Sunset Marquee. 'John was pleased as punch that he could bring them back from America,' Pearson recollects. 'They were having a fucking horrible time over there.'

Weller was typically self-conscious in his reaction to their chart-topping success, commenting in *Beat Concerto*: 'I was a bit sort of shocked. The other thing with me is that I try to keep calm about things like that because I get worried that I'm going to turn out like the rest of them. So I try to keep a little bit of calm about it, look at it logically. At the same time, from my own point of view, my sort of ego, of course I'm pleased.'

Nigel Sweeney: 'I think he was really proud. It's sort of ruined by today's values because record sales have dropped to a certain extent in the singles chart and unfortunately with the way the chart is at the moment it's dead common for groups to go in at number one. That belittles the fact that The Jam had three number one singles.

'They weren't the biggest group. They could sell 250,000 copies in one week but their audience didn't seem to be getting that much bigger.'

When the band returned to do *Top of the Pops*, Weller came up with the idea of wearing a kitchen apron for their performance. Nigel Sweeney: 'There were problems over that because there was this rule that you had to perform in what you were going to wear in the evening otherwise you weren't allowed to perform. So he's worn this kitchen apron with a Heinz soup logo on it [a vague reference to the pop art cover of The Who's *The Who Sell Out* album which features Roger Daltry on the cover holding a giant Heinz baked beans can], and the producer got the hump because it was advertising. In those days at the BBC it was very, very strict. So I had to say to Paul, "This is a bit of a problem." Again it's that thing of telling him one thing and he'll do the opposite, he didn't take it off, he just turned it round. But the studio lights were shining through it so you could still see the Heinz logo on it. Paul had got the hump because the BBC had told him to do something and nobody would allow him different. So he sang, "Going Underground", because it was mimed in those days, in a really wimpish, casual way. The words were being spat out on the song and he was there looking as if he was singing an easy listening ballad or something.'

Weller had always given his fans as much access to the band as possible, but now The Jam were being treated with the hysteria of a teenage pop band. Their security had to protect them from the feverish, collective mania of young crowds who were trying to touch their heroes.

Nigel Sweeney: 'We did the TV show *Tiswas* the day after playing Birmingham. Paul and the band wanted to go in the gunk cage [this from an artist dubbed Old Misery Guts by *Smash Hits* and who opened up a flexi disc by the magazine with the words, 'Hello, this is Paul Weller speaking – but don't let that stop you enjoying yourselves . . .']. They were feeling pretty shaky because Paul had been drinking and I think he actually gave up the booze that day. They got up fairly early. Kenny was dispatched to a DIY shop to get some blue plastic overalls, and they all went in the cage and were splattered. It was a really cool show to do at that point even for The Jam. We did loads of promotional work with them. It was never a "Fuck off we're not doing that", Sex Pistols type of thing.

'Afterwards we went up to this bar on the top, the nineteenth floor or something, of Central TV and we had a drink. The band's coach must have gone on. Paul didn't like flying so everything was coaches and buses. They'd gone on somewhere so we had to hire three taxis. All of the kids had realised the band were actually live on *Tiswas* so they turned out and surrounded the building, twenty deep. There were three cabs put in the loading bay but it was really frightening. Paul was definitely a bit shaky about this because the crowd got hold of the cabs and they were pushing them and rolling them from side to side. We just felt like we were going to be ripped apart.

'His girlfriend Gill always seemed fairly cool about the attention. There was some sort of pact. They kept themselves very private – no one knew where they lived and no one had their telephone number. They'd go off and you wouldn't see them again.'

These precautions didn't prevent some fans from tracking the couple down, though. When Weller was living in a flat in Pimlico opposite a school, people used to peer into the front room, forcing Weller to crawl around the room on all fours until they went away.

Paul Weller

At the height of the band's popularity, when Paul and Gill went out, Kenny was often not far away. 'Even when Paul sloped off for a quiet meal with Gill,' says Foxton, 'Ken would have to tag along and play gooseberry.'

There were two triumphant Easter gigs at the Rainbow in 1980, which blasted away their miserable experiences in the States, then Polydor reissued all their previous singles. Every single one of them charted again in the Top 75.

John Pearson: 'I came up with the idea of releasing all the singles in their original packaging. I wanted to stamp their authority on the British market. The band were a bit grumpy about it to begin with and, to be honest, we did not consult them about the reissues.

'I don't think John minded too much to be honest. He knew what we were up to. I'm sure there were some cases where John knew what we were trying to do and he smoothed it over with the band. He's no fool. I know a lot of people have criticised the choice of John over the years but who else can you trust to do the job that well?'

Following a benefit gig for Sheerwater Youth Club in Guildford on 18 April (the band had borrowed the youth club's van in the past), where Weller had been speeding on sulphates, they played dates all round the world – in Finland, Holland, Spain and America. The latter brought out fresh tensions, this time over the American record company's decision to release 'Heatwave' as a single. Furthermore, Weller was irritated by the fact that The Pretenders, The Clash and The Specials were all enjoying success in the States, but it seemed to be a painfully slow uphill climb for The Jam, despite their five-week presence in the country on this latest visit.

All the band were drinking heavily. Weller knocked back beer and vodka before each gig to boost his confidence. In France his stomach swelled up abnormally. 'My gut just came up like a hard-boiled egg. You could actually ping it.' The doctor said no more alcohol for two weeks, Weller's stomach went down, and then he started drinking again.

Foxton and Buckler were also hitting the bottle, exaggerating some of the tensions between them. Weller felt quite close to Foxton at the time: 'If there is any situation at all he would never stop to think about it, he'd always help you.'

Buckler became quieter when he gave up drinking. He took the decision after drinking eighteen bottles of wine with the band's tour manager Dickie Bell during a marathon session following a gig at the Hammersmith Odeon (where they were once again joined by Merton Parkas' Mick Talbot on keyboards). The drummer, who has a weak heart, turned very pale and shaky. Everyone was concerned for his health and the down-to-earth Buckler realised that his boozing days were behind him.

After a successful tour of Japan, the only country where Weller's icon appeal has never waned, the band were back in the studio. As usual they worked in the day to maintain a sharp, intuitive feel in their new songs. Buckler: 'We like to record quickly so it's best for us to come in in the morning and get it down as soon as possible. If it doesn't work out later in the day we'll usually come back to it the next morning and get it done in one take. In the day we're awake and full of enthusiasm.'

The band were heavily influenced by The Beatles' *Revolver* album in their use of sounds and guitars being looped backward and in the odd familiar riff. Tony Fletcher: 'When they were recording *Sound Affects*, the *Revolver* album was on the turntable all the time down at the studio, which was great because you could go down there and hear them gradually reworking each track. I don't know how they got away with it.'

The blatant 'Taxman' steal on 'Start!' was the first excerpt from these sessions, and the single gave The Jam their second number one in August. While the music stuttered around The Beatles' bassline, Weller's lyrics were inspired by another schoolboy hero, George Orwell, in particular his book about the Spanish Civil War entitled *Homage to Catalonia*. 'The main thing that struck me is the first few chapters when he describes getting to Barcelona when all the workers have taken over the city,' enthused Weller. 'I mean, there's a lot of talk of the "egalitarian society" where all people are equal but this was it, actually in existence, which for me is something that's very hard to imagine . . . even though it was for a short time.' Orwell's experience of a brief moment in history when people from different backgrounds and countries united together against the fascists, stayed with the author until his death. It's directly echoed in the lines from 'Start!', 'It doesn't matter if we never meet again/What we have said will always remain.'

Paul Weller

Weller's adoption of an Orwellian voice in this song is far removed from the Big Brother authoritarianism of 'The Combine' and 'Standards'. Orwell's left-wing humanism, common sense arguments and tight, journalistic detailing were all part of the young songwriter's approach.

At school, like most of his classmates, Weller had not been a big reader. However, over the previous year this 22-year-old publisher had absorbed a lot of ideas from books, movies and plays: 'I started reading more in '79,' he explained. 'I dunno, I was really thick and I couldn't talk to nobody.'

He leafed through the pages of 60s books, *The Loneliness of the Long-Distance Runner* and *Saturday Night, Sunday Morning*, alongside the kitchen-sink film dramas of the era, in particular *Billy Liar* and *A Taste of Honey*. Karl Marx, Gandhi and the Italian author Alberto Moravia were sources of inspiration and Weller also read several books concerned with 'mysticism and raising the spiritual and intellectual level of people'. These included *The Doors of Perception* by Aldous Huxley and William Blake and Geoffrey Ash's *Camelot and the Vision of Albion*. 'The ideas behind the lyrics were influenced by Ash's book,' he said, 'which were that we had lost sight of our purpose and our goal as human beings; the material goals had hidden the spiritual ones and clouded our perception. There were also religious overtones. I suppose, on reflection, the ideas and philosophies are quite "heady" and "hippyish" but it was just a phase I was going through.'

When the new Top Five album *Sound Affects* came out in October, Shelley's 'Mask of Anarchy' was reprinted on the back sleeve. Weller was trying to reclaim Shelley's romantic vision of revolution for himself and his audience, taking him away from the dull school reading lists. Although Weller was wearing his literary influences on his sleeve, he still fretted about being seen as arty and failing to communicate directly and passionately with his audience. 'We could never get away with doing anything avant-garde,' he said, 'or even vaguely avant-garde . . . even if we wanted to and I'm not saying that we do.

'The whole punk thing started because people were alienated by crappy music, obscure lyrics and references and everything. We don't want to get into that. That's what everyone was fighting about. Some people might not have meant it but we did. But also we don't want to suppress anything that wants to come through naturally. We've overcome it in the past, so maybe we can keep on doing it. It's difficult. The day we stop being accessible is the day we die.'

The album's title hinted at the positive politics of the songs which followed up on the socialist humanism of Orwell. Weller was trying to motivate people directly through music. 'The English audience demand a lot from you which is good,' he said. 'If they could carry that sort of demanding attitude through to when they start work, then society could change properly. If they can demand so much at gigs then they shouldn't go back and let the boss or the teachers order them around . . . Then music would be having a real effect.'

As Fletcher recalled, Weller was writing songs on the spot, coming up with lyrical collages which created more visual songs. 'That's Entertainment' was loosely written in hazy drunkenness around a poem he'd been sent of the same name, with Weller spilling out everyday images into a brilliant cross-section of English suburban life. A rehearsal produced 'Man In The Corner Shop', which mixes prosaic, humdrum class jealousies with his humanistic twist on spiritual oneness. 'Pretty Green' implied the loss of the human spirit in capitalism's obsession with money, while 'Dream Time's sense of claustrophobia is also rooted in pre-packed modern living. The forceful, funky edginess of 'Set The House Ablaze' attempts to open up away from the 'cold, hard and mechanical' vision of day-to-day life and the dreamily psychedelic 'Monday' deals with self-doubt and a stormy relationship. The concluding line at the end of the first verse, 'I will never be embarrassed about love again,' demonstrates Weller's determination to express himself freely and avoid the pinched, defensive attitudes around him. The character in 'Burning Sky' off *Setting Sons* reappears in 'Scrape Away', which seems to answer back the letter with a savage sense of hope as well as disgust at the writer's cynicism. Although many of the songs were written quickly by recording in the studio, The Jam had eaten up three months at the Townhouse, pushing the final cost of the album up to £120,000. Dennis Munday: 'It took a long time to record and just got out of hand. It just went on and on. At one stage it wasn't due to come out that year. We had to press it in France because there wasn't time to do it in England.'

After all the work, Weller was disappointed with the album's feel which he felt was 'bland' and 'smoothed out'. Munday: 'Everyone was disappointed with the final mix. I wanted to remix a couple of things but by then we'd spent enough money and there wasn't time.

'The company was never happy with Vic Smith. They didn't like him. *Sound Affects* gave them the excuse to get rid of him.' It was to be the last Jam album that Coppersmith-Heaven worked on.

In the UK, the critics ignored the thin production and quite rightly enthused about the depth of the songwriting. America's *Rolling Stone* was still stand-offish, however: 'One of the first British punk bands to have an American release, The Jam, who took to the stage in suits and ties, has always courted respectability, even gentility ... Though the relative directness of their current release, *Sounds Affects*, may seem like a bid for some kind of American pop appeal, it's merely a falling back on the easier Modishness of The Jam's early LPs ... Weller's nationalism, a thematic and musical commitment to things British, continues to limit his reach.'

The Jam's solid if unspectacular reputation in the US was confirmed with sales of 150,000 for *Sound Affects*. Weller was offended by such mediocre returns and ranted about the lack of airplay on the other side of the Atlantic. 'People won't pick up on us 'cos it doesn't sound right,' he moaned. 'Our records are rated, er, what's that phrase ... AOR. Is that right? Adult Orientated Radio – it's sorta like late-night crap. Music over there's really conservative. People talk about conservative England but America's far worse.'

As the year drew to a close, The Jam won an award for Best Single at the *Daily Mirror* Rock and Pop Awards. Weller attended but refused to go up to receive the trophy from Dave Lee Travis. He sat and watched the others shuffle towards the stage to the sound of a brass band playing 'Going Underground'. Weller hadn't consulted Buckler and Foxton about his decision and they looked embarrassed. This lack of tact or communication was characteristic. Weller often kept his ideas to himself, leaving people in confusing and humiliating situations.

Weller was, however, pleased by their clean sweep of the 1980 *NME* Readers' Poll, where they collectively and individually won Best Group, Best Male Singer, Best Guitarist, Best Bass, Best Drums, Best Songwriter, Best Single ('Going Underground'), Best Album (*Sound Affects*) and Best Cover Art (*Sound Affects*).

At around the same time, Riot Stories published the first issue of *December's Child*, which was another outlet for young poets and artists. There wasn't much censorship over the quality, but the intentions were good. Weller also talked in the press about the idea of a rock club/coffee bar run by the musicians themselves and a Jam-sponsored label. He'd been talking over the latter scheme with Tony Fletcher for several months: 'The Jam actually made it and had some money. I went up to the studio one day and by this point I would get taken over to the pub. Paul said, "I've been thinking about starting a record label. I wondered whether you would fancy running one." It was right in the middle of my O-Levels so I think he was probably aware it was right at the time when people decided what they want to do. I was in a band at school called Apocalypse – somewhere down the line The Jam gave us a gig about two years before we were ready for it. We played our sixth ever gig at the Rainbow and we had all just turned sixteen. They seemed quite into the band as well.

'It did take a whole year to work out what we were going to do with the label. In that year I went back to school to do my A-Levels but I left because there was too much going on. When I was about seventeen we actually got the label started. We decided we might as well call it Jamming! When Paul set it up he said, "OK, what we'll do is we have a spare room in our offices up in Nomis Studios; you can go in there and run the label."

'The day I went in there after spending a year talking it through, he brought me in and said to everyone, "Tony's going to be upstairs; he's cool, there's a desk and a phone, get on with it. Halfway through the day I'm on the phone, the door opens and there's John Weller. He says to me, "What the fuck are you doing here?" And I said, "Didn't Paul tell you?" "Paul didn't tell me anything. What the fuck are you here for?" "I'm, er, running a record label." "You're doing what? He's going to lose his fucking arm on that; I don't believe it." He'd forgotten to tell John what I was doing after all this time setting it up.

'The way it was set up was, in retrospect, a really bad way to do it, but I'm not knocking anyone. I certainly didn't know any better. We decided to record a band called Ruby from Ireland who'd been on Good Vibrations (home to The Undertones) and had quite a good pop punk feel. Paul got studio time off Polydor through

Paul Weller

Dennis Munday. What Paul said, which in theory sounded all right, was "I'll pay for everything on this record; I'll pay for the pressing, the recording and the sleeves and as the money comes back in you can use that for running your record label. I was straight out of school, only done O-Levels, not done any business studies or whatever, so it sounded good in theory. However, the immediate flaw is cash flow because the money took three months to come back in. It might've been better off to say, "Here's a sum of money, let's start it with this." I had no idea about cash flow. I'd been doing it for two months before anyone told me what VAT was.

'We only had three bands: Ruby (two singles), pop funky Zeitgeist (three singles) and Apocalypse (one single). All the singles were indie hits. There was a constant cash flow problem. While we were waiting for the money we had no idea who was going to pay for the phone bill. If John Weller had known about this from day one he might have done it differently.'

Weller also formed the Polydor-funded Respond Records at Nomis Studios, which remains his base to this day. The records were packaged with attitudes often espoused by Weller – idealism, positivity and the streetwise suss of youth. 'I think it comes across that way because that's the way [the artists] feel,' he said. 'They're all really young people on the label so for them it's like the first time they've made records and are actually going out and doing something. I think a lot of people are very wary of the teenage thing but I still really believe it ... The Respond label is for young people.'

Their first signing was the all-girl band, Dolly Mixture, who were streetwise, young and kitsch in their love of girlish 60s harmonies (they later sang the backing vocals on Captain Sensible's one-off solo hit, 'Happy Talk'). Saint Etienne's Bob Stanley was a fan of their 'urgent teen conviction', an element which also strongly appealed to Weller. Respond's erratic A&R policy continued with a rockabilly band, The Rimshots, and pop funksters, The Questions, whom Weller thought were the best band he'd seen since The Sex Pistols. None of the records sold more than a few hundred copies and in 1982 Weller pulled the plug on the Polydor era of Respond and started over with a new distribution deal through A&M with only The Questions retained from the original roster. Clive Banks, The Jam's plugger, was also asked to 'promote all

Respond's stuff. It was extremely hard work because I think it was a token label which Polydor had allowed him to have. So when it came down to the push, it wasn't really there. It was just a ploy to keep Paul happy. You know, pat him on the head, let him have a record label, give him a couple of hundred thousand to run it, then he'll be a happy boy and will probably re-sign his contract long term for The Jam. The money wasn't from his own pocket. It wasn't offset against his royalties or anything like that. I think it was an indulgence. He chose artists who were a bit malleable. They weren't challenging as people. He's a strong personality but I don't think he would have ever signed a character as strong as himself to work with because I think he enjoyed making all the music himself. At best the Respond artists were pop stars – they were never international stars. The structure that the label had would never have allowed it to be successful internationally.'

4 Three-Way Split, 1981–82

Paul Weller: 'We've never really sat down and talked about progression . . . Every time we met up we just all of a sudden got a bit better. I think, inevitably, there has got to be a time when that stops happening.'

Paul Weller: 'It strikes me that after people get over the age of twenty-five, once they get their house and the wife and the kids, ideals don't mean nothing.'

In March 1981, The Jam set off on a European tour with Ian Dury and The Skids, during which they played their most violent gig in France. French skinheads attacked some of the British fans, prompting Weller to tie a Union Jack around the microphone stand and sing the old ballad, 'English Rose'. When they returned the band recorded their next single, 'Funeral Pyre'. Released on 29 May it was a step backward, with the song buried in tumbling drums and feedback. Once again no one was happy with the final mix.

This was also the first Jam song to feature a band credit on the songwriting, but Foxton and Buckler were never to get a taste of a co-written number one as the song stalled at four in the UK. Dennis Munday was disappointed with 'Funeral Pyre', sensing a loss of momentum: 'I thought it was the beginning of the end for The Jam. It didn't take them in a new direction.'

The band didn't slack from their manic, stamina-sapping schedule and they promoted the song with more gigs around the UK. Tony Fletcher recalls that by this time Paul's girlfriend was an ever-present fixture at the back of the gigs where she'd sell the merchandise. 'I remember Gill was supposed to be working in the office but they had the kind of management that when The Jam went on tour everybody went with them. Gill would go with them and they'd put the answer machine on saying, "Sorry, we're all on tour."'

Gill's presence gave Bruce Foxton a drinking buddy, but she also drove a wedge between her boyfriend and the band's rhythm section. Often she'd be cuddling with Paul at one end of the tour bus, while the others got on with their own stuff. They rarely took partners on tour with them, except on the occasional 'glamorous' overseas trip to Japan or America. Weller's friend from adolescence, Terry Rawlings, who followed The Jam to nearly all their UK gigs, doesn't remember seeing Weller socialise with 'Bruce and Rick, or for that matter I never even saw Bruce and Rick go out for a night on the town together. Bruce would be with the beers. He'd drink with anyone. He could really put it back.'

The tour, which kicked off at the Rainbow, featured only one new song, 'Funeral Pyre', in the set. Munday had reservations as he watched them go through the same on-stage movements: 'They had reached the stage where leaping up and down like frogs on-stage was a bit passé. Everything was changing.' The sight of John Weller introducing them on-stage looked quaintly old-fashioned, although it was important to both father and son. 'I feel I pale in his shadow,' said Paul Weller. 'He's a hard act to follow. Yet it's me who receives the accolades and applause. Hopefully he gets his through me but that I'll never know.'

The Jam's hyperactive, earnest passion contrasted with a lazily foppish scene which had started to develop at the end of the 70s. An elite, glamorous group of DJs, fashion designers, wannabe pop stars and suburban freaks were swarming around Steve Strange's club nights, Blitz and Club For Heroes. At a time of high unemployment, Weller likened the scene to 'the last days of Rome', but the Mod also found common ground with the new romantics in their shared love of clothes: 'Well, at least they're putting a lot of thought into what they're wearing,' he said with gruff approval. 'So it's only about clothes, I know, but they're still thinking about them. All right, so that's very superficial and it doesn't really mean very much, but it's a thousand times better than thousands of brainless people flocking to Wembley to see . . . I don't even know who plays there . . . Rod Stewart or someone.'

Weller's tastes were opening up and he initially embraced a broad range of pop bands at the start of the 80s. 'I really like The Beat, Department S and The Teardrop Explodes . . . I don't know what Julian Cope's talking about but it doesn't matter 'cos the music's great.' He also described Madness as 'inspiring' and he even had a good word for Adam And The Ants. 'They've got a bit of style and do it with a bit of class.'

Paul Weller

Curiosity took him and Gill into Club For Heroes, where on one famous occasion the couple ended up drinking with Thin Lizzy's Phil Lynott and Pete Townshend. At the time The Who's song-writer was experimenting with heroin but he was out of his depth with Lynott, who gave him a shot in the club's toilets. Townshend collapsed and was rushed to hospital, where it transpired that he was lucky to survive as his heart had actually stopped for a short time. Weller claims he was 'so pissed' he can only just remember the incident, although the image of Townshend lying flat on his back with his legs splayed has, not surprisingly, stayed with him.

Although these clubs played glitzy Bowie and Lou Reed songs, black music was also an essential part of the mix. Weller drew inspiration from some of the black rap and futuristic funk records of the time, especially those by Grandmaster Flash and Afrika Baambaataa. He was also impressed by white English bands who were incorporating funk styles, including 'Papa's Got A Brand New Pigbag' by Pigbag and Spandau Ballet's collaboration with Beggar & Co. on 'Chant No. 1' which he regarded as a 'genuine English soul record'. Gill Price was also a big Spandau Ballet fan.

Inspired by his regular visits to Le Beat Route, where they played soul, funk and jazz-fusion records, Weller even thought about hiring a club once a week to showcase new groups. He envisaged a non-alcoholic night so the 'kids' could go and enjoy a northern soul kind of scene at a young age. Weller hadn't forgotten the boring, listless evenings in Woking as a teenager when he wasn't old enough to go to the few 'happening' places in town. However, this idea never saw the light of day.

Meanwhile, Weller was absorbing different sounds and changing his mind about the new bands week by week as he made regular forays into record stores to buy armfuls of seven-inch singles. Tony Fletcher remembers 1982 as 'a confusing time. It was hard to tell whether any of these bands were good or not.'

His initial enthusiasm for the resurgence of English pop soon turned to scorn as he became appalled at the glamification of punk by the likes of Adam Ant, conveniently forgetting his earlier compliments about the stripy-faced insect rocker. 'I'm sick of pop music, most of it's just crap,' he said. 'People like Adam Ant and Depeche Mode have totally lost sight of pop and it's just as if punk never happened. The argument on their side is that people are too young to remember it anyway but I think music should have some kind of sensibility, some kind of consciousness, instead of being party to this showbiz crap that people like Adam want to bring back.

'When I see all the bands who are just the same as the glitter groups and all the rest of that rubbish I think it's very dangerous because it's just used for pure escapism. That's not enough for me. I want something . . . with substance.'

Dennis Munday smiles broadly as he's reminded of Weller's sour, prickly insults: 'Paul enjoyed winding people up although a lot of what he said about these bands was true. The eighties was a crap decade.'

After the short-lived buzz around 'Funeral Pyre', the rest of 1981 was fairly quiet for The Jam as Weller searched for a fresh direction. They made a guest appearance at the Gang Of Four's CND show (they also contributed 'Little Boy Soldiers' to the anti-nuclear album *Life in the European*, released at the start of 1982) at the Rainbow, playing cover versions of Arthur Conley's 'Sweet Soul Music' and Sandie Shaw's 'Long Live Love'. The next day they appeared at a CND rally near Embankment in London, which also featured Zeitgeist and The Questions. They played two sets augmented by a horn section in the back of a lorry with Vaughn Toulouse (ex Department S, who sadly died of Aids a few years later) on vocals.

The first fruit from Weller's time away writing was a new single, 'Absolute Beginners', which was released on 16 October. While 'Strange Town's ambiguous, disjointed mix of styles had perfectly fitted with the culture clash of the song's lyric, 'Absolute Beginners' was a tense collision of horns and the old style Jam rhythm section. Weller wasn't happy with it, sowing the seeds for the band's split a year later. For the moment he kept his doubts hidden from Foxton and Buckler, although John Weller did sense there was a problem in the camp. His son had announced the band's split several times in the early days but this time the straight-dealing, pragmatic manager made it clear to him that the band were contracted to deliver two more albums to Polydor.

Weller stole the single's title (which was somewhat ironic given the frustration he was feeling inside an old, rapidly dating format) from Colin MacInnes's book, which celebrated the birth of the teenager, although Weller hadn't read it at the time. When he did

Paul Weller

finally rummage through the pages, MacInnes's hustling, exhilarated flow excited Weller, capturing the speed of youth which he'd portrayed in his own way through The Jam. On the surface too, the Mod plagiarist borrowed some of the jazz and coffee bar chic for his future incarnation as a laid-back Style Councillor. The Style Council also recorded a track for Julien Temple's film adaptation of the novel.

The nostalgic psychedelia of 'Tales From The Riverbank', which glanced back at the Woking countryside of his youth, deserved more than its B-side ranking.

Dennis Munday: 'That was the biggest mistake we ever made. We should definitely have made "Tales From The Riverbank" the single.'

The song's sentimental, romantic mood reflected a change in Weller's feelings towards his home town which he'd been so desperate to escape only a few years earlier. 'I enjoy Woking a lot more when I go back now,' he said. 'I used to really detest it but I can see the good parts now.'

At Christmas, The Jam played four shows in London – two at the Michael Sobell Centre in Islington and two at the Hammersmith Palais. Weller presented these shows like an old soul revue with different groups supporting each other and a northern soul DJ spinning the records. However, sections of the audience weren't impressed by this unconventional format and they barracked the support acts Bananarama and The Questions.

Tony Fletcher: 'The Jam had spoken to many of us who felt a bit like misfits at school and then later there was this herd mentality. And there was all the other Mod stuff which was really pathetic. The idea that you could play a song like "Away From The Numbers" to a crowd that's singing in unison, "We are the Mods", is obviously completely against what The Jam wanted to be all about.

'You end up trying to speak for the best of people. When I was thirteen and very unsure of myself and physically quite small, "Away From The Numbers" was my favourite song for the next five years. When five years later The Jam are the biggest band in Britain and every bloke that used to beat me up at school is into them, it's not quite the same. I think Weller must've also looked at that and thought, This isn't quite what I intended.

92

'There was a guy I knew from primary school and I'd always had him marked down as a David Watts, a good-looking boy, good footballer, went off to a good school as well. Anyway, he bumped into me at a Jam gig and he was like, "God, what are you doing here? I didn't know you were into The Jam," and I was running the label at the time.'

Around the time of these shows, Weller started sessions for a new album, this time replacing Vic Coppersmith-Heaven with Pete Wilson, who had worked with Weller before on demos. Dennis Munday sums up this change succinctly: 'Pete was a lot cheaper than Vic and he was more efficient.'

Weller's temper was on a short fuse all through Christmas, which he hates, spending hours in his flat working on the new songs. He only surfaced to have the odd argument with Smith. The songwriter put everything he had into the album. He wanted the record to be 'important'.

'I think I drove it a little bit too hard,' he said later. 'I think I made too much of it and blew it up in my own mind.'

Munday: 'I think he put too much pressure on himself by wanting to make *The Gift* the great Jam album. You can't do that. Great songs come naturally. Even to some extent he still does that now. He has a tendency to maybe shoot too high.'

Weller was recording all the parts himself and liked some of the demos more than the final versions, especially 'Just Who Is The Five O'Clock Hero'. He was finding it hard to achieve the progression he wanted and the bottled-up sense of frustration and ridiculous workload eventually took their toll. Midway through a casual game of pool at Air Studios, Weller had a semi-blackout, which he recalled in *Beat Concerto*. 'I felt as if I was in a dream and that I would slip away and not be able to get back. It's a really horrible feeling and I think it was stupid to go over the top. I've never been a real abuse person and it wasn't only that but a combination of things. It was going out, pissing it up and the process of making *The Gift* LP.' He gave up drink after this experience, proclaiming in the new year, 'I did a lot of clubbing last year and that's my lot . . . Rock can destroy you if you let it. Like, I don't take any drugs any more, I've even given up drinking.'

Tony Fletcher: 'Paul was going through a whole soul-searching rejuvenation at the end of The Jam and part of it was giving up the

Paul Weller

booze. He told me he'd had a couple of blackouts where he couldn't remember things and he did give us a bit of lecture about it once.'

On 29 January 1982, 'Town Called Malice'/'Precious' hit the High Street and gave the band their third number one hit. 'Town Called Malice' was a brilliant anti-Thatcher lament over the break-up of local communities due to the recession and Tory policies. The artwork of bars across the vista of the town captured the song's vision perfectly. Some of Weller's best lyrics shone through the song, flashing vignettes about lonely housewives and disused milk floats across the Motown beat, concluding with a resolve to put some 'joy back' into the urban depression. The other A-side, 'Precious', did just that with its Pigbag bassline and brassy funkiness.

The Jam made history on *Top of the Pops* when they performed both songs on the same show. Nigel Sweeney was the man behind the double-headed appearance: 'They did both "Town Called Malice" and "Precious". What I didn't realise when I booked it was that Paul was really proud of this because the last time it had happened was when The Beatles' songs, "We Can Work It Out" and "Day Tripper" were played, but only on video. So this was quite a big thing. It was the first time this had ever happened live in the studio.'

Shortly before the release of Weller's labour of love, *The Gift*, he agonised over one final detail – the sleeve. Dennis Munday remembers a last-minute conversation about the packaging. 'I can only think of about two occasions when he actually asked to do something that did cost a lot of money. One of those was when he asked to change the sleeve to *The Gift* and it was actually being printed at the time. We had to destroy about 75,000 sleeves. The original version had a jagged frame around the three of them. He came in one morning, very early, and he was clearly agitated. He said, "Look, I really don't like it." So I said, "Fine, take it off." He didn't demand the change, he just asked whether it was possible.'

Meanwhile, the northern soul dancer on the inner sleeve indicated Weller's current obsession with 60s black music.

The album went straight in at number one. Weller's voice dominated more than before but he was clearly overstretching. The

Jam's rhythm section simply didn't have the dynamics required for Weller's soul grooves and the results at times lacked the warm, soulful feel he was so obviously striving to achieve. However, there were some great moments as he pushed and pulled the band into funky shapes and experimental beats, notably 'Trans-Global Express' with its clipped, relentless train rhythm, chants and weird noises which left Weller's call for workers' rule low in the mix.

The LP's opening declaration, 'Now for those watching in black and white this one's in technicolour', followed by Foxton's scream of 'Baby!' at the start of 'Happy Together' was a great way to kick off the record but all this layering choked up songs which weren't strong enough to carry it off. There's too much going on in 'Running On The Spot' and 'Circus', while the clumsy calypso of 'The Planner's Dream Goes Wrong' was seriously misconceived. Restraint and control on 'Ghost' creates one of the album's highlights. The lyrics follow up on the emotional frankness of *Sound Affects*, as Weller calls for the song's character to 'lift' himself up and look to the future. Faded melancholia dog-ears the gorgeous 'Carnation', which also echoes the claustrophobic, bottled-up emotions which Weller attacked on the previous album in a Gemini-twin conversation between two sides of the same person. The album's title track closes the record on a positive note, putting a shoe-shuffling sense of joy back into the malicious urban climate.

'Just Who Is The Five O'Clock Hero' is classic Jam competing with Weller's desire to push the band into a Motown-based direction. The singer later commented he was happier with a demo version, although the song did become a Top Ten hit on import which underlines the band's popularity at the time. Prince Philip gets some stick in the track, puncturing the band's old reputation for royalist sympathies as the song's hero struggles in the rat race of 'scrimping and saving and crossing off lists'.

The critical response was mixed. The *NME* concluded, 'Weller's ambition is to face the pains and injustice of contemporary class society and yet remain positive which, times being what they are, is a nigh impossible task. The stress of the effort is what pulls *The Gift* to pieces, making it a collection of false starts.'

America's *Creem* magazine wasn't convinced by The Jam's new sound either. 'The Jam's most undernourished album . . . Longtime fans will find some value. Others can look to *All Mod Cons* and *Setting Sons* and forgive them their slump.'

Two days after *The Gift* was released, The Jam played a secret gig in Guildford to celebrate John and Ann's silver wedding anniversary. After this family knees-up they promoted the album with a four-month Trans-Global Express Tour around Britain, Europe, Canada, America and Japan. Shows had to be added in Los Angeles and New York, proving their popularity in the cosmopolitan areas. When they appeared at Tower Records in Los Angeles, they spent four hours signing autographs for near-rioting fans. *The Gift*'s celebration of black music was also a lot more appealing to America's radio stations and the airplay pushed *The Gift* into the US charts for a few weeks.

Once again, however, it was an unhappy tour with the atmosphere undoubtedly contributing to the band's split later in the year. Weller was off the booze, which focused everything in his mind into a clearer and more critical light. He was bored, the other band members were jaded, and the workload had left them niggly. There was a lot of moaning and the extended band, including the horn section, threw tantrums over petty details. 'Bruce's attitude in particular would piss everyone off,' complained Weller, 'because he would always be griping about something or other which was a shame because really he is a good bloke.'

Munday: 'I think Bruce had an inferiority complex. On the last few tours there was a lot of moaning and paranoia. Bruce found it difficult living in Paul's shadow. From *All Mod Cons* onward everything was directed towards Paul.'

Tony Fletcher: 'I always thought they were good mates until the end. In hindsight, you can see that Paul's comments were a bit guarded. He'd say, "As long as we're not in each other's pockets it's fine, we all get along well."

'They were both funny in their own way. Rick could be pretty sensible. Bruce had an enormous inferiority complex going on. I don't think that was obvious until afterwards when he didn't do much with his career.'

Foxton also felt isolated because he was the only member of the band still socialising after shows. Weller and Buckler kept a lower profile. The three of them now had little in common as people.

In the summer Weller and Gill went to Italy for a two-week

holiday, staying in Naples and Rome. It's a country he loves and has often returned to since. 'I just love the people ... They haven't got fuck all really but their spirituality is just so great. I was talking to some Italian people and they were saying that it doesn't make much difference to Italians who's in government over there, they still go on doing whatever they want to do anyway. And there's that kind of spirit, you know. It's just those little things, when you first go to Italy and you see a policeman slouched against the wall having a cigarette when he's on duty and whole families riding on mopeds, just little things like that. I think we need some of that spirit. The one thing I've got against the British people is that they're just so uptight about everything. And sometimes it takes them so long to enjoy themselves.'

By the time they caught the Orient Express home, Weller had made up his mind to split The Jam without consulting his father. He told the others while recording 'Bitterest Pill' at Marcus Studios (he also wrote 'Solid Bond', 'Beat Surrender' and 'Dr Love', the latter song he gave to Bananarama for their debut album in this brief but prolific period). Buckler felt like he was 'losing a limb' but he was pragmatic about the prospect and, as far as he could, accepted the situation. Foxton confessed to his wife that he hoped Weller would change his mind and 'lived with it for a month or so, just me and Pat, every minute of the day thinking about it.'

As for John Weller, he was 'sad about it because I started it ... and it's like the end of something that wasn't really finished.'

Weller later spoke about his father's reaction to the news: 'He wasn't pleased. We still had a contract to fulfil, some tours to do and some singles to make and he talked me into seeing it through.'

Despite the band's silence on the subject, some people close to Weller sensed something was going on. 'Weller produced Apocalypse's last single for the label in the Phillips Studio which would later become Solid Bond,' remembers Fletcher. 'In the course of that week we all got the vibe that it was going to be ending. He played us "Bitterest Pill' and someone in the band said, "That's brilliant, but where are Rick and Bruce on the record? It sounds like a great solo record." And he gave us a really weird look. So we weren't shocked. We had an inkling that something was going down.'

Nigel Sweeney: 'It was so obvious when it had happened. They were all so quiet at the end. The venom also came out. I never heard anything from Paul's lips but I did from the family. There was one occasion when his mother turned and said, "Yeah, well, they should have done more, they were always resting when Paul was hard at it", and things like that. I never asked but I think the Wellers were angry over a *Melody Maker* interview that Bruce had done over Christmas where he said he was amazed at how prolific Paul was at writing songs. The Wellers took this as saying Paul was just knocking out another album, or something like that, so there was bad feeling over that.'

The Jam's split is now held up as the classic case of a band who broke up at the right time. It was a brave, uncompromising decision but the right one. It's hard to imagine The Jam's music overcoming the tensions within the band or successfully reconciling the pull between their youthful, cocksure, brash origins in British R&B and punk and the soul and jazz-funk sleekness of the new decade. The image of The Jam playing Live Aid in the mid 80s sums up the compromises and ideological struggles which Weller would have faced, still burdened by such a sharply defined band history. Even so, it obviously wasn't an easy decision to make. Weller admitted at the time that he was 'tempted by the security of The Jam. It was a very secure situation but it was also that security that frightened me ... like saying to someone, "This is what you do for the rest of your life."'

His initial vision of The Jam as a vital, youthful force was a big factor in the split: 'I wouldn't like to become like The Rolling Stones,' he declared. 'I wouldn't like to be jumping in the air with my guitar at forty, or even twenty-six ... That's like trying to stay nineteen ... That's the one thing I've got against rock people like the Stones... the fact that they think they're still young rebels. I mean, you just don't cut it, it just doesn't work. After a while you look stupid just physically.'

The demise of his beloved Small Faces also played a part in his actions. 'Don't you think a lot of that is down to fucking dope?' he mused over his heroes' fall from their earlier creative highs, 'and all that shit and that end of the sixties era when the Small Faces stopped being what they were good at and tried to be something else?' He realised that The Jam would have to invert everything they represented in order to express his own changing tastes.

Munday observed the widening gulf between the band members: 'They'd gone their own ways long before the split. Once they got out of the *In the City* period they became a different band.

'I don't think he could go anywhere further with The Jam. I think that's what *The Gift* proved, that there wasn't anywhere else to go. Bruce and Rick just weren't good enough to transpose out of The Jam into The Style Council. It's obvious that they didn't share the same musical direction. I think it's difficult for a three piece to go on and on without being repetitive, The Who being a prime example.'

Tony Fletcher believes Weller saved himself from serious personal problems by walking away at the height of the band's success: 'I think Paul would've had a nervous breakdown if The Jam had carried on. There's a well-known photo of when he was recording *The Gift*, with him and Paul McCartney together. Weller looks like the old man in the picture. You can understand why he had to split up the band.'

One of the pressures on the miserable singer was the constant attention from his fans. Tony Fletcher: 'I know there was one time not long before The Jam split. He'd just moved, he always lived around Victoria way, and he came in and told us that someone had been through his rubbish, so they obviously knew that Paul Weller lived there. He'd only been there two days. He was a bit uneasy about it. I think the loss of privacy, the living in a goldfish bowl, was another big factor.'

After weeks of sleepless nights, the temperamental Foxton couldn't bottle up his feelings any more. At the video for 'Bitterest Pill' he was forced to wait around for ages. He paced about, growing increasingly frustrated, until something snapped and he stormed off. Dennis Munday took his place in some of the shots. The next day Foxton rang up and told the group that he wasn't doing the forthcoming UK tour. Then he slammed the phone down. Urgent meetings were held and Glen Matlock was talked about as a possible replacement until two days later Foxton changed his mind. Weller was also showing signs of stress. Gill took the brunt of his moods and after a big argument he moved into a hotel for a few days.

'The Bitterest Pill (I Ever Had To Swallow)', backed by 'Pity Poor Alfie' and 'Swallow', broke into the Top Five in mid September. It was The Jam's fifteenth single and featured a backing vocal by Jenny McKeown from The Belle Stars. Although a fine song, there's a tense, unresolved awkwardness to the music which doesn't quite carry off the soaring soul melody, despite the presence of strings to give it an added lushness.

Munday: 'There's two versions of "Bitterest Pill" and I've always preferred the original. This was the other time he asked for money. They'd finished "The Bitterest Pill" and gone into the studio on a Sunday with a huge string section. Then he phoned me up a couple of days later to say, "It sounds shit, I want to re-record it." I said, "What, the strings?" and he said, "No, all of it." So the whole thing was scrapped and started again. That cost about nine grand and in the end it was their costs. If I remember correctly the original was slightly slower and had a cod sixties break in the middle which was taken out. The final version was OK but you can hear in that it's straining a bit. It didn't have a feel to it.'

The song's over-the-top humour was the first hint of how Weller's in-jokes would be misunderstood by the critics. Lines like 'Autumn breeze blows down summer leaves' may have left the writer smirking ironically over a cigarette but critics and fans took them at face value. 'Some of them wankers wrote, "Well, it's Weller's sojourn into introspection and all this crap," ' he complained. 'It means nothing. Maybe in some ways we might even have put ourselves into that position. I'm not really sure.'

The band kept the impending split a secret as they set off on the Solid Bond In Your Heart mini-tour. They got rid of the horn section and were backed up by a keyboard player and backing vocalists, Afrodiziac, who included Caron Wheeler, later vocalist in Soul II Soul. The pressure was clearly affecting the frontman, despite his surface cool, and some dates had to be cancelled when Weller contracted shingles.

The Jam had intended to announce their break-up on a new Channel 4 music programme, *The Tube*, but the tabloids got there first. 'It was all very messy,' remembers Nigel Sweeney. 'Paul was going to stop halfway through the set and announce the news.' Instead the trio made individual statements in the *NME* before their 5 November 1982 appearance on *The Tube*, where they played 'Ghosts', 'In The Crowd', 'Town Called Malice', 'The Modern World', 'Move On Up', 'The Great Depression' and 'Precious'.

The band's final single, 'Beat Surrender', followed in the same

4 Three-Way Split, 1981–82

month, featuring backing vocals from Afrodiziac and a teenage girl from Chelmsford, Essex, called Tracie Young. This nineteen-year-old hopeful had sent Weller a demo on spec. She was shocked to get a phone call from an enthusiastic Gill Price a week later. After signing her to Respond, the A&R boss, in-house producer, songwriter and director enthused, 'I like her because she's a realistic pop star. She's not a wimpy type and she's not overtly sexy like, say, Madonna. She's resilient and mouthy and unreasonable. Some people don't like that but that's what nineteen year olds are like.'

Her contribution to 'Beat Surrender' was a way of giving her some easy exposure as the label prepared to launch her as a solo artist. In 1983, a week after The Style Council's first single, 'Speak Like A Child', Tracie scored her only major hit with The Questions-penned 'The House That Jack Built'. This was a fresh-faced but flimsy pop sensation which took Tracie on to *Pop Quiz* but failed to make her a fixture on bedroom walls or in the pop charts. Meanwhile the girls were out in force for 'Beat Surrender', with Gill Price featured on the sleeve waving a white flag. Perhaps Weller also saw Tracie and Gill as representing the 'young boys and girls in and around the West End, the way they look and the energy there. So it's partly about that and also about music. Some of the lines in it are about what music can do for you; get you off your arse and make you feel really powerful.'

Although there was an ironic twist to the title, 'Beat Surrender' plundered the Motown groove with greater success than some of the over-egged tracks on *The Gift* and ended The Jam's career with the feel-good, dance politic first expressed in 'Non-Stop Dancing'.

Dennis Munday liked the song but wasn't sure about the performance. 'A Style Council song like "You're The Best Thing" has a great feel to it. That's one of the things that The Jam couldn't capture. The cover songs on the B-side ["Move On Up"/"War"/ "Stoned Out Of My Mind"] didn't work particularly well either. Once you get into that soul area people start saying, "Well hold on, this doesn't sound right, it doesn't feel good." Paul realised he could do it but the others couldn't follow. I would have loved to hear The Style Council play "Beat Surrender".'

There was, however, a more successful hint of a fresh direction with the slow, jazzy Weller song, 'Shopping', which was on the B-side of the seven-inch single.

Paul Weller

The Jam made one more baffling appearance on *Top of the Pops*, with the chart-topping climax to their singles career. Sweeney recounts: 'We did *Top of the Pops* and Paul was at the back. It was like, why? He was pushing Tracie like crazy, so she was singing backing vocals at the back with Paul. Then it was Bruce and then Rick down the front. It was a bit odd but actually on the day it did look cool. There was a strange feeling of anti-climax though. The TOTP performance seemed a bit pointless really. His mind was on The Style Council at that point. No one in the Weller camp wanted to talk about The Jam.'

A two-man horn section returned for the farewell Beat Surrender tour, which included five nights at Wembley Arena. Louise Wener from Sleeper was one of the young fans there. 'I remember this incredible band coming on-stage, this huge hall with everybody screaming. It was an almost magical thing. It had a big effect on me, made me want to get on stage. I thought, Imagine doing that, it must be the most fantastic feeling.'

Weller was caustic about his own performances on this last tour: 'When you go out to play a concert knowing that it's going through the motions, that's one of the most degrading things ever, you know. It reaches a stage where you can't face the audience – can't look anyone in the eye. Those last few Jam gigs, it was like that. It was fucking awful.'

Nigel Sweeney followed the band's countdown to their final gig: 'The last concert was supposed to be down at Guildford at the Civic Hall. We all went along. There was me and Crowley (who was working for Modern Media as well by this time). Bananarama were doing some ridiculous dance routine. Mike Reid was the MC of the event. It was all good fun and I think they should have left it there. Unfortunately, there was a decision made by John [against the wishes of Foxton and Buckler] that they were going to do two more gigs at the Brighton Centre and that was the lowest point of The Jam. The Mod thing and the scooters made it seem like a natural end at the time but it was such a disappointing concert. It was a big, cold hall. There were people fighting down at the front. It was horrible really.'

Munday: 'The atmosphere on the last Jam tour, well, there was an undercurrent. I've always thought that Brighton was a mistake. They should have finished at Wembley. The atmosphere at Brighton was really bad. It was like being in a torture chamber.'

4 Three-Way Split, 1981–82

Fletcher: 'The last tour was a nightmare. They did Brighton and it was obvious that Paul just wanted the thing to be over with. Somebody from the audience might have thrown something and Bruce went up to the mike and gave this big lecture – "We've had a fucking great six, seven years, we don't want anyone to ruin it now, it's been brilliant" – and I remember so clearly that Paul went over to his amp, sat down and lit up a cigarette and you could see this distance between them.

'At the end of the show we were back in our little support band dressing room and Paul came offstage and he didn't walk into his own dressing room at the end of The Jam, he walked into ours. He was also completely sober, remember, because he'd given up the booze. He said, "What are you boys up to tonight then?" He didn't even say, "Oh well, that's that done with" or anything. He just came out with these comments like, "Are you boys driving back to London tonight or what?" And we were like, "Paul, you've just split The Jam." I can't remember his exact words but it was something like, "And I'm fucking glad I have too." It was definitely one show too many.'

At the end of the year they released a live album, *Dig the New Breed* (the title was a tribute to the James Brown classic of the same name) which included a cover of Eddie Floyd's 'Big Bird'. Although charting at two and offering a thoughtfully selected and packaged live memento, it was essentially a contract filler. Foxton: 'We still owed Polydor an album and Paul was in no mood to record any new songs.'

In January '83, Polydor re-released all thirteen singles and they all charted in the Top 75, an impressive way to bow out by anybody's terms. However, on a personal level the split was so absolute it inevitably left a sour taste in the mouth. When Rick Buckler spoke to the *NME* on 30 October he commented, 'We're all still friends and I think we'll stay friends. You don't work with someone for ten years and then suddenly forget them, do you?' Weller has completely blanked his old band mates ever since that gig in Brighton. They weren't the only ones who were left confused.

Tony Fletcher: 'When The Jam split up Paul did decide to change a lot of things in his life including the decision to stop funding the Jamming! label. I was given forty per cent of it but that doesn't mean anything. When it ended I remained confused for a long time on a personal level – I was still only eighteen. I guess he made the decision that certain relationships were in the past and I wasn't actually aware of that. I was never really told, it was more sort of hints, like John Weller saying you've got two weeks to vacate the office, that kind of thing. That made it a bit of an odd conclusion.

'Paul called me over Christmas. There was a rock week at the ICA and we did a Jamming! night and we put on Everything But The Girl's first concert and Paul played with them and that was the first thing he did since leaving The Jam. So we had this thing that carried on over Christmas into the new year but somewhere in the middle of that he said, "You can have the label, I don't want to do it any more." I was like, OK, but it didn't hit home until I realised I'd got a bit of debt on my hands with it and I was no longer part of the Weller set-up.

'The thing with John was that his son came first, always, in front of anyone. He was very good while I was part of the team. Then I had the rude awakening when I walked into the office and was effectively kicked out. I realised that I wasn't wanted any more. At all points in between I was family.'

Fletcher's experience paralleled those of Foxton and Buckler. Weller had put the shutters down on that particular phase of his life in order to make a fresh, uncompromised start. Although hurt, the 'other two' at first shrugged their shoulders and got on with their lives, but were soon knocked back when Polydor decided not to pick up on the option of signing them for solo deals. Foxton had a short-lived answer when his cod-funk single, 'Freak', was a Top 30 hit in 1983, but within a year he'd been dropped by his label, Arista, and he ended up joining the Irish punk band Stiff Little Fingers who made a living in the nostalgic backwaters of a minor punk revival in the 90s. Buckler had his own band for a while, Time UK, and lost money on various business ventures which included his own studio. He ended up restoring furniture for a living. At no point did Weller offer to help them out. As far as he was concerned, they'd had their time together and they didn't owe each other any favours. The overnight disappearance of Bruce, Rick and Tony Fletcher from his life would be echoed by other lost friends over the next few years.

As for The Jam, John Weller continued to regret the fact that the band didn't achieve the worldwide success he'd hoped for. In particular, he'd dreamt of playing some of the big prestigious venues in the States.

'I knew that Paul didn't really want to do it, so in a sense I was a little bit constricted. Another manager who wasn't involved personally would have said that's what we're doing and it probably would have worked. Maybe because I was his father that was one of the holdbacks. But with regard to them playing prestigious venues they never really achieved quite what I wanted to see. In the UK they did, but not really abroad. Filling Madison Square Garden, I would have loved that. They couldn't have got any higher and that would have done me.'

Over a decade after the split, Weller is more dismissive: 'I only listen to The Jam if it comes up on the radio or something and it sounds really dated now, I think. It sounds sort of funny.

'When I look back at some of those lyrics, some of them are really dodgy. But I was eighteen or nineteen then, a different person. That would be like saying you regret being eighteen or something. Everyone goes through those silly phases.'

He's rarely performed Jam material since the break-up and when he has he's often changed some of the lyrics. Nevertheless, the band's place as a classic British outfit has been underlined by the success of a series of compilation albums after 1982. A double album entitled *Snap!* was released a year after Brighton and became their first platinum disc. A straightforward singles compilation, *Greatest Hits*, was another big seller in 1991, and a collection of B-sides, demos and unreleased material called *Extras* the following year was one of the best cross-sections of Weller's songwriting so far. It was an intimate flashback to the young songwriter's ambitions in The Jam. The songs also seemed to belong to another world – an urban, working-class existence which has become increasingly fragmented due to technologically led changes in lifestyle. *Melody Maker* journalist David Stubbs touched on this when he wrote of *Extras*, 'It reminds us, alongside the temporary wave of Madness nostalgia and The Specials' *Greatest Hits*, of an entire musical genre that no longer exists – what you might call the "Sound Of The Precincts", the soundtrack to a world of endless Saturday afternoons in which lads in Sta-Prest trousers ate chips and stared wistfully at the girls on the checkout desk through the

Paul Weller

glazed windows . . . This was Weller's constituency and while he stuck to it, The Jam were strangely affecting. For while today's supposedly prole bands are deliberately small, cynical, listless and self-degrading (The Beautiful South), Weller was always at least perky and Mod-ishly "natty".'

5 Cappuccino Kidology, 1983–85

Paul Weller: 'My sense of humour is incredibly funny to me but probably non-existent to other people.'

Mick Talbot: 'Some people thought that Paul Weller shouldn't be funny and maybe they were right. It depends on the jokes.'

Weller's first appearance after disbanding The Jam was his one-off gig with Everything But The Girl in London's ICA, where they played The Jam's 'English Rose' (a song that Watt and Thorn had already covered), 'Fever' and 'The Girl From Ipanema'. Ben Watt from the Hull-born duo recalls, 'This was before The Style Council. He split The Jam up and two weeks after he phoned us up in Hull and he said he wanted to do something with us. I remember we did an afternoon's rehearsal with him and he came down in a white trenchcoat and desert boots. The thing that most concerned him before we went on-stage was what we were going to wear.'

After the venomous, suburban feel of The Jam, Weller's Mod dandyism was pushed to another level with his new band The Style Council. The band was essentially a duo, with Weller calling on former Merton Parkas Hammond organ and occasional Jam keyboard player Mick Talbot to found his new group which would push guitars into the background.

Talbot was born in Merton, south London, on 11 September 1958. He grew up in Tooting and took an early interest in the piano: 'One of my earliest memories of my interest in the piano was when I was a small boy and my mum took me to the circus. Towards the end of the show the clowns started smashing up a piano and I started crying because I thought it was the old white upright piano that we had at home.

'My dad used to play a bit and my nan did – I just used to mess around on it – and my nan, I think, thought it'd be a good idea to send me to music lessons.'

Talbot went to lessons for three or four years and passed up to

Paul Weller

Grade 5 in Royal Academy exams – 'not bad considering practising the piano often came second to playing football.'

He stopped lessons when he was twelve as he discovered rock 'n' roll. The first record he bought was 'Baby Love' by The Supremes and his tastes soon expanded to rock 'n' roll and blues artists like Muddy Waters, Chuck Berry, The Beach Boys, Howlin' Wolf and Little Richard. 'This wasn't being played on the radio at the time and some of my friends thought I was living in a time warp,' he says. 'The current music of the time that I had the highest regard for was soul stuff on the Philly, Motown and Atlantic labels.

'I've never really consciously listened to keyboard players. I got into playing along to records even though they mightn't have keyboards on them, just getting into more of an improvisational thing on the piano. I was fascinated that all these classic rock 'n' roll tunes could be played with three chords.'

Inspired by listening to his blues records and going to see gigs by bands like The Feelgoods and The Kursaal Flyers, Talbot began to play on a cheap Italian electric piano at pubs and working men's clubs in a band called The Sneakers, with his brother Danny. The duo turned into The Merton Parkas and became closely associated with the Mod revival in the wake of The Jam (who discussed the idea of producing Talbot's new band) and *Quadrophenia*: 'We never really changed as a band for three or four years. It's just that we got picked up on with all that Mod thing. I suppose the name didn't help – we just thought it was a joke because we were from Merton Park – but we became like an in-joke with the music papers and after a year the record company decided to drop us.' In the summer of 1980 the band broke up. 'I think we were quite realistic about the stigma that had got stuck to us and the whole Mod thing and we decided we had to split up.

'The weird thing was a week after that I got offered the Dexy's thing – they'd remembered me from a gig we'd done.'

Dexy's Midnight Runners had supported The Merton Parkas in Liverpool in the summer of '79, a year before the Parkas split, and the two bands had hung out together talking about soul records backstage. The Parkas included a Ray Charles song ('What I'd Say') in their set while Dexy's played Zoot Money's 'Big Time Operator'. However, Talbot's role in Dexy's Midnight Runners was short-lived. He played with them for one tour in October 1980 and then they broke up.

Meanwhile, the six foot south Londoner had splashed out on a Wurlitzer: 'I got a Wurlitzer because Ian McLagan used one and I liked that sound. I was a bit frightened by synthesizers. I thought the mini Moog looked like something that should be in a plane's cockpit.

'I used to associate synths with hippies, which was a bit stupid considering people like Stevie Wonder and The Isley Brothers, whom I admired, used them.'

Although he also enjoyed Jimmy Smith's pioneering organ playing on Blue Note records, the more 'second-hand influences' had a bigger impact. 'A lot of people might think I have loads of Hammond records but I've always liked the Small Faces and stuff – and I know that might be a bit second hand because Ian McLagan was influenced by Jimmy Smith and Booker T – but I liked the Small Faces as a group. I never listened to keyboard players just for the sake of it.'

Meanwhile, Talbot wrote and arranged one album by The Bureau, forming the band with four ex-members of Dexy's and three others to create a soul and jazz influenced sound fleshed out with a three-piece brass section. They released three singles (including a minor hit with 'You Need Wheels') in the UK by WEA but their debut album was only released in Australia and Canada. He also made cameo appearances with The Chords but his musical career was in the doldrums when he received the call from Weller: 'With The Style Council I definitely had that Hammond sound in mind and he was the only person I knew who had one, so that was a good enough reason.' Not that he was completely alone on the Hammond in 1983. The Truth's Chris Skornia was also around at this time and Talbot himself was enthusiastic about the piano player in JoBoxers, whose 'Just Got Lucky' was one of Paul Weller's favourite songs of the time. Weller felt he'd found someone who was on his own wavelength. 'It was his attitudes,' he recalls. 'He was bored with the rock scene, he disliked all that macho thing and the drink and the drugs and all that shite. We were both more or less the same age, we both used to go to clubs at the same time and we knew records from the early seventies when we were both skinheads and suedeheads.

'I do like Mick a lot. I like working with him. I like the way he looks; his knowledge of music. I don't have to explain my ideas or justify myself to him. If I say something a bit off the wall, he knows what I mean.'

Although he was lumped with the unflattering nicknames Piggy and Spiv, Talbot shared his new associate's fanaticism for clothes. He was into 'anything from Ivy League to zoot suits, smart, smooth, modernist or casual, with youth individuality thrown in, together with a dash of Noel Coward or Max Miller, not forgetting Bogart's mac.'

They went around together all the time when they formed The Style Council, with observers noticing Talbot's 'calming influence' on the former Jam singer.

Weller: 'I don't have that many friends; the implication, obviously, is that I trust the people I've chosen as friends. I value the friendship highly and the relationship between me and Mick, you could say, is very friendly. Rick Buckler, Bruce Foxton and myself led completely different lives. We didn't have the same friends so we saw each other only when we were with The Jam.'

Sara Silver, who worked at Polydor International in the 80s, gives her impression of Talbot: 'He is a very relaxed person. He wasn't weak in the Council. He was a calm figure, a well-centred sort of person. It was almost like having a proper English gentleman around. He wouldn't interfere with anyone else's life. If Paul was on one he would be very defensive. He was completely protective.'

Talbot was a genuine music fan, easy going and witty. The pair constantly tried to beat each other to the punchlines of their in-jokes and the atmosphere within the band was often good humoured. Silver: 'The early days were very arty in a fifties way, but those guys had the best parties down the studio and everyone was having fun. They had annual fancy dress parties which were the best. I don't think I've enjoyed parties as much ever since. There was one at the London Dungeon, one at Hampton Court and prior to that they were at Solid Bond Studios. Everyone would dress up. At the end of every tour as well they'd have a big party. It's funny because that's a side of the band that people often didn't understand.'

In many ways Talbot was a good foil for Weller. Both of them named the Small Faces, 'Tin Soldier' as one of their all-time favourite records. When Mick was asked to name his favourite records in a fanzine, he came up with a list that Weller would have approved of: 'Let's Stay Together' (Al Green); 'Let Me Down Easy' (Isley Brothers); 'Band Of Gold' (Freda Payne) and 'I'm On My Way' (Dean Parrish). There was clearly a natural musical connection between them. They also enjoyed a 'cleaner' lifestyle together, with Weller maintaining his abstinence from alcohol. 'When I used to drink, I was such a slob. I didn't like myself so I stopped. I think it's important in this life to act as dignified as possible.'

There was, however, another side to the new partnership which was obviously uneven. Talbot's musical suss didn't transfer into his playing. He was solid and had the advantage of being able to interpret Weller's ideas very quickly because of their shared pop and soul roots, but he lacked the intuitive feel and passion of his partner's guitar playing. His track record as a songwriter was also poor and for all his sartorial enthusiasm he was hardly a style guru. Weller had not put himself into a partnership with the spark of a Lennon/McCartney. Clive Banks argues, 'It's very difficult to bring someone as strong as you into the unit. It's either there at the beginning and you have that synergy of fighting all the way through or you don't and you never allow it. Paul missed that point at fourteen or fifteen when he might have bumped into that partner, whereas Lennon and McCartney right from the start had that yin and yang. He's a control freak, obviously, so by the time of The Style Council it was too late to bring in an equal.'

Because Talbot wasn't a rival talent, Weller happily allowed him to make a big contribution to The Style Council's material, often to the detriment of the band. In the band's seven-year history the affable keyboard player didn't come up with any memorable songs. Some of Weller's fans were also appalled at Talbot's second-rate Mod credentials and regarded him as an embarrassment compared to the 'Modfather'. One fan noted: 'I went off Weller when he brought Mick Talbot in. We never rated him. The Merton Parkas were a really sad group.'

Weller brushed aside these mutterings from his fan base and defined The Style Council as a pop band with a stylish twist. 'We want to speak in a language that's easy to understand but don't always say what people expect to hear – in terms of style, that is.' He even, somewhat playfully, set out the band's manifesto in programme notes for their autumn '84 tour:

Paul Weller

The – 'because there's only one.'

Style – 'is an expression; each individual has their own style. Style isn't just clothes and cosmetics, it's soul, it's attitude, it's spirit and thought. It's also care.'

Council – 'is a bond of people, a collective. People working together because they have a common interest. Showing that people can do it if they want to.'

Weller decided he wasn't afraid of being conceptual. 'We used to think concept albums were only made by people like Jethro Tull but I suppose everything we've tried to do has been conceptual in a way.'

The 60s Mod influences were still at the roots of the band's crease-sharp, tailored thinking. He continued to draw inspiration from the Small Faces: 'I still sit there staring for ages at pictures of the Small Faces,' he revealed. 'I think my other favourite group is The Modern Jazz Quartet because they really come across as being a group and inside the group they all have kind of separate roles, like one takes care of the business and one looks after the transport . . . That's a proper group.'

Musically he was determined to express himself without relying on established rock clichés: 'I saw U2 on *The Tube* and I just think it sounds old-fashioned. I think U2 are a load of wallies – if they had long hair and wore headbands no one would look twice or write about them.'

Weller continued to trash most of the big contemporary pop bands, – Duran Duran, Spandau Ballet and Depeche Mode: 'When I was about eight or nine I used to like groups like The Herd or Amen Corner and Love Affair who were . . . the pop groups of that time, but I just think that the people in groups then were better looking. I've got nothing against pop music because if you accept it for what it is it's quite good. I just don't think the quality is as good these days. There's far more cynicism now – there was more innocence then.'

He also dismissed the 'smug', 'art school mentality' of up-and-coming bands like Echo And The Bunnymen. 'Wankers,' was Weller's curt appraisal of the Bowie and Doors-fixated Bunnymen. The equally outspoken Ian McCulloch flashed back, 'Paul Weller? He's like the kid at school who was in remedial class and he'd 'ave spit between his top two teeth and then flick his cigarette over the school fence as a sign of rebellion. It's all very well maturin' at twenty-six but when yer just maturin' into a fifth-form remedial, what's the point?'

Weller separated himself from these bands by drawing inspiration almost entirely from black music. 'Just because I'm not hammering away at my Rickenbacker and my amp's not full up . . . people get the wrong idea. The intensity is there. If you listen to some of the early Temptations records – 'Papa Was A Rolling Stone' – well, there's so much tension without all that power-guitar. There's loads like that – Curtis Mayfield, Isaac Hayes, Bill Withers, Al Green.'

Paul's enthusiasm for funk and soul had overstretched Foxton and Buckler in The Jam, so he was now determined to take these influences much further. This passion was fanned by a more streetwise sound coming out of black America in the early 80s, after the death of Philly and the disco boom which had left Weller cold. 'When I was a kid in the early seventies all the old Motown classics were being revived and were getting into the charts again. I went away from soul for a while. I didn't like all those super-smooth acts like The Stylistics, but then, at the beginning of the eighties, the funk stuff started getting a lot harder and that revitalised my interest. I like that real dirty funk sound, the kind of thing Sly Stone and James Brown were doing in the sixties.

'There's been a resurgence of black music recently. Stuff coming out of New York that's exciting. I think that's what's missing now – that intense excitement in clubs.' He was also listening to James Brown, Aretha Franklin and Curtis Mayfield, whose influence on The Style Council grew over the next few years. 'Look at people who've been totally underrated like Norman Whitfield who did all The Temptations stuff and Curtis Mayfield, Isaac Hayes . . . the rock intellectuals look down on black music. I think it's been totally underrated and a lot of these geezers were writing about really heavy, serious subjects and dealing with things a lot more important than "My Coo Ca Choo" or something. And I think it's the same now – good records from black artists with brilliant messages.'

He named 'Get It Right' by Aretha Franklin, 'Times Are Tight' by Jimmy Young, and 'Music' by D-Train as inspirational records. 'What they were trying to say was really positive; saying don't give up, though I realise a lot of those records are directed at fellow black people in America, the ones who are bearing the brunt of the recession. But obviously it applies to a lot of working-class people over here.

'My ideal audience is the sort of soul boys and girls that you see. Pringle jumpers and all that stuff ... While everyone else goes through their different phases they're the people who will still be there ... a lot of them just do what their parents do. But I'd much sooner it was them, whether they're radical or not.'

Weller admired the look of the casuals who were rapidly adopting more European styles of Lacoste and Fila polo shirts, Diadora trainers and tight Italian jeans. They were interested in details but it was also a mass, conventional and working-class movement. According to one fan, Weller was also entering the heart of mainstream fashion as a high street guru: 'He was often actually ahead of his time. There was a time when all the mannequins in Oxford Street had Paul Weller haircuts.

'In Carnaby Street there was a shop called Melanddis. They used to knock out all sorts of stuff which was really badly made but they had a picture of Weller with a Melanddis bag so he'd obviously shopped there. The Lonsdale shop in London's Beak Street used to alternate its window between Paul Weller and Frank Bruno. The Cavern in Carnaby Street also used to make Paul raincoats and Paul hipsters which you'd have to diet to get into.'

Part of Weller's love of music and style ethic also extended to vinyl – in particular the seven-inch single. In 1985 the compact disc format was creeping into the marketplace. The vinyl zealot preferred to listen to music by thwacking a heavy needle on to the grooves and sitting cross-legged on the floor next to his old music machine. 'I've a huge record collection but it's nearly all singles. To me there is still something really magic about a 45. I've still got an old Dansette multi-stacker record player at home.'

The Style Council's musical career began impressively in March '83, with the Weller-penned debut single, 'Speak Like A Child', which was only released as a seven-inch single in a simple black sleeve. 'This for me has so much life and vitality,' Weller enthused as he spoke up about the song to journalists. 'The simple message of "growing up" doesn't have to mean "getting old". It's also about myself coming to terms with the swiftness of the passing years but a bond with myself to never grow old as in square. An open mind can always learn more.' Weller's descriptions of young people in the West End had closed the Jam's career with 'Beat Surrender'. He'd opened his next chapter with a resolve to keep a firm grip on this youthful spirit.

The recording featured 'honorary Councillors' like bass player Joe Dworniak and Orange Juice drummer Zeke Manyika, establishing the looser format of the Council.

Weller's declaration – 'The Style Council, is it a pop band first, a political instrument second? Frankly, I can't separate the two' – was reflected in their 'official' live debut at the May Day Show for Peace and Jobs at the Liverpool Empire which was organised by Merseyside Trade Union in aid of Merseyside Unemployment Centre where they played four songs to backing tapes. Bassist Joe Dworniak, additional singers and a fill-in drummer joined the Council when they played again on 7 May at the Brockwell Park CND Festival. Their two-song set went down 'slightly disastrously' with the fans who wanted more. They slung mud at the band in retaliation.

Weller asked Dennis Munday to find the Council a young drummer who could join the collective for more than the odd one-off gig. 'I received a call that a jazz/soul/funk orientated band, on Polydor, were looking for someone,' remembers Steve White, who was a teenage drummer known to Munday through some work he'd done with Squeeze. 'I didn't know who it was at all,' says White. 'I only found out shortly before I was about to audition. I was never a fan of the Jam; more a fan of Mick Talbot's in The Bureau. I found out that they already had someone but they let me audition as I'd bothered to turn up . . . I got the Kid Jensen session the next day, then the first live gig, then the Paris EP. It's been like that ever since. Very casual.'

White's youth appealed to Weller. He was also a talented player whose musicianship was well beyond his years: 'I was always interested in drums from about six onwards. I used to watch the parade bands and Boys' Brigade stuff. But when I got my first kit I just smashed it up.

'My biggest influence for showmanship was Keith Moon. When you see that manic grin on his face, pushing them along . . . Brilliant!'

Paul Weller

He was later inspired by Art Blakey, who he describes as the first 'jazz/punk drummer'. From an early age his father took him to clubs to watch other drummers. He watched in awe when he saw Louie Bellson playing for six hours in one club and met him afterwards. Bellson told the young hopeful that he practised seven or eight hours each day. 'Well, that was it for me. School work, social life, the lot . . . I didn't give a shit. All I did was practise for six hours every day.'

He had lessons with Bill Bruford for two years, then, at the age of seventeen, played for Squeeze's musical *Labelled With Love* for three months. When he joined the Council as another floating regular, the drummer opened up fresh areas of music for Weller: 'Steve White's playing, from bop to funk, is a revelation. It's opened up a whole new world, all these different things. 'Cos I mean I've been brought up on pop music and it's quite a sheltered world really. I used to dismiss jazz and classical music . . . but I've woken up to a lot of different music in the last two or three years apart from rock music and heavy metal.'

The first song Steve White played on was the anti-Thatcher single, 'Money-Go-Round', which was released in 1983 and missed the Top Ten by one place. Weller and Talbot adopted a stereotypical rackateer look to satirise the Tories and they also raised money for Youth CND through royalties from the hit. At the time the song was written they had no idea that a General Election was only weeks away. In the event it came out a week or two before the election which, much to their bitter disappointment, gave the Tories another term in office on the wave of jingoism fuelled by the Falklands War.

'Money-Go-Round' also featured a young black singer who would play a major role in Paul Weller's life – Dee C Lee. However, she was not credited as a permanent member of the Council until later in their career. By 1985 she was doing interviews with Paul as a Style Councillor although technically she was still a 'permanent session' rather than a fully fledged band member. Born on 6 June 1960, Diane Sealy grew up on a housing estate in Leytonstone, east London. 'Most of our neighbours seemed to be either pushers, pimps or prostitutes. I was determined to get away from that sort of life . . . I talked myself on to the books of a local model agency [her nickname is Motormouth]. I reckoned I'd be the face that would sell a million products but the only thing the agency were interested in were my hands and my feet.'

Sealy was a big fan of 70s pop and soul music like The Jacksons, The Osmonds and The Sweet, and later she got into Cameo, Parliament and Brothers Johnson. At seventeen she started singing sessions with rock bands, then did some cabaret in the Middle East, and after she returned to the UK she became a backing vocalist for Wham! She sang on their hit singles 'Young Guns (Go For It)' and 'Bad Boys' in 1982 and 1983. 'They didn't want me for my voice. I was just there to look good on the videos.' By this time she was calling herself Dee C Lee, which was a play on her surname. Weller was initially a fan of Wham! and a further connection was Dee C Lee's session work with Animal Nightlife.

Although she'd often listened out for her own sessions on the radio she'd completely missed The Jam and claims she had no idea who she was working for when she turned up to record 'Money-Go-Round' at Solid Bond Studios, the old Phillips studio which Weller bought for £200,000 after re-signing to Polydor in '82. In the large, elegant building in Stanhope Place near Marble Arch (which also had offices where John Weller worked, alongside his daughter Nikki who acted as secretary and manager of the studio) in central London, Lee recalls 'there were gold discs all down the hallway. I didn't recognise him from the pictures. At the time he had the long hair with the little curtain look. I said to him, "Who's this group The Jam?" as I came back from the toilet, and he said to me, "Some crap group that record here." I didn't think nothing of it.'

A few days later a friend told her about Weller's career. 'I felt a right prat but he wasn't bothered at all. Most people are overawed when they deal with Paul which is totally unnecessary because he's not the sort of person that you do need to be overawed with.'

When they married a few years later Lee sometimes caught up with Weller's past for her own amusement. 'He's got his private room upstairs with all his Jam videos and if I'm really bored I drag one out and have a bit of a giggle looking at him when he was really young.'

The Council's next studio session was one of the happiest of their career. Between 12 and 17 June 1983 they recorded the 'A Paris' EP in the French capital's Grande Armée studios, an idea inspired by The Modern Jazz Quartet who liked to record in different locations. 'We went to Paris for a week and the sun was out and it was hot every day you got up,' says Weller with summery nostalgia. 'We'd walk down to the studios each day and check out the shops on the way and stuff like that and in the evenings we'd finish at about ten or eleven and eat outside in the restaurants. All that was just brilliant.

'Paris is probably the most pretentious place I've been to! When me and Mick went over there we were attempting to outpose the French. I like the way they look, the way they carry themselves. The French have got a lot of style.'

Weller claimed he didn't know what existentialism meant but his holidaying approach to a romantic idea of Paris dictated the sound of new songs like 'Paris Match'. 'Close your eyes when you listen to this and you are in rainswept Parisian streets,' he said with ludicrous, camp exaggeration. 'Like all cities, the loneliest places in the world, even though there may be hundreds of people around, are at times like this. When I suggested that the girls' vocal at the end switched to French lyrics, our producer done his crust but what a charm it gives it!'

Sara Silver, their international contact at Polydor, found herself in the studio with the band on this trip. 'On "Paris Match" Paul asked me to write the French words. Paul made me sing in the studio so that he could then record over it. Of course I got to the end of it and I couldn't see them any more because I'd sung the whole thing flat and they were on the floor laughing. Recording to them has always had a great sense of enjoyment.'

Nigel Sweeney: 'Kenny Wheeler wasn't too keen on "Long Hot Summer" and preferred "Paris Match". I put the idea to Paul of doing the other side, "Paris Match", for *Top of the Pops*, and I have to say he was really proud of that.'

They later re-recorded "Paris Match" for their debut album, with Tracey Thorn on vocals. 'He got us down to record "Paris Match",' says Ben Watt, 'and the next thing I knew the album was out and there he was in his white trenchcoat and all the photos were in Paris.'

Tracey: 'And it sounded like Everything But The Girl and we thought, Oh!'

Watt: 'If I'm being really honest it does frustrate me. Paul obviously, to be generous, listened hard to us.'

The three ages of Weller
Clockwise from above:
The face of The Jam, 1979
(Erica Echenberg/Redferns)
The Style Councillor
(Howard Tyler/Retna)
Paul Weller, 1995
(Niels van Iperen/Retna)

Jamming at Reading, 1977
(Ian Dickson/Redferns)

Weller, Buckler and Foxton in 1978 *(S. Morley/Redferns)*

Blokes backstage
(Ian Dickson/Redferns)

(Erica Echenberg/Redferns)

One of The Jam's better ve▶
(Ebet Roberts/Redfe▶

Weller and Tracey Thorn a▶
ICA, 1981
(Erica Echenberg/Redferns

e tie remains but the style is sharper -
e Style Council, 1984
et Roberts/Redferns)

An unremarkable performance -
Live Aid, 1985
(K. Thandi/Redferns)

Dee C Lee singing at the Vienna Jazz Festival *(David Redfern/Redferns)*

Paul Weller and Billy Bragg launch the Red Wedge tour, 1986 *(Steve Rapport/Ret*

The Modfather as Pied Piper, London *(Steve Pyke/Retna)*

Weller finds his own voice at Glastonbury, 1994 *(Steve Gillett/Redferns)*

Paul Weller plays with Noel Gallagher and his legacy is assured,
1995 *(Des Willie/Redferns)*

Paul Weller in *The White Room*, 1996 *(Des Willie/Redferns)*

Two greats together. Paul McCartney and Weller at the recording of the *Warchild* album, 1996 *(Martin Goodacre/Retna)*

The soft, cool style of both acts mirrored a resurgence in jazz in the early 80s, which included Sade's multi-platinum *Diamond Life* album, Carmel, the Zoot-suited club cool of Blue Rondo A La Turk, Animal Nightlife and Working Week's jazz fusion.

Meanwhile, Sara Silver's debut experience in the studio followed an earlier baptism of fire. 'Before I started at Polydor I was at Stiff Records,' says Silver, 'where the type of artists were steeped in English tradition in the rock 'n' roll sense and I was very friendly with everyone from Madness to Tenpole Tudor. I get to Polydor and nobody had any relationships with the artists. No one could introduce you so I didn't meet Paul for a long time. The first time I met him, he was sat in Dennis Munday's office and I barged in and said hello. Dennis was their main – in some ways only – point of contact with the record company.'

While Munday was an essential link between the Council and Polydor UK, Weller was chatty with many of the London office workers. 'Paul knew everybody in the company from the postboy up. They were always in the building, especially through the Council. It was a nuisance because I was trying to work. I had a piano in the office so they'd always be in mucking about with tunes and silly cover versions.

'The only MD he had any time for was A. J. Morris. A. J. was very untypical for the music business. He was so straight he looked as if he was a bank manager. But Paul could get on with him because he didn't start talking about Paul's music.

Silver: 'For all intents and purposes they didn't like change, especially within the record company. They like their family around them. So I walked into that situation where they were a bit suspicious.'

When Silver took them out on their first promotional tour of Europe for 'Speak Like A Child' she faced a grilling from Weller which was characteristic of his initial response to new faces at Polydor. 'The first time I went out with them, I remember we had dinner and I was sat opposite Paul and it all started when he said to me, "So why are you working for a fucking record company?" That was the pitch. I pitched back with, more or less, it's none of your fucking business. We sort of had a row and everyone around the table pretty much sat back. I don't know why but somehow this row got us friendly. It was terrifying, very intimidating, but it was no different to Robert Smith who walked straight past me when I said hello, and Siouxsie Sioux. It all took time.'

The Style Council had declared their 'internationalist' flavour from the start with their first-ever photo session in Boulogne on the French coast. In Paris, Weller exaggerated his dandyism and clean, continental lifestyle to the extreme. His love of Parisian culture was partly rooted in the Mod scene of the 60s. In *Mods!*, Richard Barnes writes about one of his friends, 'He used to wear a striped jumper and a beret and eat garlic. He started to learn French . . . There was even a time when we saw him walking around wearing his beret and striped jumper and carrying a loaf of French bread under his arm.'

Although the duo tried to add a bit of English vaudeville humour – Talbot always had the air of a 40s music hall comedian about him – to their pseudo posing, the look was copied by some of their fans with initial seriousness. 'I went to Paris once with my parents and posed a lot in a grey trenchcoat and blue and white bowling shoes.' recalls one devotee. 'The French probably thought, Who's that idiot?'

Some fans also believed Weller's story about writing 'Paris Match' for a 'French chanteuse, Suzanne Toblas', which was one of the first Council in-jokes. The sleeve of 'A Paris' also claimed that the piano that dominated 'Le Depart' on the EP was going to be used in a new French film called *The Golden Lama* starring Alain Delon. There was more rib-tickling humour in France when Weller dressed up as a museum guide alongside a short-trousered Talbot in a 'hilarious' spoof TV show. Over the next few years they dressed up as angels, plucked shuttlecocks from their trousers, and chased each other around a field full of sheep, all for the sake of making 'humorous' promo videos. But for all the costume changes and thigh-slapping puns, the pair's jokes usually fell flat.

Nigel Sweeney often grimaced as he listened to the interviews he'd set up for the band: 'Mick wasn't the greatest interviewee ever – he was as difficult as Terry Hall. Maybe it was because he felt he shouldn't really be speaking at that point because Paul should be speaking, but of course then you've got Paul not speaking because he thought Mick should have been speaking. So they came up with this sort of dead two-man act. They were both silly with each other because they knew what the other was saying but it was no good as interviews. It did cause a problem. They were a comedy duo who weren't that funny.'

Ironically, the Council's Mod appropriation of Gallic cool was later adopted by Britain's affluent, Thatcherite go-getters – dubbed Yuppies – who would fill the new brasseries of London with filofaxes, mobile phones and Paul Smith suits. They too enjoyed the illusion of boulevard watering holes and clean, design-conscious jazz clubs where soft funk and easy listening jazz complemented their lifestyles.

This wasn't, of course, through any fault of Paul Weller, although by attempting to play with different cultural references and manipulate propaganda with a mixture of parody and earnest intent he was setting himself up for ridicule and misinterpretation. Quite simply, this was a game that he wasn't very good at. In the designer madness of the 80s, images were flipped, reinterpreted and disposed of at such a rate that nearly every cultural reference was caught in the cross-fire, leaving an aggrieved Weller flapping on his belly like a fish out of water. For instance, journalist Julie Burchill interpreted a right-wing reading of the absolute beginner in Colin MacInnes's novel, whose clean, sussed, modern lifestyle had clearly influenced Weller. 'Pop was the sound that lulled the young to sleep in the fifties and when they awoke in the sixties the young adult became the teenager – and freed from the politics of class, the teenager revelled in his lack of responsibility to history. The teenager was smug and superior to the few young adults who stuck by their class and their Labour Party; the stepbrother of the absolute beginner in MacInnes's novel says to the verbose sprog: "It was the Atlee administration who emancipated the working man and gave the teenagers their economic privileges ... and are you grateful? Not a bit." When he accuses MacInnes's hero of having no social conscience and of being a "traitor to the working class," [the kid replies] "You poor old prehistoric monster!" '

Clothes, books and pop music were being debated with greater sophistication in the 80s, as the media became obsessed with every detail of British culture. When Weller, the born-again propagandist, found he didn't have control over the interpretation of his messages, he backed off, complaining about the dandyfied pseudo-intellectualism of the times. 'There's too much written about the meaning of clothes,' he complained. 'There's a whole spate of journalists like Peter Yorke and all the junior Yorkies like Robert Elms and old Jon Savage. It's like they've found an alternative to the gossip column. Spout loads of rubbish, write three thousand words on the significance of ties and send it to *The Face*.'

In simple terms, of course, Weller's overt cosmopolitanism was a reaction to the overt Britishness of The Jam. He was undermining the knee-jerk image of a 'socialist' artist as a slovenly dressed, bearded figure with an acoustic guitar or a spiky-haired punk. 'It was revolution without having to dress like a naff punk,' declares an old fan. For good or bad, his boho tourism contrasted starkly with the ugliness of the times.

After their stylistic indulgences, the Council talked politics. 'Maggie and gang have sold us all out. They are the traitors; the true patriots are the women of Greenham Common,' flashed Weller angrily. He described his home country as a 'floating US missile carrier' and spoke out for the protesters at Greenham Common. 'The real rebels are the people that are actually doing something; it's not groups and it's not music, it's people like the women at Greenham. The CND marches, they're the people that are trying to do something about it, not just singing down a fucking microphone – and I'm not putting myself outside that category either.'

The situation at Greenham Common had started as a protest against the siting of nuclear weapons in the UK. In 1981, a march set out from Cardiff and arrived at Greenham, one of the proposed sites for NATO Cruise Missiles. Rather than returning home as they'd originally planned, women put up tents outside the gates and set up camp as a peaceful demonstration of their beliefs.

'Cruisewatch' was started to prevent Cruise Missiles from entering the area and eventually, in 1987, after the signing of the INF agreement, the first Cruise Missiles were shipped out of the Common.

In the face of such brutal political realism, Weller gave up writing his own poems: 'I wrote all kinds of wimpy things and real introspective stuff which is good to get out of your system but it's probably boring for some poor fucker to read. So I don't bother any more.'

On 12 July 1987 the 'A Paris' EP was released and climbed to number two with (Kenny Wheeler aside) everyone's attention focused on one song. 'Long Hot Summer'. Its accompanying video, which was shot on the River Cam in Cambridge, also caused a stir. According to Weller, 'Everything in the video is done in a really suggestive way. The pole Mick uses for punting is used as a phallic symbol and there's a shot of us lying on the grass caressing each other's ears.' The promo was censored by *Top of the Pops* and the magazine *Gay News* rang up for a quote. At the time Weller was also fluttering camply, 'French boys are the most beautiful in the world. I think there's an undercurrent of tension in Paris that, oh, say Singapore, just doesn't have.' That summer Weller and Talbot often flirted with each other in interviews as a way of winding people up. They succeeded in annoying the lad core of their audience, but some journalists believed there was no smoke without fire.

Neil Tennant, then assistant editor at *Smash Hits* magazine, posed the question directly: 'Are you gay?'

Weller: 'Am I gay? No, I don't think I am, not in the conventional sense, but I can appreciate people of my own sex as well. Some people I see I sort of feel an attraction for them but whether it's a sexual one I don't know ... I don't know about actually having gay sex but sometimes I think ... well, I wonder what it's like. I'm actually open-minded on the subject.'

This was as far as Weller went with bisexual imagery which was rooted in Mod dandyism. Richard Barnes wrote, 'The boys were effeminate and used to fuss about and preen in front of the mirror, but they weren't homosexual. There might have been a homosexual element but then there might also have been amongst the rockers and it wasn't particularly important. There was a time when Mod boys used make-up and mascara.'

There was certainly a streak of sexual androgyny in the attitudes of some Weller diehards. 'I never took any notice of the girls,' remembers an old Council fan. 'I was too busy strutting around, although in retrospect I probably looked a right idiot. I was the only student in my halls of residence who would iron his clothes and polish his shoes. I spent my grant in two weeks on cardigans, loafers and jeans. Short, spiky hair. I also had a couple of long macs – a grey one and a cream one.

'I remember going to Style Council gigs and there were complete Weller clones. They also had a knack of being able to dance like he does as well. He's a crap dancer so how they managed to affect this dancing I don't know. There were also people who were able to follow his haircut. It's one thing to look like a fan but another to think that you are Paul Weller.'

The Style Council were also very much a pop group with a young, fanatical following. Nigel Sweeney witnessed this first hand: 'They were a more commercial group. I remember trying to get on a bus going back from a gig in Manchester. Weller was still a big hero at that time and we had trouble getting in the bus. It had to be parked right up close to the backstage door and there was a big scrum going on. There were security guards three or four abreast holding on to each other and forming a little tunnel so that we could get in the back. I remember nearly losing Mick Talbot who was just behind me. Paul came through and it was mayhem. This was a gig where there was a radio broadcast car outside with an extended aerial. We were up in the second-floor dressing room and had the window open because it was a hot evening and all of a sudden we saw this guy swinging backwards and forwards past the window. He'd climbed up the broadcast aerial. He was literally on the little whip bit and he was trying to get into the dressing room on this aerial. It was madness. Once we actually got into the coach we were driving along and there were loads of traffic lights, and there were six or seven hundred kids chasing us. I was in the back seat looking back and I just remember coming up to a red light and Kenny saying, 'Keep fucking going' at the driver. Eventually we get on to the motorway which is like ten miles away and there's still thirty cars milling around us. They were that mad.'

The Style Council made a concession to their young fan base by starting their own Torch Society fan club, described by a subscriber as 'basically just a newsletter with a few pages of Paul sitting in Hyde Park, a badge, a poster every few months and an apology about printing problems.'

Meanwhile, Weller's topless cavorting in the 'Long Hot Summer' video stirred the hormones of female admirers during a sweaty, hot summer. Eugene Manzi: 'I did notice more girls at Style Council gigs. It was certainly a softer sound but one theory I suppose is that The Jam fans had grown up, mellowed out a bit, taken their wives or girlfriends to see The Style Council and the girls got into it. He's an attractive guy, good tunes, maybe that was it. I think he's always been seen as sexy. Maybe not in The Jam but the Council certainly, especially in Europe. I used to talk to girls years ago who used to fancy the arse off him.'

Sara Silver: 'Weller has never been a teen idol. All these people that find him so gorgeous – it's quite funny really because he's not. He's got a wacky way of dressing. He became very dapper so you have to be into all that to appreciate his looks.'

At the end of October the band set off for a tour of Europe, playing six dates in the V.U.B. University of Brussels, the Palace in Paris, the Volkhaus in Zurich, the Trinity in Hamburg and Meervaart in Amsterdam. Sara Silver joined them on the tour. 'I always considered them as a small British island that used to move around the world. It was very self-sufficient, very sane, but was also occasionally like an iceberg and it would just bump into things and didn't actually connect with anybody. My job became the connection point, explaining things.

'There hadn't been a tremendous amount of communication in his international career about why you're doing something and what you're doing it for. I actually went on the road and toured with them to ensure that communication went through properly. The other thing is that if you talked to Paul he'd say, "No, talk to John"; if you talked to John he'd say, "Talk to Kenny" and so on. They were great at this. You'd run around in circles and never get an answer.'

The crew around the Wellers were incredibly tight and protective, if a little intimidating. Silver: 'Kenny is an incredibly kind-hearted person, incredibly straight and good at what he does. He's given a good part of his professional career to Weller. Steve White was eighteen and we had a bass player on the early tours, Anthony [Harty] who was sixteen. I remember the first time we took him out drinking I had to hold a bucket by him all night. So these old guys looked after all these kids. But everyone was always frightened by Kenny. People don't always ease up with him either. It's fascinating because, perhaps through experience, he's understood everything and never stepped out of his place. He has no delusions of grandeur but what he knows is phenomenal. He even has a programme of when he's going to get shit-faced, and boy, when he drinks he really puts it back. Litres and litres would go into Kenny and he wouldn't go and pee. It was mind boggling. But he'd always be alert and you'd feel safe. He's the sort of bloke that if the coach got stuck on a corner he'd lift a car out the way.'

Paul Weller

In Hamburg, the 'British island' invaded the city's Reperbahn red light district while Sara Silver and the other girls on tour were left behind. 'On tour they all used to go out and have a lot of fun,' says Silver, 'but they're not the sort of men that you'd worry about losing. They're not philanderers on the road. It's all boys' stuff. Even when the guys went down the Reperbahn and the girls were left behind you knew it was all innocent stuff. It was just a bunch of guys really. That's why there was so much humour. Out of boredom comes a jokey sort of humour. It was mostly cards and reading but there wasn't much else.

'Despite the closeness of Paul and his father they do have independent lives. I don't know how they've sorted their relationship except for the fact that I've never heard the word money cross Paul's lips and as for John, I've never heard him talk about music. It's almost as if by mutual consent they have a dividing line. I mean, John never went down to the studio. I think because Ann was involved enough she has this level of understanding. Then away from the touring and music business they can go back to their own normal lives.'

The Council deliberately kept this trip short to keep things 'fresh', a policy which they maintained throughout their time together. 'Paul was very sensitive about not touring to the point of complacency,' recollects Silver. 'That was something he really instilled in himself, that he never wanted to get bored by his live gigs or act. Every night he meant it.

'The other thing was they didn't like flying. They'd nearly died in a small plane during a storm and that had affected them. Paul and his mother both hated flying. I took Paul's mum, Ann, out on tour once and she was so scared she nearly broke my hand and he was the same.'

On their return they started recording their debut album, *Cafe Bleu*, and a single, 'A Solid Bond In Your Heart', which peaked at number eleven in November. As a response to the MD's criticism of the promo for 'Long Hot Summer', the band couldn't resist a bit of tomfoolery at his expense. 'We got into trouble for the "Long Hot Summer" video with the head of Polydor, A. J. Morris,' says Nigel Sweeney. 'He asked John, "Is Paul turning?" So what they did on "Solid Bond" was a special edit for him of hardcore porn.'

According to Weller he called up Morris and said: 'There you are. This one's got lots of women in it. Plenty of birds for you.'

The following month they performed at The Big One, a fund-raising show at the Victoria Apollo for various peace organisations, and played a live set on *The Tube*. Tour dates had been scheduled for the UK around the same time but these were moved back to March to coincide with the album release date.

The new year began with yet another single, one of their finest – 'My Ever Changing Moods' which broke into the Top Five. 'It's all about the adaptability of human beings but not with a quiet resignation,' explained Weller. 'No, these changing moods are nothing to be proud of, not while thousands starve and millions are killed 'cos of power playing war.'

While it was still in the charts, *Cafe Bleu*, also hit the High Street, debuting at number two. Weller described the record as 'romantic in a funny and pretentious way', a spirit which was expressed through the extensive Cappuccino Kid sleeve notes courtesy of Weller and journalist Paolo Hewitt and a quote on the back cover from Jean Paul Marat, an 'eighteenth-century visionary'. There was a clear anti-nuclear message in Marat's quoted text: 'Watch out, for as soon as it pleases them they'll send you out to protect their gold in wars whose weapons, rapidly developed by servile scientists, will become more and more deadly until they can, with a flick of the finger, tear a million of you to pieces.'

The album was certainly brave, with Weller only singing on half the songs. 'I remember playing Rick Buckler some tracks off the first Style Council album before it came out,' he claimed, 'and he was stunned. "Are you taking the piss?" I suppose it must have been the same for a lot of Jam fans but I couldn't see the point in forming another three-piece power trio.

'People complained that *Cafe Bleu* was a jumble of styles – that there were so many things going on it got confused. But it wasn't that confusing to us – it just wasn't what people are used to, that's all.'

For many fans Weller's decision to play jazzbo guitar on instrumentals such as 'Me Ship Came In!' and 'Dropping Bombs On The Warehouse' was the hardest to understand. He was sounding more like George Benson than Pete Townshend. 'The first side is supposed to be almost like a live sound, like a combo playing in a club with minimal backing and production.

Paul Weller

'My understanding of jazz is not because of musical proficiency, 'cos I don't understand those things. If someone plays a brilliant solo I don't know whether it's good or bad; the only criteria I've got is if it sounds good to me.'

Weller's enthusiasm for incorporating jazz into The Style Council's sound was shaped by his Mod tastes. Black American jazz was at the root of Mod cool, as Kevin Pearce describes: 'You are fondling an exquisite Bluenote sleeve . . . and you know it would be against your nature to loll around any more in the relics of rock, so it's only right to seek out a new look and lifestyle. Something suitably razor sharp and streamlined.'

A year later Weller confessed: 'Some of the jazz instrumentals are a bit dodgy really, but you don't know until you try.'

Instrumental work-outs aside, there were some great Weller compositions on the album, notably the positive thrust of 'Headstart For Happiness', expressing 'real joy and optimism. Much more than just a love relationship song.' A stripped-down, piano-led version of 'My Ever Changing Moods' showed his determination to avoid the limits of The Jam through restless experimentation. The swinging, skip-along rhythm and Bobby Valentino's violin playing on 'Here's One That Got Away' was also a success: 'The Whole Point Of No Return' was an enjoyable steal from 'Everything But The Girl' which didn't glimpse much daylight between the band's styles; 'You're The Best Thing' echoed the gorgeous, dreamy glide of 'Long Hot Summer' and 'Blue Cafe' was a lazily captivating soundtrack to a Parisian boulevard stroll. On the downside, 'A Gospel' was horrible cod-funk and 'Strength Of Your Nature' was a dull motivational chant which dated within a year.

Critics were divided. *Sounds* dismissed the record as 'dispensable dross' but others picked out stuff they liked from the musical jamboree, reflecting the confusion of many of Paul Weller's fans.

The rescheduled UK tour ran from 13–20 March 1984, featuring a ten-piece on-stage band including a horn section of Billy Chapman, Chris Lawrence and Stewart Prosser. Weller also played out an irritatingly muso role in the proceedings by switching between guitar, bass and keyboards. Although the comically challenged promise of levitating strippers called Dick And His Two Swingers never materialised, conceptual tomfoolery was present as Weller dubbed each gig a 'Council Meeting' and put together the shows as a Respond package (Tracie's debut album *Far From the Hurting Kind* came out in the same year, as did The Questions' best single, 'Tuesday Sunshine') with the headliners on first for half an hour, then the support acts Billy Bragg and The Questions, followed by a second Style Council set which lasted for an hour and a half. They usually encored with 'One Nation Under A Groove' signalling Weller's enthusiasm for the sci-fi, black politics of George Clinton's sprawling, interplanetary funk. Four days after they'd completed their jaunt around Britain, the Council headed off for another brief trip around Europe, playing dates in Belgium, France, Holland and Germany, where Weller fell over and broke his arm after chasing the backing singer, Jayne, down a corridor in Berlin. The band's guitar roadie, David Liddle, a portly man with a striking resemblance to The Grateful Dead's Jerry Garcia, took over from Weller on guitar. 'That was one of the funniest things I've ever seen,' says Sara Silver. To this day Liddle still gets on-stage with Weller to play the odd guitar part, including a TV appearance on BBC's *Later Special*.

After taking a few weeks off for Weller's arm to heal, the Council played four dates in Japan. Sara Silver: 'In Japan, Paul broke as a teen idol. The stage got mobbed by young girls which freaked everyone out. It was unprecedented because they broke through territory by territory which hadn't happened before.' At their peak the Council were selling around 100,000 of their new releases, not bad for a country where international acts only account for about 20 per cent of the total market. The tour was later captured on the *Far East and Far Out* video which was released in September '84.

This trip was followed by their first shows in the States, where they played two at the Savoy in New York and two at the Wiltshere in Los Angeles to a 'mixed reaction'. Nevertheless, 'My Ever Changing Moods' crept up the American charts to number 29 and *Cafe Bleu*, which was renamed *My Ever Changing Moods* for the Stateside release, entered the Top 40. By the end of the year The Style Council were voted the best new band of 1984 by *Billboard* magazine. Weller's own feelings about America had warmed a little since The Jam.

Sara Silver: 'Paul likes aspects of America. Everything he'd ever say about it being crap and rubbish is true but there's also a lot of good things there. But they're very superficial things; the important ones are the targets for his attacks.'

Weller: 'The things that appeal to us from America have been the trivial things, really, like deluxe fridges and all that shit, and the freewheeling Cadillac kiddies. It's been no great cultural gain at all – totally the opposite I think.'

Mick Talbot underlined the Council's determination to pursue American success only on their terms: 'We got asked to do *Soul Train* twice but we didn't go and do it because that's against our nature. We didn't want to fly to LA to do one TV programme, however credible it might have made us.'

Silver: 'Kenny Wheeler loves America – he has holidays over there and his brother lives in the States. They're not your standard English family that goes nowhere. These guys travel around the world more than anybody and enjoy every aspect of it. I think they grew into that. They did it together.'

Throughout the Council's history the relationship between Weller UK and their American label, Geffen, went through plenty of ups and downs. Sara Silver recalls one such occasion. 'We had one of those experiences when we put together a two or three week tour of America and some people came over. They walked into Solid Bond Studios, as if they owned the place like Americans would. By the time they'd left this meeting, which was to discuss the tour, Paul had turned round and said, "I'm not going."

'They can shut down. At any particular point, they'll turn their backs and walk away. The question of understanding and timing is probably never more critical than with an artist like Weller. But the record industry isn't always thoughtful about the nature of the people involved in a big tour. That's why everything goes wrong all the time in the music industry. Dee didn't really like travelling either. There was a lot of stuff that she didn't like.

'There's always been this thing about Paul where you're stopping your own success. He's kept his very sane world and he's done everything on his own terms but on the other hand if you were looking at it from the record company's perspective, he should be a lot further down the line.'

In May they released another great single, a revamped version of 'You're The Best Thing' from their 'Groovin' ' EP, featuring a sax solo from Billy Chapman of Animal Nightlife.

The Council played a Youth CND benefit gig in Coventry, then after a holiday (Weller in Capri, Talbot in Crete), they made their first official visit to Italy, appearing on several TV shows and performing at some open-air festivals. 'I don't think anything had really worked out in Italy in terms of touring in The Jam,' says Silver. 'The tents were the only places you were playing, the facilities were weird and you always felt like you were being ripped off. I could speak Italian so when I started working with them I could bridge all those gaps. Those sort of experiences could open your mind up. It was a learning curve for Paul.

'He'd had an extreme nationalistic view at the start of The Jam. Now it suddenly started to hit in Italy and he'd be talking to communist papers. Or you'd have *Italian Elle* magazine doing a photo shoot with Mick, which was one of the funniest things I've seen. There was this hairdresser going at Mick with some hair gel and he was like, "Get off, you wanker." '

The Council's communal, mutually supportive spirit was in stark contrast to the fragmentation of British society taking place at the time. In particular, Arthur Scargill was leading the miners into what he saw as the last great industrial battle. Thatcher set out to destroy the miners' union which she saw as 'the enemy within'. Scargill didn't wait for a ballot and led the union into a national strike when Thatcher's American axeman Ian McGregor proposed to close half the country's pits. There were violent clashes on the frontline between miners and riot police, the most savage coming at Orgreave in May '84 where TV cameras captured some of the most disturbing scenes of rioting, mayhem and police brutality ever seen in this country. Union assets were frozen as the strike continued and miners became dependent on the fundraising efforts of artists like The Style Council who became increasingly politicised by the urgent requirement for constructive help.

Weller: 'In the early eighties it was pretty clear cut which side you were on, you know what I mean.'

Over the next few months Weller played benefit gigs for the miners in Liverpool with Bronski Beat and Madness and a GLC organised benefit alongside Arthur Scargill. Not all of his fans went along with the Council's radicalism, even as a temporary, youthful call to arms. Mick Talbot: 'I've been followed into toilets and called a communist by mobs of furrow-browed youngsters who've told us they used to like us before we turned communist.'

Paul Weller

Sara Silver: 'Paul came from a harsh background and some people identify with that. There's the real British bulldog mentality in the street sense and Weller has that behind him. There's a whole borderline of violence and male machismo that trails behind him and is still part of him. Even though he's grown up and can have the most sophisticated life he wants, the roots are still there.'

Eugene Manzi: 'I always felt that among the old Jam fans who went to see the Council there was an element of sort of football hooligans. It's funny, he's got that image of being a bit tough, and because of his accent I suppose they identify with that. But he's not really like them and I think it's a pity because you go to his gigs and you see some of these herberts and they're a bit hard.'

A former fan notes: 'There was a well-known time at Wolverhampton, during the miners' strike and Greenham Common protest. He had Anna Joy David from YCND come up on-stage in between a set and she was heckled beyond belief. Paul Weller came back on-stage and sang "Money Go Round" to great applause. He said to the audience, "You like that song and yet half of you wouldn't listen to Anna Joy. It puzzles me." I should imagine that he was quite disappointed with elements of the audience.

'At the time I thought I was completely left wing but only because I didn't know any better. I'm not now. You have to make up your own mind. I'd vote Tory now. I remember reading a magazine article and the interviewer said, "What do you think about the fact that most Jam and Style Council fans turn into bank managers?" and he dismissed it. He said it wasn't true. But I think it's more true than he would like to admit.'

Weller started putting together a fund-raising single called 'Soul Deep' under the name The Council Collective, featuring Dee C Lee, Vaughn Toulouse, Leonardo Chignoli from Animal Nightlife, Junior Giscombe and US Motown artist Jimmy Ruffin. However, Weller was ready to ditch the project when South Wales cab driver David Wilkie, who was ferrying workers through picket lines, was killed by two miners who dropped a concrete block on his car. Weller was shocked by this act of violence and his decision to delay the project while he made up his mind about what to do left thousands of singles discarded in his record company's warehouses. It was a revealing insight into the artist's approach to politics. He was not an ideological purist, but a man who ultimately empathised with normal working-class people on both sides of the picket line. He recognised that the 'scabs' who continued to work during the strike were usually motivated by a need to support their families. Although he disagreed with them he was appalled at the murder of Wilkie. After further discussions with Polydor he decided to give part of the proceeds to the victim's widow and the rest to Women Against Pit Closures and the song was released in December, raising £10,000 through its Top 30 placing. 'The aim was to raise money for the striking miners and their families before Christmas. In the light of the tragic event last week we will also be giving some of the money to Mr Wilkie's widow. We still support the strike – because if the miners lose it will mean the end of the trade union movement.'

In October, The Style Council released what would prove to be Weller's least favourite single, the strings and piano led 'Shout To The Top', which was also the first time he'd self-produced. Self-evidently upbeat, the song was in the same vein as 'Beat Surrender' and The Jam's cover of 'Move On Up'. It's not surprising that Weller would adopt the uplifting anthems of garage house at the end of the decade. The song also featured in a new American movie, *Vision Quest.*

In contrast, the B-side, 'Ghosts Of Dachau', was a stark portrayal of the concentration camp. Weller was proud of the song: 'It's about a couple who still try to carry on their love affair amongst the death and degradation in Dachau, a Nazi concentration camp. I went to Dachau in 1978; it's just outside Munich in Germany and still the place haunts you. I really think everyone should be made to visit any of those Nazi death camps. It would soon put a stop to a lot of the racist bullshit around.'

Weller also announced his ambition to take the Council's visuals a lot further. He wanted to make a film. 'An idea we have got is to make a film, not because we fancy ourselves as actors 'cos I certainly wouldn't be able to act . . . I don't think any group's ever made a great film with the exception of maybe *A Hard Day's Night*. It's always been rags to riches, all that cliché shit. I'd like not to be cast as musicians. It's just the question of finding the right story.

'Joe Orton wrote a screenplay for The Beatles which they never used and I thought the idea of teaming up Orton with The Beatles was brilliant. Someone else told me about Andrew Loog Oldham trying to buy *Clockwork Orange* for the Stones in the sixties. It's that idea we're looking for. That pairing up.'

Fans who shivered at the prospect of a Weller film would later see their worst fears brought to the screen with his involvement (alongside budding thespian David Bowie) in Julien Temple's *Absolute Beginners* and the Council's own *JerUSAlem* project.

The band set out on their second tour of the year in the autumn under the banner 'Council Meetings Part Two', with a DJ, Vaughn Toulouse, Dee C Lee back on vocals after a brief break and a half-hour play instead of the usual support band. Playwright Tony Marchant, whose new work, *Lazy Days Ltd*, had recently opened at Stratford East's Theatre Royal, was commissioned to direct the piece, entitled *The Three Musketeers Go Wild* by Aiden Cant. However, this half-hour work about two youth training scheme trainees who take their boss as hostage was pulled at the last minute when one of the actors broke his leg. The UK dates were followed by more in Italy – in Rome (where Steve White's drum kit collapsed), Bologna (voted concert of the year in 1984 by an Italian magazine) and Milan, where the demand for tickets forced a last-minute switch to a bigger venue, the Lampugnano Tenda Theatre.

In spite of his own self-criticism, Weller's Riot Stories was still trickling out new works by unknown writers. In October he announced, 'We've got a new book coming out this month. It was put together by this bloke from Manchester called Dave Potter and it's not just an anthology of poetry, it's got a more direct theme to it. It's called *Spongers* and it's about people's attitudes to being on the dole.'

The year ended with dates in Margate and London, where the Council played two nights at the Royal Albert Hall. They also made another live appearance on *The Tube*. Steve White also had a solo single on Respond called 'Never Stop (A Message)' which was credited to The Mighty Eltham Funk Federation. Described as 'a tribute to Art Blakey', it was a Latin jazz track with a big drum solo. He also played drums live with fellow Respond act, The Questions. However, Respond was dying on its feet. The early commercial promise of Tracie's 'The House That Jack Built' was never repeated and the distribution deal with A&M broke up after White's single. Only Tracie was retained on the roster, which returned to Polydor, although there were plans for more Steve White projects and even a covers album by The Style Council. However, Tracie only managed two poor-selling singles before she disappeared for good to domestic bliss in Birmingham and the Council never got round to the covers album. At the end of 1985 Weller let the label die, another failed pop-star-run label following in the footsteps of Elton John's Rocket and The Beatles' money-burning Apple. 'Most of the records were really weak', admitted the label's boss. 'There was only one good record that was really fully justified in being released and that was Vaughn Toulouse's one.'

In 1985 Paul Weller accepted the position of English President of International Youth Year, together with actress Julie Waters – an odd decision given his previous determination to avoid the tag of 'spokesman for a generation'.

'I'm still a bit unsure about my involvement, really,' he confessed. 'I think it's more of a media thing in a way – I'm sort of a figurehead. There are lots of hiking clubs and Brownie groups which is fine, but there's also the people whose interest is more political. That's more the side I'd like to be involved in. I think the aim should be to create a circulation of information among young people through all these groups, then use it in a political way.' The Youth Year celebrations culminated in a 'Physical Chemistry' show at the Queen Elizabeth Hall on London's South Bank, where Weller played a nervy acoustic solo set, sandwiched in between catwalk fashion shows and art exhibitions.

At around this time, Weller was inadvertently dropping hints which suggested he'd hit a rocky patch in his relationship with Gill Price. 'At times I do feel tied down,' he said. 'Sex complicates everything . . . It's always on my mind, I suppose, but I've got quite a warped view of it I guess. I still yearn for the way sex was when I was fifteen or sixteen: the innocence of that time. The trouble is sex can never remain innocent because there is so much to lose, especially for women.' He made it clear he didn't think highly of fidelity. 'What does it mean?' he flashed back. 'I don't believe anyone has the right to own someone else's mind or body.

'When I was younger I just fell into the same mentality that you

Paul Weller

should try and lay as many girls as possible and also treat them badly. I don't know if that's changed with the fifteen year olds today. And I'm not saying everyone grows out of it,' he added.

In spite of his seven-year relationship with Gill, he still didn't want to get married or have children: 'I can't see the point of it. A piece of paper doesn't mean you are going to stay with someone.

'I want a vasectomy because I am sure I never want any kids and I haven't got any paternal instincts at all. So I was trying to have the operation – you know, the little snip – but the doctor said I was too young.'

For someone with parents who were still together – and happily so – Weller's cynicism was surprising from the outside. However, his relationship with Gill had been going through a painful and protracted break-up for some time.

'We couldn't see why they stayed together for so long. They were hurting each other and it was very painful to watch,' said one friend. 'She was pretty down to earth. She didn't take much crap but she did like a drink. It was really sad, because she was really nice, really normal. He was becoming this star and going through all these changes. She was his other half and obviously not coping with it. Often evenings would would end up with her sobbing, crying and being carried out by Kenny Wheeler. And it was obvious that what was between them wasn't working. You just wondered why the horrible bit went on for so long. Then suddenly she wasn't there any more.'

Sara Silver also watched the relationship gradually fall apart. "It's a bit sad really. She had some problems. On the one hand she was very sweet and an ardent person. She was a real activist on animal liberation and vegetarianism to the point where it got uncomfortable. We could sit at this table and if there was anything remotely dodgy which she hadn't ordered it would be spat out in front of you. You know, it was what you were wearing on your feet, all that. But it overstepped the human thing. In many ways, because of who she was and where she was, she could have converted a nation to vegetarianism, but for some reason she had a blockage in dealing with people and only cared about animals. Subsequently the animosities set in. She was very pretty and very sweet, but boy, when she had a couple of drinks we all ended up in trouble. It just got worse. You know how people think that all artists have to suffer to write good music? Weller did suffer quite badly because he wasn't a malicious person at all. He'd just try to hide but he couldn't. So she'd come out with us on tour but invariably it wouldn't last very long because she'd get in such a state and everyone became miserable.

'Paul actually smashed a phone up once. We'd all been kept up by her phoning every single one of us in a hotel and eventually Paul completely trashed the phone.' Little of their tempestuous relationship was picked up on by the press, although the tabloids did run a report in the summer of 1985 which described a girlfriend wrecking his hotel suite in a Melbourne hotel during a tour of Australia.

Terry Rawlings: 'I used to get on with his girlfriend, mad Gill, who used to look after our coats behind the T-shirt stand. I think he was right to break up with her in the end. He was getting more and more famous, so the rider was getting bigger and bigger. She was nice but pretty nuts. There was always rucking towards the end. He was very keen on her. He used to spend a lot of time with her. They were always cuddling at the back of the tour bus. She used to like the touring side of it.

'The last time I heard of her she was running a bistro in north London somewhere. I bumped into her on Tottenham Court Road and we had a quick drink. She looked quite smart and sensible. I think she got the flat. She was just not there ever again. People just disappear. When Paul falls out with people they just disappear and you never see them again. Everyone follows Paul's lead so if you're out of favour with him, everyone blanks you.'

Gill quit her job at the Solid Bond Studios where she worked on the accounts and disappeared. Another acquaintance of the band remembers: 'After watching their problems go on for months Gill suddenly wasn't around any more. We assumed she'd gone back to her parents and no one heard from her again.'

By March 1985 the miners' struggle had ended in defeat, dividing families and the National Union of Mineworkers. There was a noticeably edgier, harder feel to the Council's next single, 'Walls Came Tumbling Down', when it came out a couple of months later. In addition to its placing in the UK charts, the single also became one of The Style Council's biggest sellers in Europe. Their new fourteen-track album, *Our Favourite Shop*, came out the same month, debuting at number one.

The sleeve featured an imaginary shop crammed with books, records and clothes which either belonged to Weller and Talbot, or defined their tastes. The books included the *Ragged Trousered Philanthropists* by Robert Tressell – 'one of my favourite books of all time,' says Weller – *Prick Up Your Ears*, a biography of the playwright Joe Orton, some Orwell, Shelley, Oscar Wilde's *The Soul of Man Under Socialism* and, according to the foppishly wedged frontman, 'things I grew up with like skinhead and suede-head.' Talbot's contribution was *The Raymond Chandler Speaking Book*. There was also a cappuccino maker, the top of an old pinball machine, a snooker cue, a Rickenbacker guitar and Weller's plastic belt with 'soul' written all over it. 'Actually, it's my favourite thing in the whole picture. I've had it since I was about six – I used to wear it around my head.' A Sex Pistols hanky, a Small Faces EP, 'Mick's Otis Redding T-shirt on a nice Twiggy hanger' hinted at musical eclecticism, while the singer's 'old record player I got as a present from my family' sits on the floor. As for the duo them-selves, Weller is reading a book by photographer Philippe Charbonier while Talbot is flicking through some old EPs.

'The original idea was a kind of parallel between a shop where all our favourite things are jumbled up and thrown in but in a way that worked,' said Weller. 'The same way that our music has a lot of different styles but what comes out makes a lot of sense to us.'

In spite of his mixed feelings over *Cafe Blue*'s instrumentals, jazz still exerted an influence on the album. 'I like more groovy modern jazz . . . The stuff that is blues and gospel based. My faves are early Donald Byrd, Herbie Hancock and Art Blakey. It's really all still soul music I think.'

'Paul was beginning to show an interest in Blue Note records and was buying jazz albums,' remembers Steve White. He would come up with a song but instead of coming up with a conventional rhythm we were trying tracks with brushes or with more jazz beat. It was a lot looser in the earlier days – anything went.'

Weller was filtering these Latin and jazz styles through his guitar playing, resisting the desire to thrash any power chords. 'I'm without doubt a guitarist even though lately I've played other instruments too. Some time ago I got bored with the guitar. My way of playing wasn't progressing so I thought it was necessary to take a rest and think it over. I have quite an eclectic style, a fusion of different sound sources. I consider myself a fairly good guitarist. I believe my best quality is that of not taking everything too seriously. I'm an economic guitarist, I think it's better to play few notes, the necessary ones, but in the proper way, I think it works out.'

The Council found time to rehearse and demo the album first. Steve White: 'The preparations for this album were much more thorough than on *Cafe Bleu*. We demoed and re-demoed songs, changing certain things and planning our method of attack well in advance. A week or so before we began recording we went into a rehearsal studio and got familiar with the arrangements, something which helped us greatly. We recorded for two weeks. All the preparation paid off and we put down an average of a song a day.'

For all the thorough preparations they were still pouring out material at a prolific rate. White: 'We just always seemed to be recording for two or three years, culminating in *Our Favourite Shop*, which was the peak for me. At one point there was a single coming out every eight or nine weeks. Not only that but "The Lodgers" single [which came out in September of that year] had something like thirty-four minutes of music on. I remember at the time a Duran Duran album was like forty minutes long and we were putting out as much music on a single.'

The Council's determination to do the unexpected created some inspired highlights. Deceptively jaunty Latin jazz on 'All Gone Away' was juxtaposed with a lyric about a ghost town ripped apart by economic depression, as Weller underlined the growing gulf between rich and poor under Margaret Thatcher's government. His tender tribute to Dave Waller ('A Man Of Great Promise') avoided maudlin sentimentality via a softly sung, musically upbeat treatment. The picket line violence of the miner's dispute was dramatised by the stark, string-led 'A Stone's Throw Away', one of the prettiest songs of Weller's career and the jazz-funk of 'The Lodgers' was a damning attack on the government. There was a brassier feel to 'Internationalists', which along with the passionate fire of 'Walls Come Tumbling Down' gave the easy-going, Latin feel of most of the songs something grittier to work against. 'Boy Who Cried Wolf' was another achingly beautiful song which focused on a broken

relationship and 'Everything To Lose' featured Steve White's first
lyric, an attack on Youth Training Schemes. The YTS schemes
were designed to provide employment opportunities for school
leavers but the Tories also realised they could massage the unemployment figures by discounting everyone on one. This initiative
also gave unscrupulous employers a cheap and plentiful labour
supply, but the inexperienced workers often received poor training,
little supervision and no guidance on safety. As a result, if you
worked on a Youth Training Scheme you were twice as likely to be
killed or seriously injured than the average mechanical engineer.
'Down In The Seine' was a lovely, lushly ornamented song which
signalled Weller's discovery of the Belgium singer Jacques Brel via
Scott Walker's 60s cover versions, and 'Shout To The Top' replicated *The Gift* by ending the album with a star-gazing
determination to fight the twin demons of self-doubt and destructive government.

Of course, the band's eclecticism inevitably misfired on occasions, with the Mick Talbot vocal on 'Homebreakers' getting the
album off to an uninviting start, while the Lenny Henry novelty
track, 'The Stand-Up Comic's Instructions', is best skipped.

Despite some mixed reviews it was widely considered to be their
best work to date. The *NME* declared, 'If nothing else this album
makes it hard ... for any Style Council fan to say they follow
Weller just for the clothes and the music. He's made politics the
first item on the agenda ... I don't consider him the fountainhead
of all wisdom on the subject, but I've rarely heard these views
conveyed with so much passion and panache.'

Over the next twelve months the album was given a substantial
push overseas, topping worldwide sales of over a million. This was
partly through the efforts of a new MD, former manager of The
Motors, Richard Ogden, who gave Sara Silver a lot of support after
his appointment in 1986.

Richard Ogden: 'I thought there was no real reason why Weller
couldn't sell overseas. I found out he had a terrible reputation –
unreliable, wouldn't turn up, didn't do television or interviews.
Thanks to Sara Silver's drive and input we got him out there. On
Our Favourite Shop we translated the lyrics into all the European
languages and we really went after the political thing.'

As well as receiving worldwide acclaim, the band were enjoying themselves. When they headlined the Glastonbury Festival in the summer of 1985 everyone in the band was drunk, even Steve White who doesn't usually drink. 'That was one of the most memorable nights of my life,' says White grinning. 'It was total utter mayhem, to see Paul flailing away on his guitar with his white Levis, trying to keep them clean as the mud was flying. It was brilliant.'

Weller: 'We played "Long Hot Summer" and I got pelted with mud. All over my white trousers. It was so bad that I had to put down my guitar. I was so drunk I couldn't even play.' Weller fell over on to his back and couldn't get up. Radio One broadcast the performance on a Saturday night and it's also a much-loved Weller bootleg.

In the same month they released one of Steve White's favourite songs, 'Come To Milton Keynes', as the next single. 'I liked the wackiness of it,' says White. 'The Glenn Miller horns, and I loved the fact that it wound the Milton Keynes residents' association up. I couldn't believe the controversy – the calls we were getting to the office saying, "You've got to come to Milton Keynes because it's a great place really." ' Few fans shared his enthusiasm for this over-egged, messy mix of kitsch horns, squealing synths and twee orchestration.

Back in 1984 Weller had sung on the Band Aid single, 'Do They Know It's Christmas?', which topped the charts in December.

'Remember that time before Live Aid when everyone hated each other in bands? I was very involved with Bob Geldof in Boomtown Rats,' says Nigel Sweeney. 'Bob rang up and said, "Spanner, I'm making a fucking record in ten days' time, get Paul Weller on the phone to me." And it's like, fuck, these two don't like each other. Anyway, the conversation took place and Paul put whatever had happened behind him – and there were things – and he also said, "Do you want any other help?" And he sat down there at the studio on the Saturday just in case they needed any other help on the backing track. He did a little bit of guitar which actually wasn't used at all in the end.

'I arranged to meet him at Sarm Studios on the Sunday. He was walking down the road, he had a long coat on and a cane or a walking stick and there were loads of press down there. But he was like, I don't care any more, I'm just me. I just thought he was completely different to how he had been. Just little things like that meant a lot to me because this was a man who wouldn't have gone anywhere without Kenny Wheeler or his dad. That was the point where he started to give people his home number. Nobody had it up to then apart from Kenny and John and I guess Bruce and Rick must've had it. He was starting to become a little bit easier with himself. They were little things but they must have been big in his mind.'

A few months later he was one of the first artists approached by the single's organiser Bob Geldof to play Live Aid.

Sweeney fast-forwards to the eve of the live event in aid of Ethiopia. 'We did the rehearsals for Live Aid on the Friday. They were running really late. I'd got Mick Talbot on Radio One's *Round Table*. He was good in those situations; when he was on his own he was good. There was no way we were going to remove ourselves early, so *Round Table* was at 5.45 and we only just left Wembley at 5.30. We left and we were scrambling along the A40. I had one of the first car phones and we did the first two links from the car.

'The next day we all piled up to Wembley. It was sunny and it was just unbelievable. It was such a big show. Everyone was getting ready for it. It had taken over England and everyone knew what was going on. The Council were the second or third band on after Status Quo had done "Rockin' All Over The World". I think they did two or three numbers. I'd organised for them to do a completely separate TV thing, so we all went down to Maidstone to do this programme, to promote "Come To Milton Keynes". We had the orchestra – sixteen strings players with monks outfits – again, Paul Weller's idea. It was a really hot day and they were sweating their guts out. While we were waiting around we were watching Live Aid on the telly. We did the TV, finished at about six, went back to Wembley and Paul got up for the finale.'

Not long after Live Aid, Weller and Dee C Lee started seeing each other. Steve White: 'It was a real surprise when I first cottoned on they were seeing each other. I remember I was out walking on a beach in Norway when we were doing a festival just after Live Aid and I'm up the beach and there's Paul and Dee walking hand in hand and I thought, Oh, what shall I say here? I didn't know what to say because they were obviously very much in love at that time. Eventually, I went up to Paul and said, 'What's going on then? Are you going out with her or what?' I just had to find out what was going on. And once I knew there was something that was fine, you know.'

Sara Silver recalls, 'It wasn't a long time after Gill, no. The two relationships almost ran into each other. But you've got to remember that Paul and Gill had been seeing each other for a long time.'

Inevitably, the relationships within the band were changed by the new couple, who married in secret two years later. Weller: 'I don't think it affected what we were about – I just think it kind of distracts you whenever you fall in love with someone ... that happened to me in '85 and at around the same time Mick had a kid. These things kind of take away from the band but that's part of growing up, I guess. It's different when you're a teenager in a band because that's all you've got and nothing else matters.'

Weller admits he acted like a 'dickhead' towards Talbot when the keyboard player had his first son, Gene. 'I remember around the time of *Our Favourite Shop*, Mick had a kid and I can see now the way I was behaving towards him was ridiculous.'

The year ended with a re-recorded version of 'Lodgers' being released as a single. Dee C Lee featured heavily and received a full credit for the first time. She also wrote her first (and last) solo Top Five hit in the UK with 'See The Day'. Dates in Australia included four nights in Sydney (the first two sold out immediately), and there was also a tour of Japan and Christmas shows in London's Wembley Arena.

Steve White: 'On the tour after *Our Favourite Shop* we had Camille Hinds, Helen Turner, Mick, myself, Dee and Paul, and essentially I'd say that was The Style Council in its best form. They were the musicians who I think understood what Paul wanted and complemented his writing better than any other musicians. Possibly there wasn't enough attention paid to the fact of how good the band was at the time because we never had a rhythm section that was as good as that one and I don't think we ever had a better band. We did Live Aid, then Australia, and we were playing the same bills as Joe Cocker and U2. We were up there with those groups, we were giving them as good as they got. Maybe Paul didn't realise just what a good band he had at that time ... that's the one that should have been carried on into the next record.'

6 Beaten Surrender, 1986–90

Paul Weller: 'I can understand the people who've got a vested interest – the moneyed classes – supporting Thatcher, but the working class just makes me despair.'

Paul Weller: 'Hopefully if Labour can open up a bit more – let the general public have a say in how a Labour Party should be – they maybe could become more revolutionary.'

'Red Wedge has nothing to do with my hairstyle,' quipped the Labour party leader Neil Kinnock at the birth of a new campaign which brought together politics and pop music. Announced at an uneventful session in the House Of Commons in November '85, the coalition of Labour MPs and socialist musicians was a response to the low youth vote at the previous election. In America Memphis promoter Phil Waldren had organised rock shows to give Jimmy Carter a helping hand into the White House in the 70s, but the British political system had always responded to pop music with a stiff-backed awkwardness. In the 60s Harold Wilson posed with The Beatles in an attempt to gain credibility but there was no organised co-operation between the political left wing and its sympathisers at the top of the charts. The love and peace, tune in and drop out sloganeering of that decade didn't get into the bowels of the political system by joining hands with the men in suits at the House Of Commons. In the 70s Rock Against Racism and the Anti-Nazi League festivals had a broad political manifesto which gathered all sorts of people under its banner. Punk's nihilism was alien to all the political groups, even the anarchists whose predominately middle-class conceptualism was hi-jacked and converted into trashy, garishly loud, youthful rebellion.

Socialist pop singer Billy Bragg was the man who brought together Labour MPs with pop musicians in 1985 with his Jobs & Industry campaign which toured around the country with politicians getting up on-stage each night to show their commitment to Bragg's cause. Neil Kinnock had also appeared in a Tracey Ullman video and Ken Livingstone, the nasal-voiced left-wing leader of the Greater London Council, appeared on a record with The Flying

Pickets. The GLC's Jobs For A Change festival in Battersea Park, an all-day freebie in front of 100,000 people which featured OMD, The Pogues, Billy Bragg and Derek Hatton's Mersey Youth Festival, also signalled a growing bond between socialism, music and the youth vote. Bob Geldof's successes with Band Aid and Live Aid removed some of the barriers to co-operation, as it had proved that musicians could work together for a common social cause. This was also the mid 80s, a time when the increasing sophistication of the media had left the Labour Party behind. While Margaret Thatcher called in the slick advertising of Saatchi & Saatchi to revamp her scolding, matronly image, Labour MPs were still associated with the ancient stigma of cloth-capped socialism conducted in smoke-filled committee rooms. There was a creeping sense of panic in the left-wing ranks and pop music was seen as a direct, youthful medium for the party to explore, which would also, they hoped, ditch the old-fashioned stereotypes.

As for Bragg and Weller, they sat face to face with party officials across a table at Labour's south London base because they were appalled at the growth in youth unemployment and the lack of freedom and opportunities for young people. The pair felt they had a collective responsibility to their audience and had to do something positive to change the situation. Bragg reasoned that the best way to respond to this was to educate, spread left-wing ideals and make a very public demonstration of their beliefs. The light at the end of the tunnel was that by mobilising the youth vote they would help to push out the Tories at the next election and put Labour back into power. When this happened Red Wedge would have established an infrastructure of contacts between the new ruling party and British youth, which would keep their audience's problems at the forefront of social change.

From the start, Weller – who was hardly a great talker let alone political orator – was uncomfortable in these meetings, but in Bragg he found a charmingly articulate foil who was a great motivator of the people around him. Weller was also critical of the state of the Labour Party's leadership, telling one interviewer, 'I still think there's some quality [Kinnock] hasn't quite got. He's not quite strong enough, that's what frightens me – that he's not quite able to do it.'

By the end of the informal talks, a rough idea had formulated which would become Red Wedge, a poor choice of names in many ways as it suggested some of the old-style socialism which had cost the Labour Party dearly over the previous years.

In the run up to the Red Wedge tour in early 1986, the speeches started in earnest. Neil Kinnock declared, 'We're not interested in using performers just to add razzmatazz to politics. That is not what we want and Billy and the boys would not let us get away with it. The people involved in Red Wedge are serious about their politics and they want to make sure that Labour listens to young people and responds to what they say. We are delighted that so many people have given their time to get Red Wedge on the move.'

Billy Bragg outlined the basic argument of the musicians. 'Pop music has always paraded itself as a radical means of change but has never come up with anything. It's always been about selling radical chic – from Presley to The Clash onwards. It's never been pro anything.

'We can also make an impact on the Labour Party policy concerning things they know little about, like pirate radio and the marijuana laws. Four-fifths of all people that go to prison on drug offences are there for smoking marijuana. There is nothing in the Labour Party manifesto about setting music co-ops for young people. There's nothing in their policies that allows young people to have their say: it's always older people making decisions for the young.'

Ken Livingstone supported Bragg's dream of changing the Labour Party from within, when he argued, 'What I hope is that if you bring youth into politics those politics will change.'

Weller also espoused this view: 'My own hope is that we become important enough to be able to apply power and influence on the Labour Party and change the way they think. I feel perhaps we can radicalise them in some way.

'I think you can overestimate the public. The *Sun* is the most popular paper, Steve Wright is the most popular DJ, and all those horrible little aspects of our lives like us losing the miners' strike and Thatcher getting elected twice all go to prove you can.'

The seven-date tour kicked off on 26 January at the Manchester Apollo. The audience were seduced with the merchandised disposabilia of a Red Wedge T-shirt which declared 'Now That's What I Call Socialism' and brown paper bags on their seats which were crammed full with a selection of political pamphlets which discussed women's rights, apartheid in South Africa, unemployment, CND and other social issues. When they'd flicked through the leaflets they were lavished with two and a half hours of music, performed by the likes of Billy Bragg, The Style Council (who sometimes played Gil Scott-Heron's 'Johannesburg' as an anti-apartheid protest), The Communards, Jerry Dammers from The Specials, Madness, Lloyd Cole, Tom Robinson, The Kane Gang, reggae singer Lorna G and Prefab Sprout. The artists also gathered together for a special concert at London's Hammersmith Odeon as part of a farewell festival for the GLC.

The media reaction was typically divided along the political lines of the newspapers. Julie Burchill touched a nerve when she wrote a characteristically opinionated piece for the London listings magazine *Time Out*. She highlighted the sense of unease created by such an organised link between pop and politics, which seemed to patronise the fans with a mix of sugar-sweet music and medicinal political reality. 'This month the Red Wedge tour kicked off. Red Wedge are the Moral Minority of Britpop; join the Party and see the Promised Land (or at least Gary Kemp's ego in the flash flesh). Too young/dumb to remember the Labour sell-outs of the 60s, it seems they have also learned nothing about the limitations of pop. Red Wedge, in relying on the razzle and dazzle of entertainment rather than the beef of realpolitik (politics has been banned from the stage), are in danger of becoming the Saatchi & Saatchi of socialism. The young must learn to take their politics straight, like adults, and not like fidgety children who must be cajoled into thinking by concerts and singalongs with the Red-coat rockers.'

Nevertheless, pop and politics continued to co-exist through the summer with Jerry Dammers organising a free anti-apartheid festival on Clapham Common, featuring Elvis Costello, Peter Gabriel and Gil Scott-Heron in front of 250,000 people. The Style Council's involvement in causes reached a prolific scale in 1986, unmatched in its mix of causes even by the inspirational James Brown in the 60s – although he instilled more charismatic fire in the American black community than Weller's numerous activities could muster in his loafered look-a-likes, many of whom treated the fight against Thatcherism with doe-eyed respect rather than passion. As for Brown himself, Weller was disgusted by his hero's decision to support the Republicans in the 80s. 'I wouldn't go and see James Brown play now because he supported Reagan in the last election – I'd boycott him.'

After contributing the song 'Bloodsports For All' to an Artists For Animals album (which also featured Madness and Robert Wyatt) in August Weller appeared with Dee C Lee and Lenny Henry on 'This Is My Song'. This instantly forgettable song was written by Leee John and Ashley Ingham of Imagination in order to raise money for SCAR (Sickle Cell Anaemia Relief) and CCE-TSA (Canon Collins Educational Trust Of South Africa), an organisation set up to meet the needs of former political prisoners and refugees from South Africa.

In 1987 Red Wedge organised a twelve-date tour which ran up to the eve of the election on 12 June. When the Conservatives won their third term in office the compromised, teeth-gritting determination of the pop fraternity was killed off overnight. The Style Council played their last benefit gig in March '88 at the Hackney Empire, organised as a protest against proposed anti-abortion legalisation. A disillusioned Weller revealed his frustrations with Red Wedge: 'On the Red Wedge tour we were made to feel guilty for talking about each other's shoes. It was like, "How dare you? Clothes are a bourgeois trapping." I love clothes.

'The main thing I regret is becoming tied to the Labour Party. There are some good individuals but they always get pushed to the back. I began to wonder what I was doing. These people weren't the type I would normally hang out with, so what was I doing smiling and shaking hands with them?

'We had to go to all these bloody boring meetings. I had reservations about joining in to begin with and I wish I'd just stuck with my instincts from the start. All the politicians I met on the Red Wedge tour, the Derek Hattons and the Cuddly Kens, they were just celebrity figures out for themselves. I'm just not interested in anything political any more.'

Dee C Lee: 'As an outsider looking in at what was happening to him it used to really freak me out and I used to say, "You shouldn't really do so much, so many interviews. Make your music." '

Weller: 'I wish I hadn't got involved in it now ... It kind of soured it all for me. The idea was OK ... but I think we were used ... it really put me off politics and I really don't have much interest in it at all. I'll be very reluctant to get involved with anything like that ever again.'

Behind the rhetoric and counter attacks, Greater London Radio DJ Phil Jupitus, who performed as a support act for Billy Bragg in 1985 under the name Porkie The Poet and worked from the start on Red Wedge, gives his first-hand account of Red Wedge. 'Billy Bragg galvanised the whole thing through the Jobs & Industry tour the previous year. This was the first national tour by a rock band which Labour had sponsored. There was me reading poems, the Sid Presley Experience, who weren't very political, and Billy. There were a couple of leaflets and a couple of local MPs every night. Then Billy wanted to take it further and came up with the idea of Red Wedge.

'I went down to the Labour Party's south London office and at our first meeting Weller was across the table. He was cool about it because there were a lot of his peers there, like Bragg and Jerry Dammers. They were good motivators. Weller also let us have some meetings down at his Solid Bond Studios. None of the artists discussed how to make money out of it, except for one afternoon when Green from Scritti Politti turned up with his manager, who was asking all the music biz weasel questions: "Will there be an album?" "What are the royalty rates?" "How much do you get each performance?" Green was obviously interested in performing but after this meeting I don't think we heard from him again.

'In fact, there never was a Red Wedge album which is amazing when you think about it. They couldn't get it organised. At the time I thought that was a big mistake but I'm relieved we didn't now. It would have been awful.

'The whole thing was so patronising when you look back at it. I mean the bass player from The Blow Monkeys turning up at a youth club to talk about politics with young people is so condescending. There were all these meet and greet the community events where pop stars were just out of their depth. All that would happen is that you'd have all these oiky kids come up to you and ask for tickets for tonight's show. The artists shouldn't have been put in those kind of situations. Red Wedge was a well-intentioned mistake, which sort of summed up the mid eighties.

'The MPs were the worst aspect of the whole experience though. We realised they were just using the musicians. They'd appear for

Paul Weller

a quick photo shoot and then fuck off. It was a brilliant piece of manipulation which left me vowing never to work with MPs again.

'The Labour Party also became less militant in the late eighties. I remember The Housemartins had stated their intention to have the royal family's heads put on spikes and the youth party organiser, Annajoy David, told them they couldn't say that. Things like that completely took away the enthusiasm of the bands involved.

'There were some good moments. I used to do a shit poem with a Casio synth before The Style Council came on and I remember seeing Richard Coles from The Communards, Jerry Dammers and Mick Talbot all gathered around this toy which this fat boy from Basildon had bought from Woolworths a few months before.

'After the first tour there was an '87 election tour which had gigs and comedy nights running parallel. Again I remember bright moments of optimism that you get when you go and see any band really. There was the odd time when I really thought we were going to win the election and it was such a kick in the teeth when we didn't.

'Red Wedge just sort of petered out after that. They tried to keep the magazine, *Well Read*, going but it would just be the same advertisers, like the record company Go! Discs, in there all the time. I think it folded after fourteen or fifteen issues because they just couldn't afford to make it any more. Billy had to stay involved but it really drifted apart. Club culture was taking over and the idea of these guys who were getting older, getting up on-stage and saying, 'Don't do this, do that,' seemed horribly old-fashioned.

'We helped to get rid of some of the cloth-cap stereotypes but we invented new ones – the trendy parents and – worse – MPs trying to be "with it".'

Phil Jupitus was initially hurt by Weller's criticism of Red Wedge: 'Paul was so cool about the whole thing that at first I was surprised when he started criticising it afterwards. He's right though. I can see now that Paul wouldn't have enjoyed the experience from the start. He cares about people. The thing with the "Soul Deep" record where he stopped half the money from going to the miners shows what kind of man Weller is. He's not going to say, "Fucking scab, he got what he deserved." He cares about people. So he was never going to fit in with all the political

150

theorising and boring meetings that we had going on with Red
Wedge. Whenever you're tied to a big campaign there's inevitably
a lot of hot air and a lot of compromise. Neither suited Weller.'

A year on from Live Aid, nearly all of Weller's aims and
activities were crumbling into mediocre results and growing frustration with the right-wing press who he felt were somehow colluding
to undermine his efforts. 'All that, "How can you be a socialist and
wear a suit?" ' he moaned. 'That's propaganda, misinformation. I
sometimes wonder if there's more to it.' The dark spectre of a
conspiracy theory was ludicrous but symptomatic of Weller's
discomfort and isolation as an artist at the tail end of the 80s.

Apart from this, however, 1986 was a quiet year for The Style
Council. At the end of March a new single, 'Have You Ever Had
It Blue?' was released from the *Absolute Beginners'* soundtrack, a
project which ambitiously attempted to portray the fusion of black
culture and white adolescent energy in Notting Hill, London, in the
1950s, through the kinetic flash of a fast-cut, pop video format.
However, the Julien Temple directed movie was an expensive flop
which destroyed confidence in the British film industry. A cast
which included David Bowie, Ray Davies and, ahem, Patsy Kensit
failed to buoy up the project, as they were thrown into a swirl of
brilliant set pieces and a tacky script. Weller had been offered the
part of Dean Swift in the movie but turned it down because he
didn't want to waste several weeks on filming. Temple rejected the
singer's offer to write the whole of the soundtrack.

Weller collaborated on 'Have You Ever Had It Blue?' with
maverick jazz arranger Gil Evans, who had worked with Miles
Davis on the landmark album, *Sketches of Spain*. The song had
been rewritten into the Steve White lyric 'Everything To Lose' for
Our Favourite Shop. Now it received a fresh jazz treatment but this
latest top twenty incarnation of the two-year-old tune was poorly
received by the critics. The *Melody Maker* dismissed it as 'allowing
Weller to croon and scat-sing his way through a piece of wretchedly
half-baked cool jazz.'

At the time Weller still saw himself as part of a fight against Tory
repression which echoed the efforts of the black emancipation
movement in the 60s, and as a lone voice of 'good taste' in the
British music scene. The vinyl fanatic dug heavily and knowledge-
ably into his collection of Stax, Motown and Muscle Shoals

records, passionately devouring songs which expressed individual identity as well as the wider struggle for racial equality. The resurgence in the States of veteran soul acts The Drifters, The Tams and General Johnson from Chairman Of The Board also fascinated him, as he sensed the time was right for a new soul sound. He actually remixed Chairman Of The Board's 'Loverboy' for a reissued single later that year. The positive, gospel-rooted thrust of Curtis Mayfield's music was another key element, fuelling his determination to create a distinctive English fusion of soul, R&B, jazz, funk and politics which signalled a move away from the Latin and Hammond pop elements of *Our Favourite Shop*. For the first time in the Council, Weller was ditching the eclectism of the band's albums by focusing and directing their music around a specific sound. He aired some of his favourite soul and R&B influences when he DJ'd at three Sunday Soul concerts in the Shaw Theatre, July 1986, also reaching out to the contemporary jazz and soul underground through the bill which included the radical twist on reggae and funk played by ultra-hip jazz saxophonist Steve Williamson and his quartet. Dee C Lee played a solo set, Steve White played with tenor saxophonist Alan Garnes in The Jazz Renegades, and the dance troupe from *Absolute Beginners*, The Jazz Defektors, also appeared on the bill a few weeks after their performance in the video for 'Have You Ever Had It Blue?' (The original Council duo mixed the Defektors' self-titled debut album in 1987.)

One final significant development for the band in 1986 was a fresh deal with Polydor, set up by the newly appointed MD Richard Ogden, who had worked up through the ranks of the company for the last five years after managing new wave band The Motors at the start of the decade. Polydor pledged their faith in the Council by offering a million pounds per album. Ogden, who had been encouraged by the million worldwide sales for *Our Favourite Shop*, believed that, although Weller hadn't completely broken through outside the UK, he'd laid down the foundations for a major international career. The band had total artistic control and were now bankrolled in whatever they wanted to do. It was an enviable position which showed how effective John Weller was as a negotiator over money.

Yet Ogden was concerned that Weller and his father were cutting financial corners to keep Solid Bond afloat. 'They bought that studio and generally in the business everyone thought they'd been ripped off,' he says in his office at Sony Records, with Michael Bolton platinum discs lined up along the back wall. 'It was a bit of a white elephant. They virtually didn't use it for anybody else except themselves and it was expensive to run. As a result guys in the group were not being paid much money and they sounded like they were being paid £50 a week. I went to see them at the Albert Hall in 1987 and they were dreadful. The drummer Steve was great but Mick Talbot for me was always a negative influence. He seemed like this cynical bloke and I never saw him as someone who was going to say to Paul, "Come on, let's do our best and go for it." And the more control he was given in The Style Council the worse they became.'

Although the American record company were satisfied with the production on *Cafe Bleu* they were putting pressure on Polydor to fatten up and enrich the sound of Weller's records. At managing director level the executives in the States felt *Our Favourite Shop* hadn't competed in the R&B and pop markets because its production was too one-dimensional, lacking the expected depth. Ogden, a level-headed, pragmatic man and, despite the hovering presence of the Bolton CDs, a genuine music enthusiast, often talked over this 'problem' with John Weller and Kenny Wheeler. There was nothing more he could do. Contractually Paul had the final say and ultimately John was there to follow through his son's wishes. John had never claimed to be a great industry tactician and Ogden found it impossible to exert any influence. 'On the basis that Paul was trying to make smooth soul music, why wasn't he making records that sounded as good as David Bowie when he did *Young Americans*? Paul was recording music in a style that you were used to sounding wonderful on your stereo but he was making these scratchy little records in his own studio, using engineers that no one else had ever heard of and who never made another record that was any good. I love old man Weller but I always thought he didn't have a bigger vision,' he says. 'I really felt that what Paul needed to do was to take a major step in his career by getting a producer and making a record that sounded good.'

Ogden set up a casual introduction between the Wellers and soul producer Phil Ramone, but as he suspected the informal chit-chat failed to spark into a collaboration. 'The old man was never going

Paul Weller

to hire anybody because he wasn't prepared to pay them,' he says.
'John would say, "Yeah, all right, but you have to pay for it," and
I said, "That's not fair, you already get a huge royalty and I'm
talking about something that's of benefit to both of us so why don't
you pay half and I'll pay half?" But he never went for it.'

Clive Banks: 'There's good and bad in the relationship with the
father. There's a lack of experience there which might suit the artist
but it certainly was inhibiting. It was always, "How much money
is it, how cheap can we get it?" You've got to put your own money
back into this thing if you're going to make it work. At the end of
the day I don't think they were ever prepared to put their own
money back into it. A producer would cost money. It's a naiveté
really. The money thing was quite restricting.'

Miles Copeland, head of IRS records and brother of Stewart
Copeland from The Police, interpreted the Weller camp's hard-
headed approach to money as an ideological contradiction to the
left-wing politics Weller espoused. 'He is a small businessman,' he
stated in 1985, 'and when he goes to negotiate his deal and talks to
his banker he thinks in a Conservative, free enterprise mentality,
yet when he writes his lyrics his experience simply isn't used. He
talks about the class struggle and perpetuates the myth that people
are different. It's a derisive, destructive thing and that the pop
world helps to encourage it is just an appalling situation.' In reality
the firm line drawn between John Weller and his son in terms of
their fields of operation reflects an independent, free-thinking
contrast in the politics of the two men. John Weller has never
joined his son on the soapbox because he has never professed to be
particularly interested in politics. Obviously there have been over-
laps and they have privately discussed money and politics, but
Weller joined Red Wedge because it was an active way of helping
people – not because he had a clear, focused ideology. Copeland's
criticism that the singer's encouragement of class awareness actually exaggerates differences between people has an element of truth.
There's no point pretending that Britain is a classless society but
Weller had drawn the lines so clearly in his songwriting that he has
occasionally perpetuated the stereotype that all working-class
youths have fur-trimmed dashboards and that public schoolboys
are inherently crass, superficial people. There's certainly a streak of
counter-productive rhetoric in both The Jam and The Style Coun-

cil, which also includes their constant attacks on Margaret Thatcher. In the end they contributed to a process of transforming a shopkeeper's daughter into a larger-than-life, formidable, evil figure, which actually made her appear almost inhuman. Through this she embodied a perverse, strong-willed charisma which helped her to dominate the political scene for over a decade. Weller can hold up his hands and say 'At least I tried' but by the end of the 80s he realised that politics by their very nature are not as black and white as he first thought. He was pulled into a deceptive, manipulative, contradictory circus, full of paranoia, back stabbing and power games which as a young musician he simply didn't have the experience to use effectively. It's not surprising that in the 90s he expressed his political beliefs more obliquely through the soulful, personal charge of his songwriting which set out to connect with people directly. The problem for The Style Council was that they started to lose this link with their audience, undermining the humanistic beliefs at the core of all Weller's music. By 1986, distracted by his relationship with Dee C Lee and the demands of his political work, the songwriter was showing signs of losing interest in his own music.

Steve White, singled out by Ogden as the exceptional musician in the Weller camp, felt his loyalty stretched by a growing carelessness in the singer's choice of people around him. What hurt and annoyed him was that this contrasted startlingly with the man's previous attention to detail. 'I can always remember some of the people we got in were totally wrong,' he says with irritation, 'and I really thought, can't Paul see that two years ago he really would not have entertained this guitarist or this bass player? That really bugged me because I've always had a higher standard for myself and the people we worked with and, well, some of the musicians that were playing in the band stopped me from playing well.'

The young musician also had an intuitive grasp that Weller, for all his passion for the originals, was cornering himself into a contrived, pre-meditated soul style. 'The thing with the musicians was symptomatic of a more general change of direction that Paul was going through. Paul was more conscious of wanting to make something that sounds very soulful and I don't know how you can do that, to consciously try to make something that sounds soul-ly ... I think for a while there he lost interest.'

Paul Weller

'It Didn't Matter', The Style Council's first single off their forthcoming album, *The Cost of Loving*, had fired a warning shot that something was wrong when it was released in early 1987. It was a lumpen, half-paced track, sweetened on the chorus by Dee C Lee's backing vocals. The critics hated it but the band's following papered over the doubts in the UK by pushing it into the Top Ten. It was a flop overseas – a major blow to Ogden after he'd signed them on the dotted line for a million pounds. The Council's fan base in the UK wasn't enough to justify that kind of figure, especially as it was declining slowly but perceptively.

When Ogden heard masters for the new album he realised his worst fears had been confirmed. 'I paid him a million quid and then he delivers this bloody album. I thought it was terrible. A terrible sleeve and an awful record.'

Sara Silver was lying ill in bed when she received an urgent package from the MD. 'Richard Ogden sent the first monitor mix of the album with a message saying, "Help, you've got to go and see Weller." I went down there and Weller was saying things like, "neither me nor Dee can sing".'

According to Dee C Lee, it was Weller who was encouraging her to take a bigger share of the vocal duties in the band. Despite her chatty, outgoing personality, she was often unsure of her abilities and certainly lacked the confidence to force herself into the spotlight.

Silver describes 1987 as the 'Dee C Lee period musically'. She adds, 'It was taking him into The Isley Brothers thing but from a Paul Weller standpoint. Everyone expected the big Jam & Lewis sound but Weller wasn't into that. In many ways it was almost a precursor to acid jazz. So I don't think people understood him at the time. I don't think it was a question of recording technique.'

Weller's own vocals didn't help the new material. His voice hadn't the richness or sweetness for such blatant soul phrasing and the results, he now concedes, were too self-conscious and 'mannered'.

In February 1987 *Cost of Loving* was released, a homage-paying, nine-track album, packaged in a DJ format of two twelve-inch singles which played at 45rpm. Weller was trying to find new ways of keeping the vinyl format alive in the face of the new competition from CD. DJ remix culture may also have influenced Weller's decision to split the mixes on the album with Curtis Mayfield and

The Valentine Brothers (whose song 'Money's Too Tight To Mention' was covered by Simply Red a couple of years previously), shaping some of the songs at the studio desk.

There was no room for Talbot's jabbing Hammond sound in the streamlined soul music and he made an uncomfortable switch to electric piano and synths. It was a plastic-sounding, uninspired and surprisingly short – given their prolific output up to this point – collection, badly lacking any memorable songs or performances. In fact the band had recorded half a dozen other songs but the playing length of the album was constrained by the limits of the twelve-inch vinyl format. If Weller had tried to sandwich any more material into the grooves it would have sounded even more thin and brittle.

Weller's voice had none of the expected warmth of a blue-eyed soul balladeer and frequently came over as uninterested. His faith in Dee C Lee's tonsil power was also a little misplaced as she struggled to break through beyond the bland pleasantries of a session singer on the irritating 'A Woman's Song' and the tediously saccharine rendition of Anita Baker's 'Angel'. The only flash of eclecticism, 'Right To Vote', featured a declamatory rap urging people to vote at the up-coming general election from the London act The Dynamic Three, which sounded half-baked compared to the vital dynamism of American hip-hop acts of the time, in particular the pioneering Public Enemy.

Following up on the success of the mid-paced, uneventful single 'It Didn't Matter', the album went straight in at number two in the UK charts thanks entirely to Weller's 50,000-strong fan base. Once the diehards had bought it the album swiftly exited the Top 75, and followed the single's dramatic drop overseas. 'We'd like to be successful in America because we don't know where else to take it now,' complained Weller. 'But if you look at the American charts, Samantha Fox is number ten. It makes you think why the fuck are we bothering really. At the moment we're probably selling about seventy thousand to a hundred thousand copies of each LP in America which sounds a lot but it's a piss in the ocean compared to the size of the country.'

A month after *Cost of Loving*, the second single from the album, 'Waiting', became the first Weller single to peak outside the Top 40, stalling at 52. To make matters worse, *Cost of Loving* was also mauled by the English press, with *Melody Maker* proclaiming, 'The

Paul Weller

music is a surprisingly accurate imitation of that most toothless, spineless idiom, Brit-funk', while *NME*'s Len Brown simply found it 'far too lovey-dovey for these lugs'.

Charles Shaar Murray in *New Hi-Fi Sound* summed up Weller as 'one of the unfunkiest people in the world', pointing out his 'inflexible, unexpressive vocals' and coming to the damning conclusion that 'he suffers even by comparison with the likes of Paul Young, George Michael and Boy George ... He is, in the final analysis, quite the most boring and inadequate white soulboy currently under contract to a major label.'

Shaar Murray also baulked at the album's sleeve which he described as 'a massive splodge of sickly orange which will clash hideously with the clothing of anybody who is not actually a follower of Bhagwan Rajneesh'. Intended as a tribute to The Beatles' *White Album*, the original sleeve exasperated the record company who were trying to introduce the band to people outside the UK in areas where Weller was still virtually unknown. Even John Weller subsequently conceded that the cover was 'crap'.

A few months later Weller was washing his hands of the album, admitting, 'It's sometimes difficult to know when you're putting out rubbish.' Like Ogden he was unhappy with the feel and sound of the record although he blamed the problems of his choice on 'machines and sequencers and all that crap. It was a big mistake for us because both me and Mick are really into natural, acoustic sounds and I think the first two Council albums were much better because of that. The Style Council after '85 were almost like a different group.'

Despite the album's commercial and artistic slide, Weller was not ready to face a few home truths. Always a man sensitive to criticism when it broke through the protective wall of John and Kenny, he wasn't ready to listen to people outside his loyal coterie of long-term friends. Most of the people around him simply said the right thing and tagged along on the back of his success. Of the latter Ogden snipes, 'Every artist surrounds themselves with lame brains. Paul's no exception.'

Nigel Sweeney: 'He did do what other people said sometimes, but he was the boss. He was quite a frightening character in some respects because he was Paul Weller. There were lots of people around him who depended on him for their day-to-day wages. So you'll find they wouldn't say anything even if they disagreed with what he was doing.'

Dennis Munday: 'I don't think he was surrounded by yes men at Polydor. At that time I don't think he knew anyone at Polydor enough to trust them. I'm sure during certain periods of time that he didn't talk to anybody at Polydor.'

The singer's mix of ego and self-doubt responded to the situation with a barrier of cocksure, one-man-against-the-world brashness. 'It all got to me sometimes in the Council days,' he later owned up. 'I got egotistical. After a while it kind of repulsed me ... We became incredibly arrogant, me and Mick Talbot, but mainly me because I directed things.' His father's dogged devotion had anchored his son and given him security at a cost – he was becoming over-protected. 'Yeah, absolutely. Too much,' he said years later.

Nigel Sweeney also illuminates some of the problems John Weller was having with The Style Council's career: 'The Jam was a perfect band for John. It was a very basic situation; meat and potatoes stuff for a manager. The Style Council was a lot different and John wasn't as comfortable with that. It was hard for him as well because by this time Dennis Munday wasn't there any more to deal with the record company. All that John had experienced before was success and now some things were going astray. I think it was a bit alien for him.'

The tensions within the Weller camp infected Paul's relationship with Steve White. Weller pressurised the friendships around him through perverse wind-ups, sullen, uncommunicative moods and contradictory attitudes. 'There was a certain period when it wasn't really worth saying anything,' explains White, 'because if you said something pro he would say something anti. There was a couple of years where he was really, really hard to work with. Everybody was against him. There were different insecurities that maybe he was going through. It wasn't really worth approaching him about the musicians, for instance, because basically I didn't find him particularly open to listening at that time and that culminated in me just leaving.'

When The Style Council set off in the spring for a depressingly uninspired tour with their worst line-up in Europe and Japan, White skipped off to work on his own projects. He played a few intimate gigs with a Hammond organist around London and then joined up with The Jazz Renegades for a trip to Tokyo where they opened a new club and recorded an album. He did, however, return for the new album sessions the following year. Meanwhile, *The Cost of Loving* proved to be the only Weller album under Richard Ogden as the MD left Polydor to manage Paul McCartney, adding to the rapid turnover of executive staff at the label in an unstable three-year spell which culminated in the arrival of new MD David Munns in May '87. Nevertheless, Ogden kept in touch with John and thought about setting up a collaboration between Weller and McCartney, although he soon settled on Elvis Costello. 'Elvis has a producer inside him and knows how to work with an artist. I thought of Weller but I don't think he'd try to bring the best out of McCartney. He wouldn't give a shit.'

For Weller, the familiar routine of benefit projects continued as the Council played a Brixton gig for Nicaragua and appeared alongside Erasure and The Communards at the Barbican to raise money for research into Aids. He also had another project ready for release which Gary Crowley accurately dubbed Weller's 'tragical history tour'. Conceived as a multi-layered, surreal satire on America's cultural imperialism, Britain's inherent racism, the class system, the evils of the Empire-obsessed Tories and the shallow ambitions of contemporary pop stars, *JerUSAlem* – 'we liked the fact that the middle third of the word spells USA. That's probably how much of the world they own' – was 33-minute proof that, *Hard Day's Night* aside, musicians shouldn't make films. It was shot on location over four weeks at the cost of £140,000 in late 1986 with a former *World In Action* documentary maker, Richard Blefield, as director and The Communards' Richard Coles in the role of plummy accented narrator. The Style Council had always struggled to communicate their insular humour to a wider audience but *JerUSAlem* left viewers even more perplexed as Weller appeared on a throne in green wellies attempting, King Canute style, to stop the waves. In addition to the image of a black English queen, affluent black villagers were shown playing croquet in the picturesque village of Aldbourne, a rather obvious inversion of the class system, although it succeeded in stirring up some tabloid controversy. Meanwhile, all the Council members got together for a fictitious interview as a band called The Very Tall Buildings, using – so Weller claimed – 'real' quotes from pop bands. In a scene which revealed just how clumsy and cliché-ridden Weller can be as a cultural commentator, Talbot played a drunken scally, Weller flirted with Nazi imagery in a German helmet and White took the role of a coke addict who performed at drug benefits.

The film was screened by some cinemas as a support film for *Mona Lisa*, then released by Palace (the company who were ruined by the failure of *Absolute Beginners*) on video and rapidly forgotten, although Weller boldly proclaimed, 'In ten years' time some anthropologist will find it and start showing it at all the fringe cinemas, believe me.' By the end of 1996 it was still collecting dust as a second-hand bargain-bin artefact. Terry Rawlings: 'I got it from Record & Tape Exchange in Notting Hill for 32p. It's absolute nonsense. Paul isn't naturally funny – you know how some people try hard. He tries hard but he's just not funny. I've known him for years and years but I could not tell you what his sense of humour is like.'

'Wanted', was released at the end of 1987, subtitled 'Waiter There's Soup In My Flies', which peaked at a so-so twenty. On the B-side was a new version of 'The Cost Of Loving', taken from the film *Business As Usual* featuring Glenda Jackson and Kathy Tyson, described in a Weller fanzine as a 'moral tale of unity winning over the system'.

To promote the single the Council set off on their optimistically titled 'Renaissance tour' at smaller club venues. Despite its modestly sized bookings, the tour was shortened by a couple of cancellations due to poor ticket sales. At the start of the new year the Council re-packaged some of their old material into the EPs 'The Birds And The B's', 'Cafe Bleu' and 'Mick Talbot Is Agent '88', the latter containing his Hammond organ instrumentals. They also recorded a new album which would return to the more eclectic approach of their earlier releases and flesh out Weller's acerbic view of contemporary chart acts with a contempt which bordered on paranoia.

Its first excerpt was the dire 'Life At A Top People's Health Farm', released to universal contempt in May. Images of Thatcher, bingo and dog tracks were thrown together over a messy backing track. Pumping horns further over-egg the mix which overspills into a self-parody of the band's original open-minded intentions. Weller grimaced when a journalist mentioned the song to him a year later. 'I hate it,' he declared.

Paul Weller

Launched a month later, with another jokey publicity campaign featuring the comedy duo Paul and Mick on surfboards, *Confessions of a Pop Group* was one of Weller's diluted 'concept' albums based around a 'parody of a pop group like they've become a commodity the same as a packet of Daz or a tin of baked beans.'

Weller: 'It's the hard sell to the shops and the public. That's what takes the art out of pop music. The final insult really was this new coding system, you know, those bar codes . . . We think that's just the last straw. There's no difference now between a record and a tin of dog meat.' His disgust also reflected growing tensions between the band and Polydor, with the Council reportedly delivering the finished tape of the album on a C90 tape emblazoned with a defiled picture of the A&R chief.

Thankfully, for all his bitterness Weller has never been able to follow a concept through on an album and *Confessions* actually swerved between personal songs like the elegant 'Changing Of The Guard' and 'It's A Very Deep Sea' – 'a modern surf song Brian Wilson would be proud of although he would do it differently' – and the wordy satire of 'Life At A Top People's Health Farm'. Even the funkadelic-inspired work-out of the title track was rooted in Weller's broader distrust of the witty, design-conscious sloganeering which became almost an art form on T-shirts and television in the 80s. 'All these really slick images come at you really quickly,' he says of the song, 'kind of parodying the sort of eighties marketing nonsense at that time. They're very good lines. We should have left it there. It would have been a good swan song.'

The sleeve depicted Weller and Talbot in tailored suits with the ivory tinkler sitting at a grand piano, presenting a classy, pretentious image which was both intended as a self-mocking send-up and a claim for ground beyond the instantly disposable. Cod-classicism also sweeps through some of the album, notably on the ten-minute long 'The Gardener Of Eden (A Three Piece Suite)', which closed the first side of the album – an amalgamation of Debussy, The Swingle Swingers, The Beach Boys and Donald Byrd.

Clearly trying to wind up the critics with the introduction of harp and Bond Street snazziness, Weller almost pulled it off by throwing the stand-out track 'Why I Went Missing' into the mix, which was the best song he'd written since the early Style Council days. The suggested confessional mood of the album's title is most overtly expressed on this song, where Weller owns up to bouts of unfaithfulness in his long-term relationships. 'There's plenty more I could have kissed . . . But I blame myself for this out-of-town kissing.'

For all its ambition, wit and complexity, *Confessions* remains an uneven, flawed album which, ironically, would date within a year as the first stirrings of Mancunian roughage in the baggy scene made the Council look every bit as contrived as their nemesis, Wham! and Frankie Goes To Hollywood. While Weller was following through his Mod ethics in mannered, overwrought, self-consciously adult styles, bands like The Stone Roses updated the Mod psychedelia of the 60s into shuffling, direct, happy anthems which would climax with their generation-defining gig at Spike Island in 1991.

Weller's decision not to promote the album left the album struggling in a polarised chart divided between Stock, Aitken and Waterman acts and those established artists who'd been given a fresh lease of life by Live Aid. It scraped into the Top Twenty at number fifteen and shot out of the charts after only three weeks. Although *Confessions* was a much better record than *The Cost of Loving*, it also received poor reviews. Charles Shaar Murray once again wrote about Weller in *New Hi-Fi*, opining, 'Paul Weller is deeply boring in a manner that hundreds of pop people with slightly less than one per cent of his talent will never be and that's his tragedy.'

Alan Jones in the *Melody Maker* was more vicious: 'Weller's entire career has been a history of ill-advised haircuts and lamentable musical gestures, shaped by books, manifestos and philosophies that he has enthusiastically embraced but rarely comes to grips with. He is a hod carrier, not a visionary; a tradesman, dusty and stinting, not a shaman or a seer. His insights are leaden, parochial, the views of a shopkeeper, blinkered . . . *Confessions of a Pop Group* is just drizzle turning to piss.'

After the release of the album Steve White officially vacated his role as a freelance Council member, while Talbot encountered an old problem with the Weller fan base when the band played a secret gig at the Shaw Theatre. 'I was playing a little classical thing before we went into a tune,' he recalls, 'and there were all these people down at the front going, "Whooargghh! Mickey! Essex! Essex!" '

There was one final closing chapter on *Confessions*, with the release of the '1-2-3-4' EP in July. The likeable 'How She Threw It All Away' wasn't strong enough to make an impression, and it failed to make it into the UK Top 40. As for Ogden's ambitions for global Council success, they'd now turned to dust.

In July Dee C Lee gave birth to a baby boy, Nat, who weighed in at 8lb 7oz and took over their lives immediately. Plans for an autumn tour of Britain, Europe and Japan were cancelled, with the claim that Talbot was suffering from a mystery virus. However, it's hardly surprising that Dee and Paul couldn't face the commitment so soon after the arrival of their first child, and Mick Talbot also wanted to spend time at home with his family. It would have been a pointless exercise in any case, as Weller's attention was once again focusing on a fresh club scene which was a step on from the studded funkiness of *Confessions*. This was not the strobeascopic flash of house which had combined with Britain's discovery of the drug Ecstasy to spawn the 'second summer of love'. A singularly unimpressed Weller commented, 'as for house music, most of it sounds like Stars On 45 to me; this incessant disco beat. I don't know much about it but I think it sounds like boring seventies disco music. Acid house, nah. If we made a house record we could call it a Council House . . . that would be nice.'

Weller was listening to the sounds being played by DJ Norman Jay at his High On Hope club in London's Camden Town, which according to Jay offered an alternative to acid chants of the newly born rave culture. 'The summer of love was going on,' he says, 'and I wanted to get away from all the smoke machines and the waving hands in the air to play some music with an emotional side to it. Something with feeling and soul.' High On Hope was an outlet for garage house, named after the New York gay club Paradise Garage where hard house beats combined with gospel-inspired vocals. Norman Jay had been to the club's last week and watched the DJs cut tracks together which ranged from gay disco-diva Sylvester through to The Clash, an idiosyncratic approach based on upbeat, positive grooves and a more soulful feel than the electronic functionalism of Chicago's house style. 'I went mad on garage records,' enthused Weller. 'I came from hating it to being totally obsessed by it. I liked it because it sounded rough and it sounded raw. Lyrically, it was also so positive.' Later he told the *NME*, 'At the time I really believed that garage house was the new Mod music.'

In London, Jay's club attracted gay, straight, male and female clubbers who were slightly older than those at the Essex warehouse parties, and the atmosphere was blunted rather than manic. According to Jay, 'Paul Weller was down there in the first few weeks. He knew the roots of garage music. He knew where all that stuff came from. He has a tremendous knowledge of black music – soul, Stax, Motown, northern soul, right up to contemporary stuff.' Weller began to enthuse about garage, deep house, artists like Blaze, the 'deep soul stuff of Willie Clayton' and American producer Marshall Jefferson, who DJ'd for the first time in his life at Jay's club. 'He chose the records and I put them on for him,' laughs the host.

In February '89, The Style Council re-emerged with a new garage-based sound, covering Joe Smooth's 'Promised Land' which had only been out a few months earlier. Featuring a remix by Joe Smooth himself, the track was played in American clubs and did well in the US dance charts. In Britain it received some airplay from pirate radio but only reached 34 in the singles chart. Former pirate radio station entrepreneur and DJ Gilles Peterson, whose pioneering of the acid jazz scene in the late 80s also contributed to the club-based melting pot which started to influence the Council, believes the singer was ahead of his time in this switch of styles. 'How quick was he to understand garage and house music?' he enthuses. 'I mean, he did Joe Smooth's "Promised Land" and got dissed for it. And look at how big dance music is now and everything that's come out of that.'

Others on the club scene were suspicious of Weller's plagiarism, accusing him of trying to feign street cred at a time when his sales were obviously declining. In spite of the muted response at large to 'Promised Land', the band released 'Long Hot Summer '89 mix', which was backed by a Norman Jay remix of 'Everybody's On The Run' and featured Brian Powell on vocals. 'I didn't want to do it,' says Jay. 'Paul rang me up and I kept making excuses. In the end a taxi arrived for me and I had to go. I'd never remixed anything before so I didn't know what I was doing. But Paul just got me to relax and play about with it until we came up with something we liked. Now it's a big collectable twelve inch. I just went to Japan to do some DJ-ing and people over there were asking me about the Weller remix.' There was also a remix by Detroit Techno pioneer

Paul Weller

Juan Atkins of Model 500, proving how far Weller had changed his mind after his initial dislike of the new dance forms. Once again outside of the club scene the release was greeted with confusion from the fans and indifference by everybody else and it failed to reach the Top 40.

The single followed up on the band's first greatest hits package, *The Singular Adventures of The Style Council*, which had injected life back into the band's fortunes by reaching number three in the album charts. Nevertheless, although Weller was mildly amused that the sleeve notes were reprinted in Pseuds Corner, the package made him reflect on the Council's career with a touch of bitterness, in particular about the lack of cover versions made of their songs. 'I think they are made to be covered,' he declared, hinting at a sense of isolation and disappointment which also surfaced when he commented, 'The best time in the Council was when we recorded the original of 'Long Hot Summer'. There haven't been too many highs since then.'

His modernist code was still acting as an alert antenna for new fashions and music. As well as checking out techno artists, hip hop, rap, soul (especially the likes of Omar and Soul II Soul), from 1988 onward he'd immersed himself in a scene which was close in style and spirit to The Style Council – acid jazz. Image-conscious Soho hipsters and fast-talking DJs had started running clubs and radio shows which, on the surface at least, radiated with beatnik, multi-racial cool and minimalist chic. Forty years after the original beat generation, acid jazz – the name was a cheeky steal from acid house but actually had no relation to the rival movement – began in the UK in 1987 as a fusion of Afro-Cuban jazz, hard bop, rare groove and hip hop, pioneered by Gilles Peterson at his Talking Loud & Saying Something club in Dingwalls, north London. Initially the scene was compiled into albums by DJs like Peterson and Baz Fe Jazz, which were mostly on Urban Records. These were followed by the formation of the Acid Jazz label, which was set up by Rob Gallagher from Galliano, Chris Bangs and Marco Nelson from The Young Disciples, Gilles Peterson and Eddie Pillar. 'We were doing a club at Babylon in Heaven,' says Peterson, 'and Rob Gallagher was rapping and having a bit of fun. Afterwards he said, "Why don't we go in the studio and make a record?" That was "Frederick Lies Still" and it cost £250!'

According to former north London casual Gallagher, whose style mixes hip-hop positivity with cockney rap, 'The first six months were definitely goatee beards and Adidas tops. We were having a laugh, going around clubs and shouting on-stage. Then everybody would shout back and we'd all go off and get stoned together.' Weller and his crew of friends like Eugene Manzi, Paolo Hewitt and Marco from The Young Disciples were regulars at Peterson's clubs – Dingwalls, Camden, in '88 and the Fez in Paddington at the tail end of The Style Council. 'He had a bit of foresight. I used to go with him to a club called Fez in 1989,' says Manzi, 'which was a rare groove, jazz, funk, hip hop, reggae club. We were there nearly every week and it was a brilliant club.'

'I came across Paul through Eddie Pillar and through Marco,' says Peterson, 'and he used to come to some of my clubs – the Fez on a Friday and I saw him at Dingwalls a few times. I also knew Steve White quite well through his jazz associations in The Jazz Renegades. Weller came to my radio shows sometimes on Jazz FM because he was just around the corner at Solid Bond Studios. He'd come along with some of Dee's music so it was a good vibe. He's just a quiet man who's into music. He's obviously got a very good sense of what's happening and where it's happening and he finds himself in those places, as was proven by the fact that during that period in The Style Council he had Omar and Brian Powell in the band, all the best people. He was almost like an A&R source for the new generation. Just look at who's in his band and sign them up. There's a side of Paul that's very soul and R&B, so he's obviously got a very good knowledge of that.'

In the sprawling club scene of the late 80s – Peterson describes the early acid jazz nights as a rampantly eclectic brew combining 'house, samba, hip hop, weird jazz, sixties soundtracks, all mixed together. I was putting together 808 State with Public Enemy with John Coltrane. That was the spirit of Acid Jazz' – Weller, Gilles Peterson and Norman Jay talked music with fanatical enthusiasm, sharing influences and styles. 'I always had a lot of respect for Paul Weller 'cos he's got this one record that I haven't got by John Lucien who's this kind of jazz singer who put out a single on Sector Records in America. I'm a huge fan and I've got all his records except for this one and Paul still is the only one who has it. It's worth hundreds of pounds on the northern soul scene and is one of

Paul Weller

those records which crosses over between Wigan-meets-Dingwalls types of scenes.'

The acid jazz crowd, like all club-based scenes, mutated and splintered at a rapid rate, yet Weller seemed to have a link with almost every shade of the movement – the casuals, the jazzbos, the soulboys – and he also sensed that this was the music of the 90s Mod. 'There's loads of Mods around in the nineties. In fact, there's more now than ever ... A lot of those kids who were into The Jam or The Specials in the early eighties will be talking about acid jazz or Talkin' Loud [the label Peterson set up after his defection from Acid Jazz]. That's been a big influence on them.'

Weller had not come face to face with his fans since he'd immersed himself in the club scene but all that changed at the Royal Albert Hall in July 1989. Taking to the stage in baggy fluorescent shorts – 'I couldn't even begin to tell you what the shorts were about. They were definitely a mistake' – he shared the vocals with Brian Powell and Dee C Lee, who was trying to fill the role of deep house diva. Given her limited range this was quite simply beyond her and the critics had a field day. They played hardly any old material and concentrated on the garage-based anthems – including the proposed single 'Sure Is Sure', which was never released – of the forthcoming album. The crowd responded in disbelief by booing and tearing up their programmes, a feeling reflected in the *NME* the following week as Stephen Dalton argued Weller was 'swallowed and suffocated' by modern dance trends and the band were 'aiming at Prince-like technicolour funk but settling for Shakatak shoddiness'.

Weller's friend Eugene Manzi was in the audience: 'It was quite funny because there were some herberts next to me going, "This is not fucking Paul Weller. This is fucking shit, man." I thought, Give the guy some space, he's experimenting and developing. Unfortunately he was growing up in public and you've got to go through a few phases before making the next step. It was ahead of its time. It was live house music and there was no one doing it at the time; it was all on the record. So it was quite clever in a way.'

'Yeah, I upset a lot of people,' remembers Weller. 'Judas! I remember two weeks later I met these two guys in a cafe, two fans who had been there, saying, "What the fuck was that all about?" They didn't understand it at all, which I can see looking back.'

There was no way that he would turn back now, however. Weller was being told by people around him that he was ahead of his time and he wanted the Council to stake their claim in the club scene. The band banked their million pound advance on the new album and continued recording. One of the new tracks, 'Hope (Feelings Gonna Getcha)', was inspired by Norman Jay's club. 'He was the only artist I'd allow to name a song after our club. Other people wanted to do it but they were just trying to make themselves look credible by association.' Jay admits, however, 'It didn't get a lot of plays down the club.'

The positive, anthemic approach of garage was reflected in titles like 'Love Of The World', 'The World Must Come Together' and 'That Spiritual Feeling' (which later surfaced on his debut solo album) but most of the songs have remained unheard after their live debut at the Albert Hall. Upon hearing the album, entitled *Modernism – A Decade* (or *A Decade of Modernism*), Polydor's MD David Munns did the unexpected and rejected it.

'Paul got very upset because I told him basically that I didn't think it was acceptable,' says Munns from his office at PolyGram Records. 'I didn't particularly say, "I don't want to deal with Paul Weller any more." I just felt the record wasn't acceptable. It was much more their choice to sever all ties then and decide, Right, we can't deal with Polydor, they don't believe in us any more. That wasn't true. I just felt we had a right to speak up. John particularly took great umbrage at this and I guess that's life. You pay for those occasions when you stand up and say what you think.

'I thought it was pretty sad that he couldn't take it on the chin, but I understand it too, the way artists feel about that sort of thing. You can go through life with everyone telling you what you want to hear or you can face some facts. Maybe Paul had never really looked for any kind of leveller like that.'

As Clive Banks points out, Weller simply wasn't used to anyone telling him what to do. 'He's a young lad who picked up a guitar, started writing songs, started selling records, had total adulation, had the money he needed to buy all the things he wanted to buy. So it's very hard to tell someone like that they can't do things when they've had success at a very early age. He's going to turn round and say, "How many records have you sold?" '

Weller: 'I was a lot more arrogant then. I'm the sort of person that, if I become obsessed by something, I can't see any other way of looking at it. But it was born out of my own arrogance I think, and I boxed myself into a corner to a certain extent. My head was up my arse. It's not an excuse; it's just a stage I went through.'

Munns: 'To be honest there were some very big Paul Weller fans in the company at the time – people who were there because Weller was on that label. There wasn't much else on Polydor. It wasn't like I had this great list of artists that I could cherry pick and decide who I felt like working with. When you're faced with only three good things on the label you'd better get your shit together. There was Level 42, Andrew Lloyd Webber ... You know, Polydor was at a low ebb at that particular point and it took a great deal of thinking to not just say, "Yeah, fine" and put it out. It was a dark moment in my life, I can tell you; it wasn't something that I slept easy on.

'When you have an artist like Paul Weller you really expect to, by and large, accept what they do within reason. I don't believe artists should sell more with each record they put out. The sales ebb and flow and you view an artist over an entire career and some sell more than others. You take it as it comes and make the best of it and if you come out ahead over a period of time then great. But there were two or three particular things at the time that I think are relevant as to why I did what I did. The Style Council's sales over a period had been going down. He'd lost the plot a bit I think. I had no desire to get rid of Paul Weller – it was his call.

'Paul Weller is always a name that people would want to have on their roster because he attracts other artists. Clearly other people heard that record and agreed with me and if that forced him to sit down and take stock then God bless him. There must have been a moment when he looked in the mirror and realised, It's down to me, I can't dodge it any more. If you do you're a fool and Paul Weller is not a fool.

'I was isolated by that decision at Polydor but there's no point in kidding yourself, is there?'

Contractually, Polydor couldn't refuse to release the album on quality grounds alone. 'To say I didn't like it wasn't enough to reject the record,' explains Munns. 'However, it did say in the contract that there must be two tracks that we thought would be acceptable singles. I only thought there was one track that was remotely suitable to get on Radio One at the time. And I said so.

'Unfortunately he just didn't want to talk to anybody any more, so he took the record back and I think he shopped around the business for a while but it never came out.'

Weller was 'astonished' by Munns' decision. 'I figured they wouldn't like the record . . . but then I thought, Well, we're The Style Council, you've got to put our record out.

'I was uninspired but it wasn't what I wanted to hear . . . It did affect my confidence after being at Polydor all those years . . . and selling all those records and making all that money and I think there should be some kind of loyalty to an artist.

'We had no relationship towards the end and I don't even think it was all their fault, it was probably a mixture . . . we all retracted more and more and started talking through lawyers and all that nonsense.'

A big factor in the ugliness and immediacy of the split was a personality clash between themselves and Munns, whose abrasive, confrontational approach contrasted with Ogden's subtle though unsuccessful negotiations and the passivity of Weller's long-term Polydor contact, Dennis Munday, who had frustrated even Ogden in his approach as simply a voice for Weller inside the company. 'We couldn't get along with the new MD – a real bolshy fucker,' smarted Weller not long after the event. 'I'm not used to people talking to me like that. Not because I think I'm Mr Superstar but I'm not fucking having it. Basically because I'm from Woking and I don't give a fuck, d'you know what I mean?'

Munns stands his ground: 'At one time John and I got on famously – when we went to New York to try and sort out the American thing. I didn't spend long enough with Paul for there to be a personality clash. I'm used to artists who are very strong willed and I'm Van Morrison's main contact at this company. I didn't see Paul Weller as someone particularly difficult but I call a spade a spade.'

Nigel Sweeney: 'If you heard it you'd know why David Munns rejected the album. This was the first person who I suspect had said "boo" to Paul. There was an incredible amount of bitterness between David Munns and Paul Weller and in some respects it was, How fucking dare he?

'I guess Munns was right to reject it. It wasn't Paul Weller – he was only singing on one or two tracks. I think that would be a

problem for any record company. It was all Dee C Lee. She was
singing four or five tracks, three of them were instrumental and two
were Paul. Especially as at that point it was starting to duck down
a bit anyway.'

Dennis Munday gives his views on the decision: 'Why did they
wait and let the relationship deteriorate to such a point that they
didn't know what kind of album they were getting? Someone has
to be there as the record is being made. So in the end it was very
poor A&R management.'

John Pearson agrees with Munday's assessment: 'Munns' reaction was bad, ill-timed and ignorant. If he was recording, go along,
talk to the geezer, see what's going on – don't wait out there in the
cold until the album's delivered and then say, "We don't like this,
we're not putting it out." '

Sweeney shakes his head in disbelief at this notion: 'That's
rubbish. Nobody used to get a look in. Paul was an incredibly
successful person. There was no one person who could say at any
point, "I don't like that song, don't put it on the album." The
singles that came out were the singles that Paul chose.'

Andy Macdonald, head of Weller's current label Go! Discs,
states, 'Would I have rejected it? Of course not. He's never flippant
about his music and if he's doing something in a certain style
there'd be a good reason for it. I think it's the most dreadful thing
you can do to someone of that talent. Stand there as some kind of
jumped-up, self-authorised censor and say, "This is not good
enough." It's not a record company's job to do that. I have no
sympathy with his decision at all. I don't think you can judge things
at a particular point in time. How does he know he can't sell it? He
thought at the time it was outside his abilities to sell it but what
about the future?'

Although Ogden believes Weller needed to face up to reality and
still regrets that he never sat down with the artist and thrashed out
his criticisms, he maintains that: 'I would never have rejected the
album. He was the most important artist on the label and they'd
still have made money out of The Style Council. It would be like
EMI dropping Paul McCartney which they would never do.'

Meanwhile Munns refutes the argument that Weller's venture
into dance music was daringly innovative and therefore worthy of
release. 'I don't think it will be treated differently if it is ever

released,' he argues. 'I am aware that some of the people that he worked with have come through – and maybe it was ahead of its time and experimental – but as an album it didn't work. They may have felt something when they recorded it but at the end of the day you have forty minutes of music that you're supposed to listen to in your kitchen. You either get it from that or you don't and none of the Paul Weller diehards got it.'

As the Council broke off all face-to-face communications and left further discussions to their lawyers, Norman Jay and Gilles Peterson talked over the idea of *Modernism of a Decade* being released through the recently formed Talkin' Loud label. 'Maybe we were too small,' he says. 'It might have worked out but who knows? I don't think Paul's dad was into the idea.'

Enthusiasm for *Modernism – A New Decade* rapidly dissipated as Weller and Talbot drifted apart. 'I wouldn't say it was Mick's fault,' states Weller, 'but I just wanted to finish the whole thing, go away for a while and think. It was strained . . . it was quite ugly. We were both trying to put this last record together and we were both uninspired. It seemed to drag on, and then, when it wasn't going to come out . . .'

The Style Council broke up after playing for the last time on a satellite show hosted by Paula Yates in early 1990. 'There was no motivation,' explained Weller. 'I didn't know why I was doing it. I just found myself there. And that's fucking wrong.'

As for *Modernism – A New Decade*, it still hasn't been released. Norman Jay comments, 'Obviously I did hear the album. He's a great songwriter so the songs were good but the production was very of its time, very '88 or '89. I don't think you could release it now unless it was updated with some nineties remixes.'

Weller recently told *Select* magazine, 'I'd like to [release it] one day. It's just about picking the right time. Or even just doing a mail-order thing. Fans only. It's not the kind of record that's going to set the world alight.'

Dennis Munday, who has compiled several Jam and Council compilations over recent years, also reveals that 'there's quite a bit of unreleased Style Council stuff. I've got demos at home which are unfinished. There's cover versions and all sorts of stuff. When he had Solid Bond he could just go in and do whatever he wanted to do.'

Paul Weller

In retrospect the bright eclecticism of The Style Council only ever had a short shelf life. The loose collective format enabled Weller to dabble and have fun, inevitably leading to an erratic mix of inspired pop and self-indulgence. If they'd broken up in 1985 their reputation as an intense, diverse and largely successful experiment in Weller's career would have been sealed for good. However, over the last four years the singer's political commitments completely overshadowed the band and his attempt to streamline them into a soul unit with *The Cost of Loving* album was a disaster. The complex, mix-and-match sound of *Confessions of a Pop Group* was too much, too late. For all its inventiveness it was too contrived for most fans. As journalist David Sinclair concluded, '[The Style Council were] a group who virtually redefined the concept of carrying on to the point of meaningless and indeed some distance beyond.'

Weller's understandable attempt to inject some humour into his career after the rather po-faced, black and white platitudes of The Jam was too forced, as the artist himself now concedes: 'We were trying too hard. I was trying to get away from the stereotype of the miserable moaner. We went too much the other way. You know we thought the videos were really funny – they made us laugh and a few of our friends laugh 'cos we all got the joke. But that isn't good enough. There's a thin line between doing what you want to do and indulgence. I guess we crossed that barrier.'

He also over-thought the parodies and propagandist rhetoric of the band which tried to have it both ways. It takes a very subtle, finely tuned wit to combine earnest, deeply felt political beliefs with slapstick humour centred around two well-dressed wannabe Marx brothers. In the end the atmosphere around the band was one of self-conscious deliberation, which made them represent some of the worst aspects of the 80s, in particular a lack of spontaneity. 'I fucking hated the eighties but now I can see that, however much we railed against it at the time I was part of it, even though I never thought I was,' confesses Weller. 'The Style Council were an archetypal eighties group without even wanting to be but I was too concerned with the way things looked to see it.'

Weller blamed some of this on the synthetic sounds they were using. 'Most of our recording was done in the control room – fucking sequences and drum machines,' he groaned. However, in the mid 80s The Pet Shop Boys showed how witty lyrics and machines could produce sophisticated, wry, modern pop music with a sense of humour.

At their worst, the Council often ended up pastiching their heroes, and this combined with their snide humour into a half-baked, smug, nouveau cool. The *NME* sniped at the Council in 1995 when a singles compilation, *The Style Council Collection*, was released. 'It was all bloody silly. The cappuccinos, the Sta-Prests, the desperate striving for *l'essence de cool Française*, the constant presence of Mick Talbot, a gormless Mod also-ran re-cast (and miscast) as hipster supreme . . . The Style Council are to blame for acid jazz, white socks and unintelligibly stupid manifestos on the album sleeves.'

Gilles Peterson nearly choked on his cappuccino when he was told the Council had invented acid jazz. 'I obviously liked the clothes but they, er, had a more bossa nova feel,' he said with bemusement. 'I was a purist really. I linked The Style Council to Everything But The Girl, so I couldn't really say they were an influence exactly. It was a little bit soft and quite poppy.'

At their best the Council confounded expectations, took risks and made some great music, especially their early singles. In the end Weller concludes, with a hint of surly paranoia, 'We could never shake off the legacy of The Jam. We could have made the best record ever and no one would have noticed.'

7 Dazed and Confused, 1990–91

Paul Weller: 'I felt awful for ages. I had no interest in music.
I lost all my direction, all my motivation. I kind of lost my
bearings in it.'

Paul Weller: 'I had a time when I split from Dee a while back and
writing songs helped me out the other side.'

The first post-Style Council album which Weller threw his
energies into was Dee C Lee's solo LP, *Free Your Feelings*,
recorded under the name Slam Slam. Dr Robert from The
Blow Monkeys and Marco Nelson contributed to this mix of
rejected tracks from *Modernism* – including 'Move (Dance All
Night)' and 'You'll Find Love' – and new songs, one of which
'Round And Round', would later surface on Weller's self-titled solo
album. Eventually released in the UK by MCA records in April
1991, *Free Your Feelings* was a bitty flashback to Weller's production work for Respond artists, with a few enjoyable moments
thrown into a plastic, synthetic mess of over-egged backing tracks
and cod house chants.

For most of 1990, Weller's curmudgeonly but energetic personality bounced off the walls of his Holland Park home in west
London, where he spent all his time with his son, Nat, and his wife.
'For two years or so after [Nat] was born I wanted to be around
to see his first steps or hear his first words and I was around which
I'm glad about. At the same time it also caused me a lot of grief
because I need to have music to stabilise me, it stabilises my whole
being . . . And I wasn't doing that.'

Fatherhood enabled him to put his career to one side for a while
but bottling up inside the familiar sleep-deprived, chaotic atmosphere of a new family was a sense of bullish resentment at Polydor's
treatment of him and a nervy frustration as, for the first time in
fifteen years, he stopped writing.

Dee took the brunt of his mood swings when her naturally wired,
ambitious and occasionally short-tempered husband had no musical outlet. 'He wasn't doing anything creative,' she says. Dee

wanted him out of her hair as he mooched about, unsure of what to do with himself. 'It was getting to a stage where he was really getting on my nerves and I wished he'd just get back in the studio.' She looks back at those days together as 'a low period . . . it affected us a lot.' Indeed, their relationship was put under so much strain by the new set of circumstances that they split up for a while. 'We had a lot going on,' is her laconic summary of their marriage during the two years after Weller left Polydor. The artist himself hinted at this when he wrote on the sleeve of his first solo album, 'Thanks and love to Dee, my (fairly) long-standing and (frequently) long-suffering wife, who's stood by me when I've been way down and hateful for it, putting up with my many moods . . .'

John Weller was forced to watch his son's self-belief gradually evaporate. 'The only thing that worried me was that he was worried,' he blustered. 'He looked to me that he was trying to get back into it and couldn't.' The barrage of media criticism had affected Weller in the second half of The Style Council but the momentum of new releases enabled him to push forward regardless. Now he was brooding. He admitted to himself that the Council had gone on for too long, finally exhausting and confusing their fan base while failing to reach out to anybody else with their later albums. They had aspired to make their mark on so many levels they'd often inadvertently focused attention away from their songs. He felt exhausted at the prospect of getting back into the same routines and certainly had no appetite for facing the press so soon after the split.

Weller had experienced short-lived writing blocks before but this was different. He didn't know what musical direction to take, and fresh from the fall out with Polydor he lacked the confidence to try anything new. According to a friend at the time, 'Paul started going into the studio every day but he was a little bit lost. He didn't really know what he wanted to do.' The Style Council had failed to shake off The Jam's legacy and he realised his next project would, once again, be compared to his first. For a thirty-something with an ageing fan base this was a grim prospect. He told himself he was 'washed up, an old has-been', and as he felt there was nothing vital or fresh in his new demos, for the moment at least Weller stayed put and hoped he could rekindle his passion for songwriting.

This passion started to flicker as he lost himself in the music that had inspired him to form a band as a fourteen year old. Like all music fanatics a lot of albums in his collection took him back to the time and place he'd first heard them. Records by The Beatles, the Small Faces and The Who provided snapshots of his adolescence and he remembered how he felt when he listened to *Revolver* or the Small Faces' 'Tin Soldier' as a kid. For all his sussed, sinewy poise and sharp-edged modernism, there's a romantic, yearning, sentimental side to Weller which now fixed on both the music of his youth and childhood memories of Woking, a place which he used to hate for its parochial smallness. Gradually, self-doubt, youthful optimism and sentimentality began to mix into the contradictory moods that would colour his songwriting over the next few years – in turn dreamy, proud, nostalgic, passionate and edgy. 'I hadn't been back [to Woking] for about eight years,' he said later in the *NME*, 'not since The Style Council started. And I only came back through here because I was going to buy a scooter in Aldershot. It's perfect, innit? Afterwards, I drove back in the car and stopped off here, and went back to a few places that I hadn't been to in years. And at the same time, I started playing a few records that I used to listen to then – Stax, R&B, the Small Faces, The Who – and everything started to make some sense again.'

Eugene Manzi, who knew Weller through the later Style Council years, observed Weller's appetite for political action fading as he struggled to get back into his songwriting. 'I think he regretted some of the political things, especially Red Wedge. People see your character and read the politics through it. Some people you just know are OK and others you think, Naargh. You can tell. He'd done his stint with politics and maybe he realised you don't have to preach politics at people. You are what you are. He is essentially a musician.'

Music was now just about all he cared about, whether it was made by sartorially challenged, bearded hippies or sharp modernists. Manzi found himself grilled about artists the singer had recently discovered. 'He would mention things like, "Have you heard of this artist or that artist?" – especially Van Morrison and Neil Young. It's a good thing to widen your vision a bit. He was a bit narrow musically, probably because he had this thing about you shouldn't listen to anybody with a moustache or long hair. Paul came to the realisation that just because you dress differently doesn't mean you make bad music. He wouldn't give those people the time of day at one time. Then he grew up, started listening to them and thought, This is great.'

When Steve Brookes renewed his friendship with Weller in the early 90s, he was amused to discover his school friend raving about music with technically brilliant guitar solos made by men with straggly chin growth. 'It's funny because I saw him a little while ago and he was raving about the Free's *Fire & Water* album which I was into in '71 and he thought was a load of shit. He said to me, "I can't believe I've got into it now because I wouldn't listen to it when you said it was great." '

Even so, Weller wasn't sagging into a dope-fuzzed haze of folk and hippy-esque electric rock. He was hanging out with DJs and musicians from the acid jazz scene who were also redefining some of the folk and psychedelic influences of the 60s into a new, modern sound. Gilles Peterson's roster at his label Talkin' Loud expressed a unique mix of hip hop, folk funk and jazz in acts like Galliano (Mick Talbot produced one album), The Young Disciples and Urban Species. A few years later Galliano's breakthrough hit was a version of 'Longtime Gone' by Crosby, Stills And Nash, one of the bands who were exerting an influence on Weller at the turn of the decade.

Eddie Pillar, who continued to run Acid Jazz when Peterson left, was well versed in the 60s pop which Weller was rediscovering. The mother of this ex-Jam fan had run the Small Faces fan club in the 60s. Pillar himself used to have a Mod fanzine in the 80s and released records on his own Mod label, Countdown, which included The Prisoners on its roster. Ex-Prisoner James Taylor became a pivotal figure at the Acid Jazz label as a solo artist, backed for a while by Steve White on drums. The label also included the kitsch retro TV themes of Corduroy, who included members of that 80s Mod act, Boys Wonder.

A further connection with 60s modernism was forged when Weller jammed on-stage with ex-Small Faces Kenney Jones, James Taylor and another one of Pillar's bands, Mother Earth, for the film project, *The History of Acid Jazz*. This collective played an old Small Faces instrumental, 'Rollin' Over', down at Ealing Film Studios, although the pseudo-documentary has never been released.

Weller's association with Acid Jazz has continued into the 90s,

Paul Weller

as his sister Nikki joined Pillar at the record company as his assistant and he played on records released by the label. Another link between the Weller camp and acid jazz was forged when the style was ironically exported back to the States through the launch of the Groove Academy and Giant Steps' 'jazz not jazz' nights in New York and artists like Guru from one of Weller's favourite groups Gang Starr. After a visit to London, Guru experimented further with rap and jazz samples, resulting in the laid-back moods of his *Jazzmatazz* album in the early 90s. Dee C Lee would eventually work with Guru in the mid 90s, before, appropriately enough, relaunching her solo career in London's Jazz Cafe.

Boosted by the like-minded vinyl junkies of the acid jazz scene and his own library-sized record collection, Weller started to find his way back in 1990, albeit slowly.

'I think he just started to believe in himself,' says Dee. 'By the time our first boy was two and a half he'd started writing a lot again.'

The next step was to play live. In November 1990 he played his first solo gig at the home of acid jazz, Dingwalls, under the quasi band name of The Paul Weller Movement, underlining that he didn't have the confidence to become a fully fledged solo artist quite yet. The clumsy retro feel of the name did him no favours but it was characteristic of a return to live performance which was often shambolic and messy. 'I hated doing it but it really helped me,' he says. 'I had no interest in playing whatsoever. I was awful, the band were awful, but all the time it was bringing me back to what I do best and now I'm really glad I did it ... What people liked about these shows was how many mistakes we made; the fact that we were getting away from the kind of slickness that The Style Council had.' The biggest plus point from the experience was his reunion with Steve White, who played drums on the tour. 'I didn't think me and Steve could have carried on after The Style Council. If he hadn't got in touch with me around that time it might not have happened. Steve had left a couple of years before the band broke up – not necessarily with bad feeling – but there was a kind of vibe between us. He didn't like the way in which we were heading and we didn't get on too well. So I didn't really think about him until a couple of years later.'

White's eclectic abilities were stretched by the untidy but enterprisingly diverse music which greeted fans in the club-sized venues Weller had chosen as a low-key springboard. There were six musicians in front of the drummer, playing saxophone, flute, vibraphone, keyboards, trumpet, flugelhorn, trombone and guitar, with only the sketchiest idea of what they were trying to achieve. Weller's own playing varied between a thrashing, passionate edge which fans hadn't heard in years, jazzbo pickings and Mod psychedelia. While many greeted the occasional Jam song with the nostalgic mania peculiar to old fans, the gigs did showcase some new material. There was no sign of the declamatory lyrics, codified swagger or wise-cracking, jokey titles of the Council in the four new songs, which were more introspective, expressing a sense of uncertainty about the future. 'Round & Round' included the words, 'Movin' up to collect our prizes/Sinkin' fast into life's surprises/Win today but lose tomorrow/Lending what we just can't borrow', which were rooted in his recent experiences. Another song, 'Kosmos', concluded, 'Who am I? What am I? Where am I to go?' Apart 'That Spiritual Feeling' and 'Here's A New Thing', which would eventually end up as B-sides, and The Jam material, the rest of the shows featured Style Council material and a cover of the Isley Brothers' 'Work To Do'. Two sell-out shows at London's Town & Country club were not matched elsewhere, with Weller often playing to half-empty audiences populated predominately by old Jam fans. Photographer Kim Tonelli followed The Movement's tours at the start of the 90s: 'At the 100 Club, Paul said to me, "Kim, go out and take a photograph of the people standing in the line to get in." I took it and I was so disappointed because a lot of them were really old and sloppy. I showed it to Paul and he wasn't very happy.'

At the end of 1990 Weller put his Solid Bond Studios up for sale to raise funds for album sessions the following year. His decision caused a bust-up with his sister Nikki (who was working at the studio) over money and the running of the building. Sara Silver: 'I don't know what happened with Nikki. It was a definitive argument. That's where the family thing went wrong. Ann's always been around but never involved. She's just been mum right the way through. But it's really just John, Paul and Kenny who have stood the course.

'If Nikki had turned out to have some talent I don't think

anybody would have tried to stop her. Ultimately, I suppose, the only thing that could have happened for Nikki was she could have been brought up to manage Paul when his dad didn't want to go out there any more. But aside from that it was always going to be a sub-plot. Maybe she just grew out of them as well and then perhaps you fall foul of it. I'm sure there are some slightly sad stories. Even Mick Talbot – I look at him and I think, there's something strange about this but nobody's talking about it. Even the thing Mick Talbot had with Galliano was an interesting kind of relationship. It was a bit non-committal and then you think, well maybe it's Mick. He wasn't actually going anywhere. I don't think Paul really falls out with people – it's more that he moves on and people get left behind. It is an autocratic regime. There is a king in this world and there always has been.'

Weller's rift with his sister has lasted for several years, and it didn't help that a few months after their big blow up he ended twelve years of vegetarianism during a tour in Germany, much to Nikki's disgust. Just as Terry Hall has turned from veggie label-examiner to chain-smoking meat and potatoes man, Weller will eat just about anything these days. As his mate Terry Rawlings points out, the singer shovels 'the worst old shit' into his stomach. 'I've seen him eat these big plates of chips and pie in horrible greasy cafes, the sort of food you wouldn't give to a dog. He'll tuck into that and then he'll go off and have a drink. I know people say he looks really healthy but a sun tan hides a multitude of sins. And he goes down to a health club in Sussex with – you won't believe this – Kenny Wheeler.'

Now that the Weller camp had a few songs to tout around, John reassumed his foot-slogging role of taking the tapes to the record companies, just as he had in The Jam days. The Wellers had already rejected a deal with Talkin' Loud, while another deal within the PolyGram umbrella had also fallen through a few months previously. 'I remember Paul coming into Island back in '89 to see Clive Banks about a deal,' says John Pearson. 'I really wanted Clive to sign Paul but they couldn't sort it out together. I don't think it was so much the money, I think it was some of the stipulations that made it difficult for a record company to concur. I think Paul thought, Fuck record companies, I'm going to screw them. They were asking for things like total ownership and control and no record company could accept those terms.'

Clive Banks had left the promotions world behind to take over as managing director of Island Records. As soon as he heard that the deal with Polydor was falling through he got in touch. 'I was desperate to sign him. I've never had any doubts that he will carry on making music as long as he wants to. There are other artists who struggle along but if the hit single isn't there they can't do it any more. If he doesn't sell records I think you'll still find him playing out there.'

Banks's enthusiasm wasn't shared by the one man who could overrule his decision – the company's owner. 'I had one meeting with Paul and John, who came up to Chris Blackwell's flat, but Chris just didn't rate him. He saw it as too British and not international. Sadly, at this moment in time it has to be said he's completely right.' Not that Banks believes Island would have been able to transform Weller's international profile. 'At that particular point Island in America was absolutely shoddy so we wouldn't have been able to change that situation for Paul.' He doesn't remember the Wellers asking for an 'enormous amount of money' or writing 'prohibitive' restrictions into their terms, 'although to be honest we hadn't really got that far,' he confesses. He also stresses that Island could afford to allow the Wellers some ego-boosting terms because the label 'was owned by the Polygram group and the whole Jam catalogue was in that group, so effectively it was the same thing. You were effectively working with two catalogues and record companies never lose out on those scenarios. When they sit there saying it's unrecouped, they're not unrecouped, they're in profit. It's just the artist who is unrecouped. That happened when David Bowie signed a deal with a major and although his new album didn't make a lot of money the back catalogue sales went up and the record company still ended up in profit.'

At least one senior A&R man did baulk at the money, however, claiming John Weller was 'living in the Dark Ages. He was asking for a million pounds.' Weller himself maintained his bravura as the record companies backed away. 'I think they're selling me short,' he blasted back. 'Some of the money they're offering I'd expect they'd offer to some new band. I don't like people taking the piss.'

'It was bloody awful,' agrees John.

A certain David Munns watched these developments with interest: 'My guess is that there was some soul searching in their camp and they thought, Let's not just run off to the next guy who pats us on the head and says, "Lovely." My guess is they took more stock of that than they'd acknowledge.'

As John continued to walk out of his record company offices still clutching his son's tape, the artist himself entered Solid Bond Studios to record a new song, 'Into Tomorrow', with former Rolling Stones, Spencer Davis Group and Traffic producer, Jimmy Miller. The increasingly erratic New Yorker was enjoying his own renaissance, working with Primal Scream on their *Screamadelica* album and a new PolyGram band, Ocean Colour Scene. Both these acts would later become closely associated with Paul Weller, but his collaboration with Miller was an unsuccessful one-off. On 26 February he re-recorded 'Into Tomorrow' with Solid Bond's engineer, Brendan Lynch. The young studio-tanned technician now took on production duties for the first time. Luckily for Weller, who has always preferred to promote from within his own ranks of friends and long-time associates, Lynch was a talented, open-minded operator who drew inspiration from the pre-digital past. He was enthusiastic about achieving a more organic feel than the Council's records and put some real soul back into the music. Lynch's favourite singer was Aretha Franklin, a good starting point for a musical relationship with Weller. He was also a fan of George Martin, The Beatles, Joe Meek, Lee Perry and Funkadelic.

Working in a backroom set-up because The Young Disciples were recording on the main desk, Weller blasted through the new song, which was the most passionate, guitar-led music he'd made in over a decade, far removed from the romantic posturing of the Council. According to Lynch, 'I'll always remember when we finally went home in a cab after those two days. Paul got out of the cab and he looked back in and shook my hand. I could just tell that he'd found it again.'

Weller was buzzing: 'I think it's quite an original song and sound. It's about me trying to get a grip on becoming a thirty-something and the great grey mass that lies between the simple black and white world of my youth.'

Weller had the song to kick-start his career back into action but there was still no deal on the table. He decided to take a different approach. 'I can't see myself ever moving back on to a major label,' he announced. 'If I put any records out they'll more likely than not be released on my own independent Freedom High label. It's been proved nowadays that you no longer need major backing to achieve success,' he added, referring to recent successes for bands like The Farm and The Inspiral Carpets. Ebullient words from an artist who had spent years at Polydor in increasing isolation, to be followed by over a year of dead time without a contract. Neither did he have a very impressive track record with his previous entrepreneurial labels, Jamming! and Respond. Perhaps if he'd had a manager with record company experience it would have been a realistic proposition, but for all John Weller's pragmatism he had no idea how to run a label. They went ahead anyway, calling in their promotions man Nigel 'Spanner' Sweeney to give them a helping hand. 'John phoned up one day and said, "Spanner, Paul's made a fucking great record, I need to see you." So I went over there. Paul had written "Into Tomorrow" and they wanted to put it out themselves. We had this conversation which was slightly weird because John thought I could not only do radio and TV promotion on it but that I would also do press, marketing and just about everything else. The only thing they'd sorted out themselves was distribution through Pinnacle's independent network. John didn't seem to quite understand how to put out a record. I'd ask him, "So what about the marketing?" and he'd be like, "Well, can't you fucking do that then, Spanner?" Then I'd say, "Who's going to do the press?" and again he'd reply, "Well, can't you do it then?" So basically I phoned around and got a guy from Go! Discs to do the marketing and a couple of other people helped out. Pedro Romanyi did the video out for nothing, just costs. It was all really low budget. The whole thing was done for, like, £10,000.'

Despite this chaos, the single – which was released in May on Weller's own Freedom High label – pushed up into the Top 40 and whet the appetite of fans who had long since given up on Weller.

'The single created this resurgence of interest,' says Sweeney. 'Virgin Records were interested in Paul but they had to drop out because of money. The Wellers were still talking about a hefty deal and you see when all the figures were added up because of the international thing people were going, "Well, we're not sure this one is actually worth it." I was also talking to Go! Discs but they weren't sure because of the record company politics – they were part-owned by PolyGram, the same as Polydor. I don't know exactly what was going on there but there were some behind-the-scenes problems which put them off at that time.'

To coincide with the single's release, The Paul Weller Movement toured again, calling the shows Live Part II. Alongside Steve White the rhythm section consisted of bass player Henry Thomas, who was formerly of music education programme *Rock School*, with Gerard Prescencer providing trumpet and flugelhorn, while Linda Duggan and Zeta Massiah supplemented the slimmed-down line-up with backing vocals. The set at Brixton Academy on 20 April included a cover of the Small Faces' 'Tin Soldier' as a tribute to Steve Marriott, who died while the group were on tour. The only new song was 'Into Tomorrow', with the remainder of the night's entertainment fattened up by the odd Style Council song and Jam tracks like 'Precious' and 'Alfie', the B-side to 'The Bitterest Pill'. As expected, the crowds still called for old Jam tracks. 'Part of me gets very pissed off with it but another part of me understands the reasons why,' said Weller philosophically. 'Let's face it, The Jam made a big impact on many people and I suppose it's only natural they'd want to relive a few memories.' However, he insisted, 'There's no way I was going to revive songs like "Eton Rifles" and "Going Underground" because they weren't really my favourite songs and they'd look pretty odd against The Movement's sound anyway.'

In the summer Weller finally off-loaded Solid Bond Studios, selling the lease and making a loss of £100,000. Nevertheless, this was a healthy influx of cash which kick-started the sessions for his debut album at Comforts Place, a Surrey residential studio bought in 1984 by Bucks Fizz managers/producers Andy Hill and Nicola Martin. He pared down his band to a core unit. 'The whole album was recorded with just me, Brendan Lynch [who was house engineer at Solid Bond], Steve White on drums and Jacko Peake on saxophone and flute. I'd never been able to record like that before and it was a real pleasure.' In fact, other players did drop into the sessions – namely Brand New Heavies' vocalist Carleen Anderson, Style Council bassist Camille Hinds, Marco Nelson (who had turned Weller on to Nick Drake and Tim Hardin) from The Young Disciples and Weller's old Red Wedge sparring partner, Robert Howard, alias Dr Robert from The Blow Monkeys. Howard, like Weller, is a shy, quietly spoken and listless character who often hid behind a veneer of mouthy arrogance. As a child he'd lived in Scotland, England and Australia, finally settling down in London in the 1980s where he formed the chic pop outfit, The Blow Monkeys. Although famous for his stylish suits and fast-talking wit, he showed the same restlessness as his new band leader in his musical adventures, rapidly moving on from pop singles like 'Digging Your Scene' and 'It Doesn't Have To Be This Way' into house music, acid jazz and a one-off duet with Algerian, Cheb Khaled, at the end of the decade. In many ways, The Blow Monkeys distilled left-wing politics, poetic romanticism, razor-tongued wit and pop into a sleeker and yet less contrived style than Weller and his Councillors, but Howard also found that his willingness to deviate into dance music frustrated his record company. Weller encouraged Howard to start over and it was no coincidence that both artists signed to the Japanese label, Pony Canyon, along with Dee C Lee who inked a new solo deal. The Modfather also played on Dr Robert's debut album, *Realms of Gold*, in 1994, which followed the raw, live feel of his friend's music, as well as revealing a romantic streak which bordered on the Shelley-esque.

Weller's deal with the Fuji film-financed Pony Canyon was for an album tentatively called *SX2000*, a title inspired by an SX model of the Lambretta scooter. 'The Japanese have the bucks,' was all he said about his new record company. More funds now poured into the Weller account, enabling them to mix the new album for a release the following spring. Meanwhile, back in the UK, a video of The Movement's gig at London's Brixton Academy on the second tour was released to stir up a little interest until a new record label could be found for a full British release. These tentative solo steps contrasted with the robust interest in Weller's back catalogue which took The Jam's greatest hits to number two in the UK charts. But Weller dismissed rumours of a Jam reunion. 'I'd have to be really down to my last pair of loafers before I'd do that,' he quipped. 'Someone asked me recently if I thought people had a right to feel let down by me and I don't think they do. I think you can only let yourself down.'

He did flash back into his past – albeit that of a childhood fan – by recording a version of 'Don't Let Me Down' for an obscure Beatles tribute record which raised money for Oxfam's Cambodia

Appeal. A self-financed trip to America provided a much-needed shot in the arm as he pulled an audience of 6,000 at the Greek Theatre in Los Angeles. Coinciding with this upturn in Weller's career was another big event in his family life. In October 1991 Dee gave birth to the couple's first daughter, Leah.

Although overjoyed, this added to the complex situation he now found himself in as he set his sights on launching his solo career in the UK while trying to maintain the family life he'd focused on in the time between The Style Council and The Paul Weller Movement. Inevitably there were pressures, and something had to give, but at the end of 1991 he was ready to return to the fray with a fresh sound and an attitude grounded in his recent experiences. 'Up until [the last two years] I'd had quite a cushy ride really and now I'm prepared for whatever comes my way. It did me good, helped me come back down to earth a little bit. It made me doubt whether I was as strong as I thought I was.'

8 Changing Man, 1992–94

Paul Weller: 'My perfect date? Raquel from *Coronation Street* probably. She's fucking all right.'

Jim White (*Independent*): 'It took The Who three years to transmogrify from Mods to hippies. Weller has taken five times as long to cover the same distance.'

At the start of 1992 Weller finalised a new record deal with the PolyGram-affiliated Go! Discs, headed by Andy Macdonald. His new MD declared he wasn't afraid to release the album because 'Paul zigs when everybody else zags'. The gutsy, British R&B sound of 'Into Tomorrow' had pulled back some old fans but Weller's music still seemed oddly redundant in '91 and '92. In the States grunge had followed rap as the latest underground scene to explode into multi-platinum sales, a change spearheaded by Nirvana's *Nevermind* album. The band's singer, Kurt Cobain, was a charismatic and visceral frontman, a mix which highlighted the pitiful limits of England's mumbling shoe-gazing scene in 1991. There was a crisis of confidence in the British music industry, which made Macdonald's deal with a struggling English icon seem a little perverse and certainly courageous.

The negotiations dragged out longer than the Weller camp had wanted, testing the nerves of the man who, as usual, was taking the brunt of the tension. 'I remember going down to see John Weller,' explains Nigel Sweeney, 'and it's never nice to see anyone worrying and he was really worrying for Paul. He has to because it's his son. He was just waiting for the phone call from Go! Discs. Andy Macdonald must've sorted out the political problems and was interested. John was waiting for the call from business affairs at Go! Discs and he was panicking because if it wasn't that label there seemed to be nobody else. It wasn't like there were loads and loads of other labels battering the door down for Paul.'

John Weller: 'It's been a gamble but it's certainly paid off.'

Gary Blackburn watched the deal come together from Anglo's office above Go! Discs. 'Andy gave them a lot of money for a label like Go! Discs and put a lot of faith in it,' he says. 'He didn't get a return until the second album. Paul likes Andy's laid-back approach to the record business. It's unusual; there's only a few people around like that.'

Andy Macdonald had worked at Stiff Records, the same place where Sara Silver developed a rapport with the artists on the label. He founded Go! Discs with some of the Stiff spirit, concentrating on British pop artists headed by The Housemartins (who later splintered into The Beautiful South, Beats International and numerous other Norman Cook dance projects) and the inspiration behind Red Wedge, Billy Bragg. The only dark if distant cloud on Weller's horizon was that he'd effectively returned to PolyGram, the mother label for both Polydor, Go! Discs (they had a 49 per cent stake in the label) and David Munns, who remains a key figure at their international offices in central London. 'Paul Weller is still part of PolyGram through Go! Discs and I have no desire to fall out with him or upset him,' says Munns. 'I think his records are fantastic and I play them at home.'

In March '92 Weller played a low-key solo date in Tokyo where his debut album reached the top slot in the international charts. A few weeks later, Polydor released a CD of Jam out-takes and B-sides entitled *Extras*. It was a fine album, revealing the depth of material Weller had written in the band and acting as a timely reminder of past glories for fans who had stopped buying the later Council records. Weller himself rediscovered tracks which he's previously dismissed. 'It kind of made me feel nostalgic,' he told the *NME*. 'I started digging out some of the old records, listening to them in a totally different way . . . I enjoyed that experience and I found that there were a lot of good songs I'd turned my back on. But I still feel uncomfortable playing some of them. I'll get a verse or two in and then I'll find two lines of a lyric that I can't really sing any more because they're so badly written.'

In June Weller played seven dates around the UK, mostly in front of small audiences in club venues. The shows included London gigs at the Grand, the Mean Fiddler, the Town & Country Club 2 and Subterrania. There were further changes in his backing band for these solo performances with Camille Hinds now on bass, alongside organist Helen Turner and ex-Orange Juice drummer Zeke Manyika. All three had worked with Weller in The Style

Council and Mick Talbot and Dee C Lee completed the reunion,
when they joined the band for an encore of Marvin Gaye's 'What's
Going On?' at the T&C2. Given Weller's time away from both the
charts and the British media, it was hardly surprising that the
audience were almost entirely old fans. Gary Blackburn winces a
little as he recalls, 'Pre the release of the first album things weren't
really as good as you might have imagined for Weller. He was
really out on the edge of the media circle. He had this anvil of The
Jam around his neck and all these dodgy Mods from the seventies
who just worshipped him and adored him. They were all thirty-odd
now and looked terribly sad at the gigs. He had that image of
somebody who was great once and had all these sad fans.'

These small-scale gigs were in stark contrast to Weller's next trip
abroad. He sold out 10,000 capacity venues on his return to Japan
and in the US former Small Faces organist, Ian McLagan, joined
him on-stage at a Los Angeles date. Back in the UK, Go! Discs
released their first Weller single, 'Uh Huh Oh Yeh', which borrowed the riff from The Beatles' 'Dear Prudence' – not for the first
time or the last – and gave him his first Top Twenty hit since 1987's
Style Council single, 'It Didn't Matter'. When he performed it on
Top of the Pops he felt uncomfortable alongside the young rave acts
and boy bands, vowing never to repeat the experience.

The song's vague title was far removed from the Council's bad
puns and sloganeering. The lyrics were personal and introspective,
conveying Weller's mixed emotions as he looked back to his Woking
childhood in the lines, 'Each memory returned to trace/reminders of
who I am.' The single's B-side, 'Fly On The Wall', was a lovely
acoustic ballad and completed a promising start on his new label.

When Weller's self-titled debut solo album was released in the UK
in September, it took him back into the Top Ten thanks to the
return of some sympathetic fans. Although his jazzbo guitar still
fluttered in the mix, the album possessed a looser, more evocative
sound than the rigid stylishness of the Council. 'Above The
Clouds'' jazzy psychedelia was soaked in the 60s influences of
Curtis Mayfield and Marvin Gaye. There was also a spiritual
undertone to the songs as the writer faced up to mortality and
self-doubt: 'Summer gone so quick/I have to wonder will I last . . .
so sadness creeps into my dreams/Scared of living but afraid to die.'

Paul Weller

'Amongst Butterflies' also distilled a spiritual mood into the understated acoustics. 'I haven't been converted to natural religion or anything,' he laughed. 'Everyone gets a bit more hippyish when they get older.'

Weller made a clean break from The Style Council's political manifestos, reflecting a fresh attitude in the father of two. 'I used to feel terribly guilty about everything. The money, the lifestyle, the hotels and stuff. Now I just think that I worked fucking hard for it all. So why shouldn't I enjoy it?'

No one in the media had the will to grill him about this change of heart. The political lines weren't so clearly drawn any more. The Labour Party was moving rapidly into the centre (a process which was speeded up by their fourth successive election defeat in 1992), eventually reinventing itself under Tony Blair as New Labour. Margaret Thatcher had long gone and her replacement, John Major, wasn't such a demonic figurehead to rally against. The arrival of the rave drug ecstasy gave youth culture a fragile, hedonistic and apolitical sense of community, later overspilling into the football terraces and pubs where some of Weller's old fans also got themselves 'sorted'. The country was still in an economic mess but the polarity of yuppies and old-style unions in the 80s had long gone. Despair and disillusionment lingered but, like Weller, most 34 year olds now had families and were looking back to their roots.

Weller: 'I still care. How can you not care? But in this last election voting was a tokenistic thing. I was casting a vote against the Tories. I hate the way they're turning the recession on to people. It's our fucking fault now. Thatcher tells us we had too much credit, we bought too many houses. She encouraged us.

'I've been some people's spokesman . . . It's all bullshit really and I think people who have grown up with me will realise that. There are people out there who are the same as me – with two kids who met their wife at a Jam gig in '79 or whatever. We've all grown up together and we've been through a lot. As long as it doesn't get too nostalgic or sentimental, I'm happy.'

Former Red Wedge activist Phil Jupitus saw a bit of himself in Weller. 'I'm glad to see him growing old disgracefully with a smile on his face. I'm sure fatherhood has changed him. I've had two kids and it's certainly changed me. You worry about doing the best for your kids and become less altruistic as you get older.'

Nevertheless, the music on Weller's self-titled debut didn't go deeply into the national psyche. The ideas and attitudes that would later elevate him to 'Modfather' status were present but the fluid feel of the best songs was overshadowed by self-indulgence on others. Cod-jazz tangents and twee hippy images conjured up by flute solos were also a little too much for some fans to take. The critics were unconvinced by the comeback. According to *NME*'s Steve Sutherland, 'Paul Weller's first solo LP is utterly bereft of virtue in the same way as a Paul McCartney record is – can't find Weller in there.' The album also got a lowly two-star rating in *Q* and a three out of ten mark in *Vox*. Adam Sweeting from the *Guardian* wrote, 'Broadly speaking, the playing is fine but the songs are strikingly devoid of shape and content . . . Play any of these songs beside "A Town Called Malice" or "That's Entertainment" and you'll wonder where the real Weller went.'

Charles Shaar Murray, now a *Telegraph* journalist, opined, 'His voice is still too small and inflexible for him to be the Great Soul Man of his dreams, but his heart is in the right place even if his wardrobe isn't.' Andy Gill of the *Independent* feigned indifference. 'This is the Post-Modern World and what, ultimately, is so interesting about Weller's disinternment of the past? And should we hang around waiting for him to get beyond 1970?'

Another *NME* writer, David Quantick, was more generous: 'Bring on the Pimm's and let's have a sing-song around the old Hammond because Paul Weller is back. Nearly, anyway.'

Nigel Sweeney admits that it was hard work generating enthusiasm for the first album. 'The reaction was OK but it wasn't fantastic,' he says. 'Nobody felt that Paul Weller was digging in really, really hard.'

The follow-up single, 'Above The Clouds', was co-produced by acid jazz stalwart Chris Bangs. However, fans who had recently forked out for the album didn't rush out to buy the single and it flopped, failing to reach the Top 40. On the B-side was an emotional, bluesy acoustic song, 'Everything Has A Price To Pay', and a version of Traffic's 'Feeling Alright', which featured vocals from Carleen Anderson and Dee C Lee. Writer Chas de Whalley wasn't alone in noting Traffic's growing influence on Weller. 'He's taken the thing that The Spencer Davis Group were doing and then moved into the area where Traffic were. I always thought that

Paul Weller

Traffic were a bit messy and never really got a grip on their material and I find Paul's stuff the same . . . Paul's solo stuff sounds like Traffic meets Humble Pie. He's followed a very peculiarly English route, almost as a mirror image of someone like Steve Winwood.'

Humble Pie were a 60s 'supergroup' formed by ex-Small Faces singer Steve Marriott with former Herd guitarist Peter Frampton and Spooky Tooth's Greg Ridley. Their mix of acoustic material with the rockier style of their Top Five UK single 'Natural Born Bugie' possessed the kind of rawness which Weller was trying to recapture after the self-conscious approach of The Style Council.

Brendan Lynch's remix of the album track, 'Kosmos', sprawled into the clubs in early '93. To many it was a more adventurous piece of music than the first album. 'We did it for ourselves really and just put it out on promo,' says Lynch with a shrug. DJ Andy Weatherall picked up on this version and made it his set-closing anthem at Sabresonic. When Primal Scream heard 'Kosmos' they asked Lynch to remix their 'Funky Jam' track on their *Give Out but Don't Give Up* album. 'At the time we were going to the northern soul night at the 100 Club,' explains Lynch. Weller and Primal Scream were both big northern soul fans and the latter covered the Small Faces song 'Understanding' for a tribute album. The track was produced by Lynch, who enthuses: 'It had quite a good northern soul vibe on it.'

At the same time, Weller's band toured the UK and Europe, promoting the solo album with sets which included covers of Aaron Neville's 'Hercules', Marvin Gaye's 'What's Going On?' and Neil Young's 'Ohio'. Young wrote the latter as a reaction to the shooting of demonstrators at Ohio's Kent State University, which made it stand out like a sore thumb against Weller's new non-political songs. He also played The Jam's 'Man In The Corner Shop' and The Style Council's 'Headstart For Happiness'. Backed by flute and bongos, Weller's return to the Albert Hall in October was semi-triumphant, although the extended muso work-outs tested the patience of some fans.

Weller was also featured on the cover of *Scootering* magazine, discussing his renovation of a recently bought Lambretta TV175, before he left for a US tour in the autumn where the album had just been released. Sell-out gigs at the Ritz in New York and LA's open-air Greek Theatre once again proved his popularity in the main American cities as he ran through a set which included an acoustic version of 'A Town Called Malice'.

The year ended with Paul Weller's debut album failing to make an impression on the critic's favourite album of the year polls, but his own choice, Blur's *Modern Life is Rubbish*, signalled a brash, confident pillage of English pop history that had begun a year earlier with Suede's cocky twist on David Bowie's back catalogue. Suede's frontman Brett Anderson was part of a long rock lineage of suburban failures (he grew up in Hayward's Heath, between Brighton and London) which included Weller and Essex boy Damon Albarn from Blur. However, while Anderson reached out for the sexually ambivalent, faded glamour of Ziggy Stardust, Albarn drew heavily on 60s pop, notably The Who, the Small Faces and the lyrics of Ray Davies from The Kinks. Guitarist Graham Coxon was a big Weller fan, naming The Style Council's performance at Ipswich Beaumont Hall in 1983 as his favourite gig of all time. 'It was the first time I saw Paul Weller. I never managed to see The Jam, which always irked me, so it was really exciting to see one of my heroes on-stage. He was great as well. Good clothes, of course.'

The sartorial guru, with reservations, was impressed with Blur: 'Not because of the Mod thing,' he insisted. 'I think that's been overstated, but because of the songs – the lyrics and the attitude. They come from Colchester, don't they? I can relate to that southern England, small-town, suburban mentality. It's a kind of escape from boredom – London's bright lights. They've captured some of that for me.'

Weller spent the first half of 1993 recording his next album in the Manor, a residential studio set in Oxfordshire countryside which had been created out of a Jacobean manor by Virgin founder, Richard Branson, in the early 70s. Vines and woodland surrounded the building, making it the perfect location for Weller's organic, rootsy R&B sound. Initially he played the new songs with Marco Nelson and Steve White but by the end of the session an extended family of musicians guested on the record: Mick Talbot, Dee C Lee, Max Beesley, Jacko Peake, Helen Turner, Robert Howard and Steve Cradock from Ocean Colour Scene. When the album was finished, the easy-going, filial atmosphere was added to by the arrival of the entire staff of Go! Disco, as the label shut up shop for the day, hired a minibus and took everyone down to Oxfordshire for the playback. The label's co-director, Mike Heneghan, remembers, 'We all went down to the Manor, which was a beautiful house. The gardens are lovely. It was a hoot playing table tennis and snooker and listening to the album. It was a very special occasion, getting everyone in one room, all hearing *Wild Wood* for the first time. The studio's quite small so you're all crammed in and it was a great experience.'

A Style Council compilation of rarities, *Here's One That Got Away*, released by Polydor on 28 June, was followed in July by the first single from *Wild Wood*, entitled 'Sunflower'. After another intro strongly reminiscent of psychedelic era Beatles, Weller launched into a big, rocky riff which blasted through without the attachment of jazz or flute doodling. It was an exhilarating return to form, the best thing he'd done since the original version of 'Into Tomorrow'. There were also hints that Weller was appealing to a wider audience as the song breached the Top Twenty.

A new single, 'Wild Wood', was released in August, charting at fourteen. Weller explains the acoustic sound of the record: 'I tried to write a folk song or at least my interpretation of one, a very traditional olde ballad one, where the chords don't change throughout the song and the only changes come from the dynamics of the playing and the lead voice.' Later in the year he played 'Wild Wood' at a gig in Glasgow and the crowd sang along with him, transforming it into a 'real folk song'. Its lilting, natural style was reminiscent of 60s artists Nick Drake and Tim Hardin, with the former part of an English post-Mod movement into folk music. The single also included a low-key remix by Go! Discs label mates Portishead.

On the surface 'Wild Wood' appeared to be a pastoral ballad, harking back to childhood memories of the Surrey woodland. Weller confessed, ' "Wild Wood" is all about these magical memories I have from when I was a kid. "The Place I Love" on *All Mod Cons* is a bit like that, too. "Monday" on *Sound Affects*, "Boy About Town" – these are the songs I like now.'

However, the lyrics worked on several levels. There's a softly stated spiritual side to the words and a harder, metropolitan layer of fast-moving images as urban commuters brave the rush-hour 'high tide' to get to where they should be going. Both layers were reflected in the video, with Weller the balladeer singing under a tree interspersed with shots of Piccadilly Circus as 'people fly by in the traffic's boom'. Weller also intercut a positive response to this urban chaos: 'Don't let them get you down, making you feel guilty about ... all the good things you deserve.' The combination of simplicity and different resonances in the words made 'Wild Wood' one of Weller's finest songs and raised expectations for the forth-coming album.

Released almost exactly a year after the debut, the *Wild Wood* album peaked at number two in the UK charts and reached gold status (100,000 sales) within two weeks. It was a more focused record than the first, which successfully stripped away the jazz indulgences to a warm, raw, uplifting sound. Weller had worn his caring, humanistic beliefs on his sleeve in The Jam and The Style Council but in *Wild Wood* they were felt purely through the music. It was real soul music – raw, urgent and inspiring, where *Cost of Loving* had been simply mannered and superficial. The emotional conviction of the songwriting was vented through the best singing of his career, which was rich, husky and free from self-conscious imitation of his old heroes. 'I got older, you know. I think it's a physical thing,' says Weller of the changes in his voice. '. . . It's like anything, the more you do the better you get at it, I think. Or at least the better the technique becomes anyway.'

Nigel Sweeney also noted a major change in the twelve months since the self-titled album: 'With *Wild Wood* I think people felt, He's trying now, and I think that's reflected in his voice, which is completely different from the first album. I think the lessons learnt on the first album were put into effect on the second album. I said this to Paul and he did agree. That album was the point where people understood him.'

Wild Wood fleshed out the sense of self-doubt, disillusion and hope expressed in his debut but with greater passion and convic-tion. 'Can You Heal Us (Holy Man)' has gospel-expressed hope and confusion in equal measure, the acoustic-based 'Food Of The Mountain' glimpses dreams which are always just out of reach, while 'Has My Fire Really Gone Out?' is a deliberate tease, with Weller psyching himself up and putting 'an end to all your doubts'. The past lingers in 'Shadow Of The Sun' as the singer reaches back into his childhood inspirations, 'All The Pictures On The Wall' outlines a broken relationship, 'Moon On Your Pyjamas' is a sentimental, father-to-son song with an isolated jazzbo guitar, and 'Country' is a hazily optimistic resolve to go 'into the light, out of the dark'. The ambiguous visions and naturalistic imagery works with the music, rather than setting up the kind of stark contrasts of The Style Council or the tight, caustic passion of The Jam. On paper Weller's lyrics appear simplistic but the voice, words and music complement each other perfectly. They are also layered with diverse influences – Eastern mysticism, R&B riffs, the hushed Californian harmonies of Crosby, Stills And Nash, Neil Young's visceral songwriting, British Mod psychedelia, soul, thirty-something self-doubt and a childlike sense of joy, expressed with the conviction Weller has been searching for since The Jam's *Sound Affects*. Brendan Lynch's spurts of analogue synthesisers also layer up the tracks with a psychedelic feel, and the band weren't afraid to jam around the tracks, an approach which signalled the live, spontaneous attitude Weller took into the studio. The pivotal player who enabled him to do this without tumbling into self-indulgence is Steve White. His inventive fills and ability to switch from power to a deft lightness of touch held the album together.

Weller's statements in the press expressed a change of attitude to a more personal vision: 'I don't believe in religion or politics,' he argued, 'just in music, pop culture. That's my religion, it's just what I do.

'The lyrics I write now happen to be a lot more personal. I tend to write them at night when it feels like everyone else is asleep but I never consciously decide what they're going to be about. When I was in The Jam I wrote about other people's feelings. Now I write about my emotions. I've come full circle.'

His friend, Paolo Hewitt, explains: 'He's still idealistic in some respects. I think he started out wanting to change the world and now he wants to change himself . . . I think he probably is more wary of making political statements but it's also a reflection of the changes everybody goes through as a person.'

Although *Wild Wood* is arguably the best album of his career, the critics still expressed reservations when it first came out. Paul Moody in the *NME* stated, 'It's not the absolute *tour de force* we may have hoped for but it's home to at least two songs ("Sunflower" and "The Weaver") that would grace any retrospective. And how often can you say that sixteen years into someone's career?'

The task of plugging the album to the media now fell to Gary Blackburn at Anglo who replaced Nigel 'Spanner' Sweeney in 1993. He knew the job wouldn't be easy. 'I think Paul and his dad had worn ... They say no to any kind of promotion. They're very reluctant to do stuff. For example, he wouldn't do *Top of the Pops* unless he played live. It's easy to just assume that he won't do stuff.

'We thought *Wild Wood* was a good record but we didn't think it was that great at the time because these things do grow with age. We met him and talked through what he wanted to do and how he wanted to go about it and the one thing he focused on was that he said if he could play live he would do anything. That was the key really.

'The singles from the previous album hadn't been playlisted. They'd only got token airplay. "Into Tomorrow" was a great single and nobody picked up on it really. He had no support from the evening session or other taste-making DJs other than old Gary Crowley. So it was like building from the bottom upwards. Jackie Brambles was doing the lunchtime programme at Radio One at the time and she's a big fan. We got Paul to play live on that show which he did. There was a bit of drama because they wanted him to do a Jam number and a Style Council song which he absolutely refused to do. But we were able to persuade him five minutes before they went on air that it would be a good idea to do a song from each era. He really didn't want to do it but in the end he did "That's Entertainment" and changed the lyrics and "Long Hot Summer". Then he played "Sunflower" and "Wild Wood". It really made a big impact. All the station heard it and soon we were on the playlist. That was the one compromise that was made.'

Blackburn recalls the first time he had father and son and Kenny Wheeler facing him in his office. 'When you meet the Weller gang, you've got Kenny, this big guy, then you've got his dad, who you think, What the fuck is he on about? His dad doesn't make any sense. When you meet his dad you think he doesn't know what he's talking about. It's the one thing I've come to learn over the period of two or three years I've been working with him – the importance his father plays in the set-up – because I couldn't fathom it at all in the beginning. His dad isn't particularly articulate or knowledge-able about the business. He hasn't got a lot of marketing nounce.

'They're very tight, very sure of themselves and they know where they've been. They're quite a hard gang to get them to treat you with any respect.

'It's an unusual relationship to have with your father. He's made sure Paul's got everything he needed since he was a kid to get him where he is. I think Paul's the one that makes all the decisions but he draws strength from having John and Kenny around him. They provide the infrastructure, the machinery of what goes on – the attitude and the muscle. But Paul calls the shots.'

Lisa Verrico remembers her first encounter with the gruff-voiced John Weller in 1993. 'I met his dad the first time we went to New York around the time of *Wild Wood*. The first night we were in New York, we all went out for a meal but his dad was like, "No, no, I'm going out on my own." Later we were sat in the bar at two o'clock in the morning and his dad comes in later than us. He's been out to all these old boxers' pubs and he was saying all these names of boxers, saying, "Guess who I've seen?" Of course I didn't know any of them, but it was brilliant to listen to. He'd gone out on his own and had a really good time, which I thought was really cool. Anyway, his dad was talking about how no English bands do well in the states and I was going, "Well, what about Depeche Mode or Radiohead?" And he'd never heard of any of these bands. He doesn't know any bands apart from his own son's.'

The next single, 'The Weaver', was a big R&B track built around a great Weller riff and powered by some impressive guitar work from Ocean Colour Scene's Steve Cradock. It was the only album track he'd played on but it hadn't gone unnoticed, by Weller and his fans, that it was also one of the best from the *Wild Wood* session. There was a definite chemistry which Weller had been searching for, arguably since he'd first discovered Steve White. Now he had White, Cradock and producer Brendan Lynch slotted into the best band he'd ever played in. There was a rawness and edgy passion in the sound which harked back to the visceral power of The Jam; he also now had a band who could bleed fresh influences into the sound and achieve the catholic diversity of The Style Council.

Birmingham-born Jam fanatic Cradock (whose surname is only one letter short of Ann Weller's maiden name), first met Weller back in 1987 when he travelled to Solid Bond Studios to press a demo of one of his Mod bands, The Boys, into the singer's hand.

In 1990 he formed Ocean Colour Scene after seeing The Stone Roses at the Irish Centre. Confirmation came a few months later when they saw the Roses again at Spike Island, an experience which the band describe as a 'pilgrimage'.

He met Weller again when his new band booked into Solid Bond in '91 to do a mix of a track with former Rolling Stones producer, Jimmy Miller. The band released one album, *Yesterday and Today*, on PolyGram in '92 and then left the label owing £500,000 due to wasted studio time and laughably expensive videos which were rarely shown.

The call from Weller came out of the blue, but it's been a tight, inspired partnership ever since. Cradock outlines the recharged confidence he felt in the Weller band: 'When I was playing with Paul I knew my playing was getting better. I'd had Otis Redding and Booker T albums when I was thirteen. I could listen to it, dig it ... but I couldn't play it. That started to change.' One moment on-stage with Weller at the Glastonbury Festival sums up how much his role in the post-*Wild Wood* band means to him. He stood with Weller on his right and Steve Marriott's autograph in his back pocket. 'It was like the friends were touching my hands,' he says.

In addition, Ocean Colour Scene's singer Simon Flower performed as a support act for Weller and the band's Damon Minchella joined the Modfather on bass. Coincidentally, Ocean Colour Scene are managed by Cradock's father Chris, a no-nonsense figure, not unlike John in his nuts-and-bolts approach and pride in his boys: 'I'm an ex-copper, right. Twenty-five years in the police force. And I have never, ever known four characters with the guts and determination of these lads. I've never come across it before in any walk of life.'

The tight set-up around Ocean Colour Scene slotted neatly into the Weller 'mafia'. Some old friends of the singer are saddened, however, by the insular atmosphere around him, which now has self-professed music groupies at the heart of the band. 'What's going on there then?' questions Terry Rawlings. 'They're fans of his. What must that be like when you've got someone who thinks you're a hero playing in your band. It's not a normal situation; it's a bit insincere and superficial.

'Paul has outgrown the everyday experiences of everyday people. I think he's genuinely sad about that. There is no one left around

Paul Weller

him who is a fishmonger or a plumber. If you've just got loads of
acquaintances with people, it's like living in a campsite.'

However, Cradock is undoubtedly a talented player who gives
Weller a youthful, uncompromising and fan-obsessive drive at the
core of the band – a potent force to feed off. Ocean Colour Scene's
own revived fortunes, which initially owed something to Weller's
patronage, have also given Cradock independence. He's clearly
followed through ambitions which extend well beyond that of
sparring partner to the Modfather. In 1996 Ocean Colour Scene's
second album, *Moseley Shoals* (a Stax-meets-Birmingham joke!)
built on the success of their hit single, 'The Riverboat Song', to
become a platinum seller before the end of the summer.

If Weller drops people with an alarming full stop, terminating a
friendship absolutely, he's also a loyal mate to those who stay in
favour. Rawlings himself admits, 'Paul has been incredibly generous to me over the years. I've heard stories about him being mean
but I've never seen it. If you're his friend he can be very supportive
and he'll always get his round in. But I criticised him once too often
to his face. Even little things like telling him that his guitar strap is
too high, just joking around, he'll be pissed off about it for months
until he finally decides he gets the joke. It can be really hard work.'

Eugene Manzi, whose friendship with Weller has survived intact
for a decade, also points out how the singer makes an effort to say
'hello' and remember people's names even if they're only casual
acquaintances – a rare trait in the music industry. 'I think it's so
unusual for someone of his status to be like that,' says Manzi, 'but
he is. He remembers people. He sees my daughter once a year and
always says, "Hello Vicky". He is well mannered. He's also quite
shy but it depends who he's with. If there's somebody he has no
respect for he won't give them the time of day. He doesn't suffer
fools gladly. I've seen that side of him once or twice. He'll just walk
away.'

In October the band set off for Japan with new bassist Yolanda
Charles and, of course, Cradock, alongside White and Helen
Turner. Much to Weller's chagrin, Polydor raided The Jam's vaults
while he was away, this time for the inferior *Live Jam*. Back in the
UK Jonathan Ross joined Weller for a rare airing of 'A Town
Called Malice' on the TV show *Saturday Zoo*, followed by a

caterwauling-free appearance on BBC's new music show, *Later*, which was hosted by Jools Holland. A few weeks later Weller kicked off a triumphant UK tour complete with 'Match Day' programmes and football styled T-shirts. Dr Robert notes with a wry grin, 'Weller's no good at football. Cricket is more our game now. It's funny because Paul used a lot of the football mania in his marketing. At gigs he'd have football shirts for sale and he never plays football. But his fans are definitely straight off the terraces.' Weller was now more at ease with the rowdier elements of his following than he had been in The Style Council. By the end of the year he'd also defied his critics and was back at the top of the British music scene. *Wild Wood* was nominated for the Mercury Music Prize and the Brit Awards' Best Album category, while Weller featured at the Brits in the final list for Best Male Artist.

In March '94 *Wild Wood* went back into the Top Five, fattened up by the addition of a new single, the introspective 'Hung Up', which gave him his first Top Ten hit of the decade. There was yet another UK tour in the spring, followed by dates in Europe and America. The festival shows at Glastonbury and Phoenix ranked alongside the best of his career.

The period from spring to summer '94 was important to Weller for other reasons. Blur's *Parklife* album went straight in at number one, sparking off a fascination among British youth for all things Mod. Albarn and co. weren't authentic, codified elitists but their love of Madness, The Kinks, The Jam and the Mod movie, *Quadrophenia* (whose star, Phil Daniels, sang on the year's anthem, 'Parklife') was wittily transformed into a fresh, cocksure and infectious style which defined a horrible new term, Britpop, and turned Weller into the 'Modfather'.

Eugene Manzi watched this development with a touch of be-musement. 'All the new bands sort of look up to him as the godfather of that movement. I'm not so sure that they're right. He's still around, making music, he's credible and he's successful. I'm sure if the Small Faces were still around and credible they would look up to them.'

Weller was the only icon referred to in Blur's pillage of English pop who was still a force to be reckoned with. Although Madness reformed at their Madstock gigs in London's Finsbury Park, these events were nothing more than a pocket-lining, nostalgic knees-up.

Paul Weller

Ray Davies from The Kinks was still writing but his biggest hit of the last decade had been the mildly amusing 'Come Dancing', which says it all really.

Weller's knowledge of British music goes a lot deeper than the younger Britpoppers. While he represented a popular lineage from The Beatles through to Blur and Oasis, he also referred back to the lesser known British R&B acts, preserving some of the gritty, emotional edge of these artists for a new generation. Gilles Peterson enjoyed passionate conversations with Weller about music, trading opinions on records and making discoveries. 'I was ignorant to a lot of that R&B thing – the more white sound of people like Brian Auger. He helped me become aware of the importance of those sort of artists, who made pure British music. Thank God there's people like Paul. There's still room for these nutters who can come along and fuck things up a bit. I mean, who else is carrying the torch in the nineties?'

The ex-Jam singer was now bristling with born-again credibility and there was even a superficial, tongue-in-cheek Mod revival inspired by Blur's *Parklife*. The Colchester band were elevated to fully fledged pop heroes, with fans noting their rampant appropriation of English pop history, including 60s Mod fashion. The band's guitarist and ex-Jam fan, Graham Coxon, was a regular at the 60s retro club, Blow Up, which had a Mod-meets-psychedelic cultural mix reflected in Sgt Pepper uniforms and dandy Mod clothes worn by the DJs and on the dancefloor. Coxon also appeared around town in a parka, while Damon Albarn made Harringtons (a casual zip-up jacket inspired by Rodney Harrington, a character in the American TV soap, *Peyton Place*) hip again. To his credit Coxon was knowledgeable enough about 60s culture to recognise that Blur weren't true Mods. 'The original Mods were office boys who only worked so they could afford speed and some nice clothes,' he stated. 'That doesn't really fit in with our lifestyle.'

There were other major changes in the music scene that spring. In April '94 the grunge scene started to disintegrate with the death of Nirvana's Kurt Cobain, followed by Hole bassist Kristin Pfaff shortly after. The worst side of grunge – its nihilistic, self-absorbed misery – began to take over as Courtney Love became a freak show and poor second-raters Stone Temple Pilots also began to fall apart through the drug problems of their singer, Scott Weiland. The 'alternative scene' created by grunge went through a long, slow decline in America but in Britain it was effectively blasted out of the system by Blur and another band rooted in English pop from the 60s – Oasis. Their anthemic take on The Beatles, T-Rex, The Sex Pistols, The Rolling Stones and The Jam made straight-between-the-eyes British rock 'n' roll cool for the first time since The Pistols and The Clash.

'Oasis are one of my favourite groups at the moment,' enthused Weller. 'They seem to appreciate all the good values of being in a pop group. They know that when it's done properly music still means something to people.'

The man who had spent years trashing rock music as a dead end now proclaimed, 'For all those people who said computer games or comedy or any of that crap were the new rock 'n' roll a few years ago, it's proved they were all fucking wrong. Rock 'n' roll . . . always comes back.'

Not surprisingly, given their mutual admiration, Weller and Oasis started to hang out together. The mood in both camps was buoyant. Journalist Lisa Verrico, who was a mate of Oasis, observed Weller and the band getting on like a house on fire. 'That summer Weller was starting to have a good time, and he had a better time with Oasis. They were doing that thing where it was that first burst of success and it's all really exciting. Weller could hang out with Oasis and have a bit of that first-time rush without all the horrible sides to it. I think they both got something out of it. When Oasis were recording "Whatever" at Maison Rouge Studios in June, Weller came down just to hang out.'

Gary Blackburn believes Weller still fights with himself over this level of success, particularly when compared to the Gallaghers' ease with their fame: 'I think he's quite uncomfortable being Paul Weller. I think he struggles with himself a little bit. He wrestles with all the bullshit that goes with being famous. There are a lot of times when I'm with Paul and I want to say to him, "Loosen up, man, enjoy it, it's great." I think privately he is enjoying it but he has a hard time demonstrating that. He's honourable. Noel's a very different character. He's so comfortable with his success. He has such a simple, clear vision of what he wants to do. He has no problem with being rich and famous.'

Paul Weller

Noel Gallagher's 'Victor Meldrew of rock' quip certainly hints at a character who will never completely shake off his tense, miserable moods. However, the more introspective Weller was drawn to the extroverted, hedonistic atmosphere around Oasis and, literally, let his hair down (it hadn't been this long since the kipper-tie phase of early Jam) and rocked out in an environment consisting of an upbeat mix of cocaine, spliffs, booze and girls. 'I think he was so pleased when all the success happened,' says Verrico. 'I didn't really know him when he wasn't selling records but from what I can tell he had to stay at home and couldn't write because he was really depressed. I suppose it meant twice as much to him when he started selling records again. Part of the reason why he's got a really good attitude now is because he's been through a down period which Oasis haven't had.

'When I went to Switzerland to interview him he was in a really good mood. He loves being on tour, getting all the boys in the band up the back of the bus, and they all play tapes that they like to each other. There's this little gang mentality. The whole time I was there he was just standing in the street, bouncing up and down because he was so happy.

'He's nothing like how he comes across in articles, where he seems to be the most sombre, boring person in the world. They've made him out as really egocentric, distant, thinks he's better than other people, has got no sense of humour, and it's just not what he's actually like. He's a little bit shy until you get to know him and then he's really friendly. He's definitely a flirt. He's probably really friendly because I'm female. I'm not saying he isn't friendly to blokes or that he's friendly to every female. But maybe he's a bit more relaxed with girls on first meeting than with men. I've been in pubs with him and these blokes come up to him and go, "You know, *Mod Cons* changed my life," and I can see he looks awkward. But if he doesn't get that off you I think he's a bit more at ease.'

Weller also became an icon of another fresh cultural shift – the return of the lad. After the 80s had spuriously invented new roles for the sexes in the format of the mythical new man, the 90s came up with the 'ironic' post-modern lad, to be followed by the full-on, all-action lad. The camp, dandy images of The Style Council were now long forgotten as Weller and his new mates, Liam and Noel

Gallagher, were celebrated as lad icons by the unabashed soft-porn-and-sport-for-geezers-mag *Loaded*. A mildly amused Weller found himself reinvented by the media once again. 'What's a lad, you know? I've got no idea. *Loaded* do like me because they think I'm a superlad, apparently, but I'm not. I don't understand any of that . . . I'm just a man. I can be a bastard, like every other man.'

This hedonistic, buzzing period in Weller's life wasn't simply a reaction to his new success. It was also fuelled by the emotional free-for-all following the break-up of his marriage to Dee C Lee in the first half of 1994. The workload that came with his newfound success had put as much strain on his relationship as the depressed period at the start of the decade. As well as throwing himself into his career, he tried to centre himself with a bit of security by leaving Lee with the house while he moved to a new place at Selsey Bill, where his parents now owned a large home on the south coast. Terry Rawlings, who first saw Weller down at Selsey Bill when they were both staying in their families' caravans, observes, 'He's still spoilt, yeah. It's a sort of family spoilt. Ann and John always used to remind me of the Pinners in *Just Good Friends* – the Paul Nicholas character's parents. They were rich but they used to eat fish and chips on gold plates. They're very much like that. Products of our time, classwise.'

Weller had one foot rooted in this rich, working-class culture clash and the other in old-fashioned rock 'n' roll. 'He was definitely avoiding stable relationships at the time,' says Lisa Verrico. 'We were having a talk about my last relationship and I asked him whether he was going out with anyone. He said he wasn't. But still that whole summer every time I saw him out he was with somebody else. I think he was going out with people but he was just having a good time. If you've been with someone for a few years and it breaks up, you just want to have a good time.'

Sessions for the next album kicked off in summer '94 – clearly a pivotal time for Weller. Noel Gallagher dropped in to add some guitar to Weller's reading of Dr John's 'Walk On Gilded Splinters'. He also joined Weller for the T In The Park festival and his annual Royal Albert Hall gig, while Primal Scream invited the pair on-stage at the Shepherd's Bush Empire for a jam on The Who's 'So Sad About Us'. This musical bond would be given its most public airing at the start of '95 with their double-headed (Weller on

Paul Weller

keyboards, Gallagher on acoustic guitar and vocals) version of Oasis's 'Talk Tonight' on Channel 4's music TV programme, *The White Room*.

When Weller wasn't recording he was on the road, blasting through sets with the conviction of a man who is absolutely sure of his direction – an unusual position for a pop star to be in when he's edging towards middle age. *Mojo* magazine touched on this in a review of his 'homecoming' gig at the Civic Hall, Guildford: 'It's ironic that a man who so passionately believed that you had to be young to have anything valid to offer rock music should have found his true style and a comfortable niche at the age of 35.'

He also maintained the momentum of his chart career in the autumn by scoring another Top Twenty hit with 'Out Of The Sinking'. It was a stop-start, stuttering Mod ballad. 'I wanted to write a great English Mod song,' he enthused. 'The middle section is pure Small Faces and proud.' On the B-side was a cover of The Beatles' 'Sexy Sadie', just in case anyone forgot the source of his original inspiration.

As the year drew to a close, the workaholic, ambitious Weller found himself reaching out to his family in the only way open to him. 'I was away (as usual) on Natty's sixth birthday. We had started another US tour but I got to play "Moon On Your Pyjamas" on the same day, live on New York radio. It's sentimental, yes, but I was trying to send out signals to my son.' However, the push and pull between family and work was stretched to the extreme by the shock of John Weller's stroke in the winter. Gigs were cancelled as Weller rushed to his father's side in hospital, where John went through a heart bypass operation. When the singer set off for a seven-date tour in Japan he was not only separated from his own children but for the first time in his career he didn't have his father at his side.

The tour was his seventeenth visit to the country and the band found themselves in front of large, quietly appreciative audiences with a high quota of jazz pseuds left over from The Style Council days. There was also some unpleasant backstabbing as Weller and co. criticised the abilities of the band's bass player, Anna Piva, not only behind her back but also to an English journalist who discovered the musician was about to get the chop before she did. This was a small but disturbing hint at the way the inner sanctum expels people who don't fit in in a manner which borders on cruelty.

Live Wood, which was culled from four different sets between late '93 and mid '94, captured some of the intensity of Weller's live shows when it was released in November, though it was hardly an essential purchase.

Then, much to Weller's amusement, he was also named by style magazine *The Face* as one of the 100 most influential people in fashion. 'I didn't realise I was,' he responded. 'I can't take things like that seriously. I've only got about fucking five or six tops I wear. I haven't really got that many clothes but everyone thinks I have. I mean, I love clothes, but I haven't really got that many. There's hardly anything I like in the shops. I'm so fussy.'

Two years after the project began, a Weller documentary put together by his friends Paolo Hewitt and the video director Pedro Romhanyi was finally released on video. Bruce Foxton and Rick Buckler were conspicuous by their absence – they refused to appear – but Bragg touched on the appeal of The Jam when he commented: 'If you want to write a song that appeals to a lot of people you have to touch their experiences pretty deeply. Weller was aware of that and used imagery that lies deep in the English psyche.' Gary Crowley also hinted at the man's fallibility, in a revealing and often amusingly candid documentary which wasn't the whitewash which Foxton and Buckler had predicted: 'The other thing that endears him to people is that he has got it wrong at times. And he's admitted it!'

9 The Streets Also Dream Their Dream, 1995–96

Kevin Pearce, *Something Beginning with O*: 'As pop stars go, Weller is one of the strangest. Intense, intensely private, endearingly human, hard, heroic, fallible. He made mistakes in public but always bounced back. As dependable as a Dr Marten's shoe, he could still surprise and wound.'

Tony Fletcher: 'He was very obsessed by youth. I think you are at that age – you want to change the world by the time you're twenty – and Paul did better than most. When I saw him in New York a couple of years ago he said how great it was to get old and he said he couldn't think of any musician who doesn't get better as they get older and it was brilliant, which I thought was quite amusing.'

The single 'The Changing Man' launched Weller into 1995 with yet another Top Twenty single. It was a driving, insistent song with dive-bombing synths and a big, churning R&B riff. Weller claimed the title came from one of his daughter's dolls whom she called the 'Changing Man', although Terry Rawlings says the singer half-inched it from an unknown band of the same name. Pedro Romhanyi's flashy, pop art promo video for the release dropped a big hint about the packaging for the forthcoming album.

When it came to designing the sleeve of the album, which Weller was now calling *Stanley Road*, he decided the ideal package for the sentimental yet forward-looking mood of the songs was a pop art sleeve. In the 60s, British artist Peter Blake made a personal form of the artistic style which wasn't as remote and coldly conceptual as many of his peers. In an interview in 1963 he explained: 'For me pop art is often rooted in nostalgia: the nostalgia of old popular things. And though I'm also continually trying to establish a new pop art, one which stems directly from our time, I'm always looking back at the sources of the idiom and trying to find the technical forms that will best recapture the authentic feel of folk pop.' Blake found inspiration in the world of his own childhood and youth (toy shops, comics, badges), pop music (Elvis, Cliff Richard) and film. He developed a heraldic, carnival style of lettering which was very British in its depiction of all-in wrestling and striptease. He also designed the sleeve for The Beatles' *Sgt. Pepper* and many of his heraldic emblems of targets and hearts became part of mainstream, Carnaby Street Mod fashion. Peter Blake's work was also perfect for Mod's stylish, clean, working-class aesthetic. 'I've always been Mod sympathetic,' explains the artist from his studio in the National Gallery. In particular, those ambitious plagiarists, The Who, defined themselves as a Mod-meets-Pop art band under the influence of their managers Pete Meaden and later Chris Stamp. 'They were turned into a British pop art band,' explains Blake. 'They went through all the art catalogues and found images. When they started wearing medals, that was based on the self-portrait I did. Their belt with black and white diagonals was also appropriated from a work I'd done. I'd used the Union Jack imagery which they started wrapping them-selves in and I'd done the first proper target. So it was a direct line from pop art through The Who to Paul Weller.

'The other thing is I come from Dartford, that bit of north-west Kent running down from Lewisham to Gravesend. It's a strange area, not cockney and not London, and it's not the country either. It produces bands like the Stones and The Pretty Things and the boxer Henry Copper; strange people with strange accents that are half cockney. It's just the same with Paul coming from Woking.'

On Blake's first meeting with Weller he found the nervy singer quietly spoken but well informed about the history of pop art. 'Paul called me to see if I'd do it,' he recalls. 'All he'd decided at that point was that the album was called *Stanley Road*, so there was obviously an element of nostalgia coming from him already. One of the things he was interested in was my cover for *Sgt. Pepper* but he was also genuinely interested in pop art because he'd already used the star motif and the heart motif which I'd explored in the sixties. So what we did was make a kind of hymn to pop art. It's very much a déjà vu, post-modern looking back at the art move-ment in a very obvious way.

'He then started coming round every so often and we talked a lot

Paul Weller

about his childhood and about pop art – not over the whole area, mainly about the images that he was interested in. So I asked him to do a list of things that he was interested in for a collage on the cover. It was a very random list and at first I did a mock-up for it and it just didn't work. On the first list he'd got Peter Osgood but in a way George Best was better because he was more of a symbol. He also added Aretha Franklin to the second version.

'I don't think anyone's really got to grips with the CD format yet but what I came up with was the idea of it being LP size with another image in the middle that was a CD size image. So the border is pop art and the middle is a watercolour of him as a boy. I thought it was a nice idea of a boy holding a picture of himself as a man. The sleeve was changed on later editions so that the painting is the front image and the other bits and pieces are inserted into the CD booklet.

'Either way, it really is a very sentimental sleeve. That's his mum on the beach sitting in the deckchair. "The Water House" is a very sentimental painting and the photograph of Piccadilly was an old shot of London. The little Small Faces models were his own and the bus is like the one he remembers taking as a little boy. He also brought along the Wilfred Owen poem, which I thought was interesting because it wasn't one of his more famous war poems. He was really only interested in one line, "The streets also dream their dream", which obviously related to his feelings about Stanley Road, the place he'd grown up in. For years I've been accused of being sentimental and I've always argued that sentimentality is a pretty good reason to make a painting. It's a very unfashionable reason but it's a strong emotion. So I had a feeling for what Paul was trying to achieve, although he sometimes found it difficult to talk because he was very nervous. He called my wife Mrs Blake and when he came he was always on edge. He's quite twitchy. He wrote a very sweet letter afterwards saying how nice it had been to work with me. No one has ever done that before. The other thing he did was phone and say, "I was really nervous of you and if I seemed rude I didn't mean to be but I was so nervous, it may have come across as antagonism." '

When *Stanley Road* was released in May it went straight in at number one, taking Weller's revival to a new level. Reviews were favourable although some writers felt that he was treading water. Ted Kessler wrote in the *NME*: 'Every few years a new influence gives Paul Weller a kick up the arse and he reinvents himself before reverting to type. It's time for that boot again, otherwise it'll be the same frustratingly patchy collection reshaped next year. If he is the changing man, then it's time to light another pyre.' *Vox* scribe Craig McLean was more enthusiastic, declaring, 'Whether slaying us with his stripped-bare soul, or making his guitar deftly creep from foot-on-the-monitors riffage, Weller is entering a glorious early middle age.' The album was also nominated for a Mercury music prize.

Weller described the new songs as English R&B: 'I suppose *Stanley Road* is carrying on from *Wild Wood* and the first album. The songs are stronger generally and I think the playing's a lot better. We cut every track live in the studio this time, so it's got a different kind of feeling to it; more of a raw, live sound. More balls to the sound, you know ... more beef to it. You know, the expressions used by young people these days ...'

He was really proud of the lyrics: 'I'll try to go more with what sounds really good now, hopefully without being banal. It's OK to write a great line but if you don't sing it right or it doesn't flow then you miss it anyway. That's what I try to concentrate on now – the instinctive side.

'You know "Redemption Song" by Bob Marley is pretty good to me. There's nothing clever about that – and it's more fucking powerful than anything Morrissey ever wrote.'

The strident 'Porcelain Gods' updates some of his feelings about fame, first expressed in The Jam's 'To Be Someone': 'It isn't as factual as me thinking I'm a porcelain god,' he explained. 'There's lines where I'm disappointed in myself 'cos I've let down my wife, but then there's other bits that go on about something else ... They're all powerful images: "Beware false prophets, take a stand/ My fortune cookie just cracked up in my hand." They're good poetry.

'This is me playing lots of roles, from phoney icon to iconoclast ... I wanted a sense of overbearance, an edge between sanity and almost losing it, and it's all those things to me.' Brendan Lynch encouraged the band to jam at the end, adding a whole new section to the song.

Paul Weller

Noel Gallagher's acoustic contribution to 'Walk On Gilded Splinters' is barely noticeable in the rocky twist which the band give to this Dr John song, sacrificing the maverick spirit of the original. The bluesy 'Woodcutter's Son' (freshly minting an old riff stolen from The Who's 'Magic Bus') and more whimsical 'Pink On White Walls' feature Steve Winwood on keyboards and piano, while the tender ballad 'You Do Something To Me' is the album's most expressive track, rivalling 'Wild Wood' as one of the best songs of his career. 'Time Passes . . .' is another moving track about a broken relationship and 'Whirlpool's End' swirls cosmically around big, circular riffs and whirling electronic squeals. Its lyrics capture the sense of flux and uncertainty at the core of the songs: 'Now nothing feels the same way/Feels like it's changing again/In a brutal world where there's nowhere/To run, hide or cry.'

Of the piano-led track 'Wings Of Speed', which builds up from blatant McCartneyisms into a full-on gospel blow out (vocals by Carleen Anderson), Weller revealed, 'I tried to describe the feelings I get from "The Lady Of Shallot" by John Waterhouse, which hangs in the Tate Gallery. I tried to make it part Afro-American gospel and part English hymn.'

'Broken Stones' was kept simple, and is almost fragile sounding. 'That's the first ever take of that track,' Weller explained. 'We didn't even rehearse it. What you hear is the first time the song had been played that way.'

One of Weller's favourite songs at the time was 'White Line Fever' by The Burrito Brothers. 'I realised it's about the road, how it keeps on going and you just keep on burning up the miles on this journey,' he said. 'I think that's brilliant, that idea of it never ending.'

According to Weller, he re-used this idea in the title track, expressing 'a kind of optimism and life's endless possibilities and the road going on for ever . . . that's what it represents for me. You get further and further away from those ideas the older you get and the more realistic life becomes but it's nice to remind yourself now and again. It's like when you sense a certain smell in the air or you see a certain light in the summer – whatever gets you off. Or just feelings that put you back in touch with when you did think life was endless and possibilities were endless. To try and get back into touch with those feelings from time to time is nice.'

Weller explored the imagery of his home town in order to reach back into his childhood. However, it's not an album about the wonderful world of Woking, which will sadly disappoint any Japanese tourists who visit the place in search of the gritty romanticism expressed by the songs.

Weller: 'Up to the 1970s it was nice, old looking ... [Stanley Road] is flattened now; the house is gone,' explained Weller at the time of the album's release. 'I drove down there the other day with my son to go swimming, pointing out that I used to live there. There's a working men's club around the corner where I did my first gig. He wasn't interested. It's funny to look at those places. Everywhere looks tiny and run down. All the reasons I wanted to get the fuck out of there.

'My main link with Woking is the area where I used to play as a kid – the woods around there, the rural side. The actual town's a dump, like most satellite towns. They've got a big shopping mall but no one's got any bread and the shops are empty.'

While fans layer their own childhood memories on to the images and colourful moods created by Weller, there are some who connect more directly – his old schoolfriends and particularly Steve Brookes. He's amused by the rural, wooded romanticism associated with Woking thanks to his mate's solo albums. 'We used to go down the park a lot, I suppose,' he says, grinning. 'If you're in a town like that and you're a kid and you don't have your own transport you normally only walk places – down to the park and to the canal. Woking is not much of a rural place. Even if you step out of Woking town itself it's still suburban. We did walk out into the countryside. To be fair we did it enough to establish a presence in our memories.

'I do identify with parts of the *Stanley Road* album. The overriding thing is the image of the zebra crossing in the title song ["amber lights flashing 'cross the street/And on the corner ... a dream to meet"]. We used to sleep in the front bedroom and that Belisha beacon thing flashed all night. He'd been sleeping there since he was a young kid so I think it was etched on his mind. That was quite evocative. The zebra crossing is still there actually.'

In July the ballad 'You Do Something To Me' gave the singer another Top Ten success. After the technicolour special effects of the Pedro Romhanyi-directed video for 'The Changing Man', which Weller had mixed feelings about, he decided to try a young female promo director, Sonja Phillips, for this latest release.

Phillips had previously worked with Weller as a camera operator. 'He only works with friends,' she explains. 'He wouldn't have called me up if he didn't know me already.' Weller had firm ideas about what he wanted to achieve with the video. 'He wanted to go back to his influences rather than spend loads of money on tricks and concepts, so he gave me about twenty Beatles videos and some Small Faces stuff. He was very keen on using Super 8 film, so we just took a camera out and spent a day going around Woking and Box Hill. He wanted something beautiful, natural and about him. It was a really intimate little crew – just three of us. We filmed on a gorgeous day in Woking, believe it or not, and it made England look beautiful.' The final edit caught the hazy, reflective atmosphere of the music perfectly. 'I had a lot of offers of work straight after,' says Phillips. 'Everyone wanted the same sort of video and they were all boy bands who liked Paul Weller. I had a lot of the indie bands saying, "Oh, we want fish-eye lens, Super 8, all that."'

From summer to winter '95, Weller was clearly in a buoyant mood. He carelessly grew a moustache for reasons only known to himself – 'I thought that was a fucking top idea. I'm gonna grow the fucker back just to wind people up!' – wore his hair long and straggly, showed off his sun tan at the festivals and gigged constantly, slipping a five-song acoustic section into most of the shows. 'It's taken some time but now I understand what I'm good at,' he declared. 'That's playing live, conveying emotion, getting people fired up and inspiring them.'

Observer journalist Sam Taylor wrote an insightful review of Weller's gig at London's Brixton Academy in late November which probed some of the contradictions in this revitalised performer. 'So, has Paul Weller become what he once despised? On the face of it, yes. At the cavernous, atmosphere-less Brixton Academy . . . Weller did things that at eighteen would have made him spit: he wore his hair lank and shaggy; he played several meandering guitar solos; he sang of disillusionment and lost love and middle-aged crisis . . . The usual line about Weller's recent popular resurgence is that he has stayed true to his audience. In fact, he has stayed true to himself – self-centred, wilful, at times preposterous – and his audience has tuned in or tuned out depending on how closely his experiences mirror their own. Despite his current hipness among the Britpop generation, most of the audience at Brixton looked old enough to have bought *In the City* when it came out in 1977. In a sense Weller is still the spokesperson for his generation – only now that generation is less sure about the world and itself.'

A year or so after his break-up with Dee C Lee, Weller glanced back over his successes with mixed feelings: 'It's been a great year for me professionally,' he commented. 'When I look back on the last couple of years, it'll definitely be a golden period. Personally things haven't gone quite so well but I suppose that's all part of the learning process . . . Playing live has been a real high this year and splitting up with Dee has been the complete opposite.'

For the first time since he'd met Gill Price as a teenager, Weller avoided getting involved in a long-term relationship, although there was a rumoured 'romance' with Paul McCartney's daughter, Mary. 'That whole thing about how he was going out with Paul McCartney's daughter was just a joke,' says Lisa Verrico. 'He's just friends with her and at the launch party for *Stanley Road* it was a set-up because they knew the press would be there.'

In September he released a new single, 'Broken Stones', which was shot through with the blissful, laid-back simplicity of its subject matter. 'I love the images in that song. I was on a beach with my son when I wrote it. He was asking me where all the pebbles were coming in from. I told him they were once part of some big rock but that time and the waves and the weather had smashed it apart and sent different bits all over the world.'

In interviews he spoke more openly about his relationship with his kids: 'Am I a good father? Yeah, I think so. I was looking after the kids for about three weeks there and it was brilliant. They make me very happy. My daughter Leah is a real performer. She's not even four and already she's right into singing. She sounds like Hilda Ogden though – really high pitched, but even more falsetto. And she's beautiful. Fortunately she gets her looks from her mother.

'At Nat's school there's a real racial mixture which is good. But you know a mixed-race kid will always be treated as black in this country.'

'Nat doesn't seem to naturally go towards [music], really. It's more my daughter: she'll definitely do something, either sing or play or dance. She's always doing it; she seems like a natural performer.'

Both of his children are aware of what their 'Modfather' does for a living.

'Nat's seven now so he's well up on it. He's been to a couple of gigs. They're both aware of what their mum and dad do. They're proud of us.

'You have to be practical with kids. You don't have time to sit around being analytical because you've got to feed them or clean their arse 'cos they've just shat themselves. I like that thing of being tapped into the earth again. And being separated from Dee, I miss that stability.

'Sometimes I feel more rounded for having kids and sometimes I don't. I don't feel wholly secure now, even for all the success. It's just not in my nature. I'm always trying to prove myself. The point about having kids is that before you know it, you just start worrying about them and their future. It's neverending.'

The year 1995 also witnessed the elevation of Britpop into the ultimate mainstream – the tabloid media. Extraordinary hype centred around the release of Oasis's 'Roll With It' single and Blur's 'Country House' in the same week, prompting the newspapers to blow up the animosity between the two bands into a full-on battle between north and south; working-class 'singing electricians' against foppish, middle-class bohemians; the 'new Rolling Stones' set against the 'new Beatles'. Bets were taken and headlines stolen as the debate raged for a week until Blur came out on top. Their moment of glory was brief before Oasis steamrolled them by achieving a Top Ten place in the American charts and playing epic gigs at Manchester City's Maine Road stadium and Knebworth in '96. Weller had been talking about recording an EP of contemporary cover versions – an Oasis track, Blur's 'End Of A Century' and two others – but the idea was dropped as the tabloids picked through the personal debris of Liam Gallagher's oafishly rock 'n' roll behaviour, Damon Albarn's relationship with 'posh bird' Justine Frischmann from Elastica and created scandals of dubious infamy to turn Jarvis Cocker into a fully fledged media star, which he spontaneously rose to by wiggling on to Michael Jackson's stage at the Brit Awards in early '96. Britpop was now too big for an EP-sized homage from one of its so-called founding fathers.

Weller loved the recharged confidence of the music scene in Britain, but he pulled back from some of the ridiculous jingoism of the media: 'I'm not being nationalistic but it's great when you can feel proud about English pop music again. Most of the American bands just sound the same to me. Which ones? I've no idea, I get their names mixed up. You know, like that lot who cut their pants off the bottom. I don't buy all that nihilism stuff. Life can't be that crap, especially not if you're in a group. There has to be a few joyful moments. It's a pretty good job.

'I probably know more musicians now than ever before. And not because I hang out in trendy bars . . . I've just got respect for more players now. And most of the time they're probably ten years younger than me. We just seem to have more in common: Oasis, The Charlatans, Primals, Blur.'

This back-slapping camaraderie spilled into a series of on-stage duets and guest appearances but no co-writing credits between Weller/Gallagher or Weller/Albarn. The ever-territorial Weller probably felt this was a bit too close to home. He's still yet to sit down and write a song with an artist even approaching his own talent. Clive Banks muses on this streak of private individualism in a twenty-year career during which he's written over 200 songs. 'He's much more likely, I would have thought, to work with Burt Bacharach or John Barry than he is to go to one of his contemporaries,' he says intriguingly. 'I'm sure if he was offered the modern-day equivalent of the new Bond theme he'd like to do that – it would be challenging and expanding to him and yet it wouldn't tread too much on his ground. The record company certainly should be suggesting things like that because those sorts of things can be entertaining for yourself and take yourself into other parts of the world. At the end of the day if you try it and it doesn't work, throw it away. You've got to be open on this but he's always been so insular and private.'

Weller is also a somewhat intimidating person to collaborate with, at least by reputation. He's a dangerous artist to cover as well, which might explain why fresh versions of Old Jam songs tend to be hidden away on B-sides, notably with Morrissey's 'That's Entertainment' and more recently Garbage's 'Butterfly Collector'.

Paul Weller

No one of any stature has dared to take a Weller composition into the Top Ten, an odd situation for a man who drew initial inspiration from The Beatles, moulding an approach based around catchy pop hooks. For all the distracting sway from punk to jazz-fusion to R&B rock, Weller has always written a good tune. There are rumours of a tribute album to be released in 1997 which might rectify this situation through cover versions by The Beastie Boys and Ocean Colour Scene, but this is still a project initiated from inside the old Weller camp – sleeve designer Simon Halfon is the man behind the album. Weller's caustic comments about other artists retain their sting in the 90s and make him a difficult artist to tackle on record. Britpop back-slapping aside, he didn't pull punches about bands he didn't like. 'I'm not impressed by people who muck about and pretend they can't play their instruments,' he sniped. 'I don't know if I'm getting old but no one seems to be able to sing any more. They talk sense like that little bird from Echobelly – she was very nice – but then you see them perform . . .

'You may think Elastica or the new whatever it is are great but I could play you a record or two – they would blow your mind.

'I don't care about Nirvana dropping their pants at the MTV Awards. I'm past all that bull. I can remember a time when people were real and I believed in them.

'I don't like stupid wimpy music. I like music with bollocks to it – which doesn't necessarily entail guitars turned up and played full throttle either. Just meat and potatoes, know what I mean?' Even REM, with whom Weller shared some festival dates in Europe, came in for some stick. 'I'd never watch a band like that,' he said, snubbing the biggest band in the world.

Weller has always taken pride in a streak of musical conservatism, which thankfully he's often contradicted in his own career. 'A guitar should sound like a guitar,' he said in The Style Council, with Luddite doggedness. 'What else can you play music on? We don't wanna do any far-out shit with fuckin' synthesisers or Swiss Alpine horns or something, we just want to play natural instruments.'

In the 90s, Weller questioned the tastes of 'a generation who were brought up on Depeche Mode, listening to people posing with keyboards. I wouldn't have thought they'd be terribly inspiring compared with the effect of hearing a really good guitarist doing his stuff.' He listed his own choice of equipment in musician magazines, and his favoured instruments had a distinctively retro feel – guitars included 1968 Marshall Bluesbreaker, Epiphone Casino, 1968 Gibson SG, Gibson Firebrand and an Ovation acoustic. The Beatles used a lot of these sounds 30 years ago.

He has also stated the worryingly Lenny Kravitzism: 'I'd sooner settle for being great than original. Originality's just what people hear in it – if someone really likes a song it'll sound original to them anyway. I'm not bothered about originality. I don't even think about it.'

His half-fantasised roots as a jobbing musician resurfaced when he was asked what he would have done if his career had never taken off. 'I would just be in Woking playing the same pubs and clubs,' he argued. 'Made the top of the circuit, making the maximum money you can earn on that scene. I wouldn't have done anything else.'

In reality, Weller's watertight, iconic credentials led to an all-star jam with Noel Gallagher and Paul McCartney on The Beatles track, 'Come Together', for an album which raised money for Brian Eno's War Child charity. Entitled *Help*, the project was co-ordinated by Tony Crean from Go! Discs with incredible efficiency and not to mention speedy co-operation from all the artists, including Blur, Radiohead, Oasis, Massive Attack and Suede, who recorded their contributions in one day, 4 September. Only five days later the album was released, selling 71,000 copies on its first day in the shops. For Paul Weller the chance to record with his old hero was 'like a dream. For someone who used to have Beatles posters on his wall when he was a kid, thinking that years later I'd be working with the geezer, not only on a Beatles track but in the same studio they all started off in . . . you can imagine. It took a while to get over it.

'Macca was jamming all day with all of us, doing "Green Onions" and "Time Is Tight", playing the drumkit, playing through one song he'd written on the way up from his farm or whatever – we were jamming on that. At one point that was going to go on the album. We ran out of time, unfortunately.' 'Come Together' was later released by Go! Discs as a single under the band name The Smokin' Mojo Filters, but got lost in the Christmas rush and failed to add to the initial impact of the album.

Paul Weller

Although the spirit and musical quality of *Help* was universally applauded, there were some who saw the Mojo jam as unhealthily retro. Former Orange Juice singer Edwyn Collins, who was also enjoying a resurgence through the 'Girl Like You' single, derided Weller and co. for creating a 'Campaign For Real Rock'. The ex-Jam singer seemed to accept this when he commented, 'I much prefer these sounds to the state-of-the-art digital sound now, and consequently my records sound that way. I'm kind of a librarian of rock music.'

When The Cure slipped back into the spotlight in '96, they also vented their spleen against the Modfather. The band's Simon Gallup declared, 'Paul Weller is a contemptible character. He revels in his Englishness and he's surrounded by a music industry that, at this moment, wants everything that's British, so he's seen as some kind of icon.'

Robert Smith was a little more reserved in his verbal attack: 'He's written some really good songs. It's what he's being made into that's the problem. It's just a shame he didn't reject it. He's made a choice – he doesn't mind being this figure. If he'd turned around and said, "This is bollocks, I don't want to be this person", I'd have more respect for him. If we were put in that position I'd say fuck off!'

'I mean, that thing at Abbey Road . . . Regardless of what was going on there [the War Child project] it was all like Big Rock History! Paul McCartney, Paul Weller and Noel Gallagher carrying on this great tradition. That sort of thing either makes you go "aargh!" or it makes you go "oh great!" And in this instance, unless it makes you go "aargh!" there's something wrong with you.'

Gallup: 'It's procreating that myth that people in groups are all great mates and every Friday night they meet up, put fags in the corners of their mouths and jam along to some old classic.'

While this was harsh, given the spontaneous nature of the *Help* project, Weller's public avowed distrust of anything beyond 'meat and potatoes' rock was irritatingly one-dimensional. It was also false, as Weller's own tastes have stretched well beyond such narrow limitations. According to Go! Discs' director, Mike Heneghan: 'Paul's consumed by music. That's his life. If you talk to him it's, "Have you heard this record? Have you heard that record?" Some might be new, some might be old. It's all sorts of stuff – rock, dance, rap. He's a total Mod because he's always very on it all the time – very alive, very alert, musically driven. And if he writes a good song he's happy to say it's a good song.' The singer's small-minded declarations were yet another example of his ability to tunnel his own vision and block out any awkward grey areas. He also, of course, enjoys the odd wind up. Unfortunately things haven't changed that much from The Style Council and these little outbursts are not exactly rib ticklers.

Weller was also attacked from some quarters for mellowing out into an adult rocker – the Eric Clapton of the 90s no less. While there are some musical similarities with Clapton's early 70s work, the on-the-ball suss of the modernist and edgy self-doubt makes him a more energetic, fleet-footed figure than the former Cream guitarist who seems to be stuck in a rut of sterile blues and expensive suits. Weller greeted such comparisons with righteous anger, a little ironic as he'd been comparing himself to Clapton a couple of years before.

'Fucking bollocks, I've still got edge in my music, hopefully always will have – and if my music ever got as laid back and mellow as Eric Clapton I'd pack it in. Or shoot myself.

'I either don't know who my contemporaries are, or they've vanished or I've got no respect for them. I don't dislike Lydon or Strummer. I don't really know either of them but their music doesn't do it for me. I don't want to slag them off because they were a big influence on me at one time as well. But I don't really think about contemporaries. I relate more to younger bands than I do to my own peers.

'Trouble is, there's hardly any examples of people who carry on and don't just become more showbiz and more and more boring. There's only Neil Young and Van Morrison.'

Weller's plugger Gary Blackburn recalls how he watched the singer back away from an attempt by ITV's art programme, *The South Bank Show*, to portray him as a great British icon – the sort of televisual status which Sting was absolutely unable to resist with disastrously indulgent results: 'I remember *The South Bank Show* was really keen to do something on him. It's not often we get the chance to do something like that and we were really chuffed about it. When I spoke to him about it he said he wasn't interested which surprised me. I said, "Well, at least meet them" – and he did after a gig. They were trying to place Paul as part of the great tradition of British poets . . . which he thought was a complete load of wank. He completely tossed it out. Paul said, "I appreciate your interest but I'm not comfortable about it." When they left he kept me behind and said, "Gary, I don't want to do this because this is the sort of thing that people do at the end of their career. I really feel as if I'm just starting." He has a better sense of where he's at than anybody else.

'In fact, I've learnt a lot about promotion from Paul Weller – the less is more route. He did *Top of the Pops* around the first album but he was so embarrassed about being on in the middle of 2 Unlimited and Super Mario. He would do *TOTP* if he could play completely live but the programme just isn't geared up to do something like that because they're recording seven or eight bands in a day.'

In summer '96, *Top of the Pops* launched their Friday night slot with Weller playing live versions of 'Peacock Suit' and 'The Changing Man'. He'd got his own way once again, giving the programme one of its most memorable moments of the year in the process.

In the first half of '96, *Stanley Road* passed sales of over a million and became certified triple platinum. Weller's audience was effectively four times bigger than The Jam's, an incredible achievement for an artist who only three years previously was struggling to crawl out from under the shadow of his old band. Nigel Sweeney shakes his head disbelievingly as he acknowledges this amazing turnaround: 'He's caught the crest of the wave again. He's a very lucky man because it could have gone the other way. He's retained a fair amount of his principles and he's become a nicer person for it. He's much more relaxed now. Five thousand per cent more relaxed. The last I saw him was at Chris Evans's television show, *TFI Friday*, and he was just hanging around in the bar and he was completely at ease. He wasn't even in the programme. Can you imagine a young Paul Weller doing something like that in The Jam? It just wouldn't have happened.'

Weller intended to take time out in '96 but it didn't work out that way. There were more triumphs as *Stanley Road*'s sales continued to snowball through the year. He won Best Male Solo

Artist at the Brits for the second successive year, and in February he played a fiery live set on the Jools Holland hosted *Later* show which devoted the whole programme to Weller. The performance was actually screened twice over a weekend at the end of the month. Weller, who was once again in a sociable mood at the after-show party, clearly enjoyed every moment, as Lisa Verrico recalls: 'There was this little crappy drinks thing afterwards. I went up to say goodbye and stuff to him and he asked me what I thought of the show and every time I tried to tell him, some complete nymph-like 21 year old would be shoving me out of the way and throwing her arms around him, saying, "Oh my God, it was brilliant." So I asked him, "Have you got a lot of female admirers?" and he was like, "I can't believe it. I'm 38 years old and I've got more people buying my records than ever before and more girls fancying me than ever before and I don't understand it." '

Weller swaggered with the confidence of a man who has found his audience when he faced 30,000 fans at his own Lazy Sunday Afternoon (a reference to an old Small Faces song) one-day festival in London's Finsbury Park on 9 June. Britpop had died with the new year, turning the event into a clannish, enjoyably indulgent celebration of homegrown talent with The Bluetones and Shed Seven providing the support slots and Primal Scream's Bobby Gillespie and Andrew Innes shuffling on stage at the end of the show to join Weller, three members of Ocean Colour Scene and P. P. Arnold on a version of the Small Faces' 'Song Of A Baker'. Guitar solos were elongated to absurd, rockist lengths as Weller 'jammed' with the band on his own songs, while the inclusion of 'Tales From The Riverbank' in the set flashed back to old glories and illustrated Weller's relaxed, cocksure ease on a day dubbed 'Modstock' by the press. He also played his new song, 'Peacock Suit', which gave him another Top Five hit the following month. The single was packed with blasts of salty R&B riffs and wigged-out solos but, like the day in Finsbury Park, there were no hints of a fresh direction for the next album, provisionally entitled *Heavy Soul*. An emotional, acoustic-based new song, 'Driving Nowhere', has also excited fans at live shows. Weller spoke guardedly about some of the new material. 'I've started writing new stuff and that's got a really different feeling to it . . . we've been listening to loads of old New Orleans records recently, like The Meters, Alain

Paul Weller

Toussant and Booker T & The MGs . . . Trouble is, I'd better not start talking about individual bands 'cos everyone will start saying: 'Oh, it's heavily Meters influenced, like the Nick Drake thing with *Wild Wood*. And that's bollocks, man. It doesn't work like that.'

Meanwhile, the *NME*, aware that the British music scene was suddenly in limbo after a fantastic two-year period, decided to marshall their forces against Weller, presumably as part of a process of letting something new in from the wings. All they succeeded in doing was once again revealing the claustrophobic pettiness of the British press. Weller's plugger Gary Blackburn, who has observed the man's revival from the inside, believes the artist has a momentum which will take him well beyond curent trends: 'In this multi-media, very clued-up world we live in now Paul won't go out of fashion,' he argues. 'He'll be ranked as one of the tastemakers, a durable icon. A lot of my contemporaries who I went to school with stopped watching *Top of the Pops* but they're still interested in music. Trouble is, they didn't know how to find out what was good, so to go into a record shop was quite intimidating for them. Now with your magazines like *Mojo* and *Q*, and the TV shows *Later* and *The White Room*, along with the progressiveness of Radio One and *Top of the Pops*, they're beginning to rediscover good music. The whole Oasis versus Blur thing last summer put pop music back into everybody's life and Paul has benefited from that. *Stanley Road* is one of those albums that a lot of people have because they want it on the coffee table for after-dinner conversation. That's what happened to Portishead the year before. It was coffee table dub and the sales kept building up and up in very much the same way.'

However, while Weller and Go! Discs bask in the upward curve of sales at home, which has gone hand in hand with his credibility, the artist is at best only a cult figure overseas. Given that the UK accounts for less than ten per cent of the world's CD sales, the singer's status is still a marginal one in the bigger scheme of things. 'Why is it that Go! Discs haven't broken Weller abroad?' demands international promotions expert, Sara Silver. 'Questions should be asked there. Nobody has changed the status quo and I don't know why. There was talk of PolyGram "fucking up" the release of *Stanley Road* in the States. I hear this term "fucking up" applied to Weller's international career a lot and that's just not acceptable at this stage.'

Former Simple Minds manager Clive Banks is familiar with the problems of localised success. 'One of the big problems is that Go! Discs has no international reputation. I wonder whether that's the structure of how a label like that is set up. At the end of the day they're at the mercy of the corporation who, certainly in America, dictate when and where to put the pressure on to promote the acts. You're not going to break America unless it's been decided that the backing is there. It has to be co-ordinated correctly and that's difficult to set up if Go! Discs aren't pulling the strings in the big corporate structure. On the one hand Go! Discs is a brilliant place for him to be because the attitude running through the company is so completely him, but I did think it's going to put him in a situation where he's limited.

The unchanging managerial set-up of the Weller camp also continues to put up barriers against international success. 'You have to have someone sitting on top of the project who has a complete overview,' states Banks, 'but who also has the co-operation of the artist. The Weller thing is very much a family business.'

John Weller is not an easy point of contact for a record company to deal with as his first concern is getting the right money for his son. After that his interest starts to wane. Banks experienced this first hand when he dealt with The Jam and The Style Council in the 80s. 'As I've said, it was always down to money,' he explains. 'Always with the manager of the artist you'd like to think of him as a partner. You're there to give him a strategy and the benefit of your experience and very often with John I felt a lot of that wasn't of interest. He was like, "Right, OK, fucking hell, who cares about that, we just want to do *Top of the Pops*." We were trying to say, "To do *Top of the Pops*, you should be doing this, this and this as well," but he didn't seem to take it in. I wouldn't know how much John wants to crack America now. Does he have the energy to spend six months over in the States, working with the record company, trying to sort out the best way of doing it?'

There are other deep-rooted problems. Weller's resurgence in the UK was certainly given a helping hand by Britpop's plagiarism of The Jam. The sense of a continued lineage to the classic reference points of English pop music gave Weller a context and a place in 90s culture which he then capitalised on with tremendous energy, soul and invention. However, The Jam's failure to make their mark internationally means that these building blocks to current success simply aren't there. Banks: 'Strategy wasn't a big part of The Jam's career. It used to fall from one thing to another. I think with more strategy in The Jam they would have been much bigger worldwide and Paul's opportunity would be so much more easy, because there's three-quarters of the world now who have no idea who Paul Weller is. If he wants to break through in certain places of the world he's got to start all over again and it's really a tough one. Coming out of doing massive shows here and then going to America and playing to 500 people in the mid-West and they're not reacting in the same way as in England. If you don't keep your career in tandem with everything happening around the world at the same time, you have this problem.'

Banks doesn't believe that Oasis's success in America has opened doors for Noel Gallagher's 'miserable' mate. 'The sound of Oasis's records is so dramatic and Beatleish, it gave them that initial impact. The on-going success will be because they'll put the work in and they are hugely entertaining. They've got great wit and charm whereas Paul is much more cynical. He's still as likely to slap a New York DJ or just walk off in a huff if he doesn't like him, whereas Noel will have charmed the man as well as having his own bit of wit and maintained his own credibility.'

The raw R&B sound of Weller's solo records is also debated by record company executives and American DJs. Richard Ogden confesses, 'I still think Paul's records are badly recorded. I can't hear much improvement in terms of production from The Style Council days.'

To many British fans, the spontaneous, aggressive sound of *Stanley Road* is part of its appeal. 'A lot of modern, so-called rock bands go for that really hard, toppy production which makes the songs sound transparent,' states the lean-limbered frontman. 'I like to hear raw emotion, the sound of human beings interacting on tape. We don't, for instance, record with a click track and that's immediately breaking the rules of modern recording. If you're playing together regularly and you're a tight unit, you shouldn't be forced into regimented time-keeping by a click. When a musical performance is truly exciting, it is bound to waver slightly in tempo – that's natural.'

However, Clive Banks is aware that this is a mixed blessing when the CD is handed over to American radio stations who, while rejecting the slickness of late 70s FM rock, are still geared towards a certain depth and richness of sound, typified by Butch Vig's dynamic productions for Nirvana, Smashing Pumpkins, Sonic Youth and his own work on Garbage's debut album.

'Even in Britain, Paul's records still sound remarkably different to everything else on the radio,' says Banks with obvious enthusiasm. 'They sound great but they don't sit comfortably because they stand out as slightly rawer on the productions – more organic than modern. They're not even like the "alternative" stuff coming out of America, where they have a station format sound. If it kind of jars then they won't play it even if they like the song. In that case you just have to hope that you make the noise which everybody thinks is the new thing. You become the leading edge of it all, but it's a bit of a remote position, that one. They sound organic more than modern. That's also what I like about it. He's not mumbling now. He doesn't care almost; he's very confident with the vocal. You hear a record of his and you think, Yep, I want to go and see him live. The Style Council never made me want to see them. It was all a bit tepid. The international situation could change,' he adds on a positive note. 'One record in a movie could transform the whole thing and there's a couple of great albums sitting there ready to sell well worldwide.'

As the singer enters the second half of the 90s, the anchorage provided by his father's management may eventually loosen. John Weller's ill health in late '95 was a shock reminder that this quiffed-up, human dynamo is entering the fragilities of old age. Now 65, it's likely that he'll find the right moment to step back from the frontline position he currently holds. Sara Silver believes he'll want to leave on a financial high. 'The next deal for Weller is going to be pretty astonishing. I would say that his father has been scheming to set his son up. You know he had the heart by-pass operation – it did make him feel very vulnerable. I'm sure if he sees things like Oasis, his father is saying, "We should be as big as that." But I think the next deal is possibly the last one that his father will do for him.

'It could be one of those shocks that could do Weller a lot of good. It depends where he falls. I talk to Kenny quite often and he's been sick a few times on tour. They're all getting old.'

Terry Rawlings is more gloomy about the break-up of the long-established team. 'I just hope Paul has enough real friends when that happens,' he says with a touch of bitterness, 'and people will be there for him. That last barrier might be removed. It must be a worry for him.'

From his more removed position as a veteran of the music industry, Clive Banks believes that Paul Weller will assume greater responsibility and negotiate for himself. 'I think the mould is set,' he argues. 'I think Paul will have experienced so many things over the last twenty years he will probably truly believe that he can make all the decisions himself. It would be very hard for someone coming in to be part of that structure and be able to influence things.'

There are dangers with this level of control. 'You look at someone like George Michael who effectively does everything himself,' says Banks, 'and he doesn't do it particularly well really. He has these strange photos taken of himself which I assume he thinks look good but they don't. Trouble is, there's no one there to say, "This is crap, this is nonsense," and give him a slap around the head.'

Of course, a similar situation already exists in the Weller camp as there isn't a character in the set-up with both an overview and the power to direct the artist in case of sartorial or musical mishaps. The divisions between the managerial input John, Paul and Kenny are constantly blurred. While John does most of the face-to-face negotiating with the record company, the others are often close at hand and absolutely nothing is agreed without his son's complete approval. Weller will probably pool his friends, experienced or otherwise, into a new set-up with him still ruling over all the final decisions. Whether they hold their collective breath and hand over some power to an 'outsider' with good American contacts ultimately depends on how keen Weller is to take his music to the US public. Nevertheless it will be a sad day for the singer when his father is no longer at his side at every turn of his career and the personal impact of that will be hard on both.

If the low worldwide sales of his solo material and possible managerial changes are a distant dark cloud on Weller's horizon, a bitter argument with Bruce Foxton and Rick Buckler hit a little closer to home at the start of 1996. The gulf between the ex-Jam members was revealed in Foxton and Buckler's oddly trivial book, entitled simply *The Jam: Our Story*. The old rhythm section complained about a one-way traffic of Christmas cards and 'casual' trips down to Solid Bond Studios which had been met with absolute silence from the Weller camp.

Prompted by the publication, Weller finally responded with chilly indifference. 'They've been whingeing in the fucking press about how many Christmas cards you can send someone. I've seen that quote reprinted so many times, and then their book comes out, so they're obviously bitter. But it doesn't make sense, thirteen or fourteen years after we split up. I don't understand it, to keep fucking harping on about it . . . we formed the band when we were kids, made it beyond our wildest dreams, earned good bread out of it, had a good time, but all good things come to an end.'

Meanwhile, Foxton and Buckler had spoken, back in 1992, of suing John and Paul Weller for £200,000 in unpaid royalties on video materials, revenue from merchandising and publishing royalties on their co-credited 'Funeral Pyre' single. There was talk of both camps being prepared to accept an out-of-court settlement but the lack of communication meant that the dispute went all the way through the legal procedure, concluding with a payment of around £70,000 to the aggrieved claimants in February 1996, a final figure which was complicated by negotiations over future rights of Jam-related material. John Weller had adopted a straightforward approach to money created by The Jam: 'I had a mandate, whereby all four of the boys signed every cheque in the Jam account – me, Paul, Bruce and Rick. Insisted on it, so they couldn't accuse me of favouritism.'

Sara Silver was surprised by news of the court case. 'His father made some very definite decisions. He will always talk about money. It's two things with him – he loves his son and thinks he's the best artist in the world. The other is money. He's not a pretentious man, he's very direct and he's incredibly smart. From when they were very young he took all their money away and stuffed it into bank accounts so they couldn't get hold of it.

'The areas of finance that go down. Once you get into the level of the touring business everything around it has some shady significance. I don't know who thinks they're doing what at any time. There doesn't seem to be a job for specific people in his outfit. They all seem to muck in together over everything, so it's quite feasible that money and stuff gets clogged up.'

Terry Rawlings also sees this financial argument as a side effect of the 'muck in together' working-class attitudes at the root of the Wellers' business set-up. 'If no one shouts about it then don't bother about it, know what I mean,' he explains. 'Don't fix it if it ain't broke. But when someone does uncover something I'm sure they're pretty up front about it. That's the old working-class ethic, isn't it? You hold your hands up as soon as you get caught.'

Nevertheless, Foxton and Buckler remain somewhat timid in their criticism of Weller. Buckler in particular has continued to bottle up his bitterness about the end of The Jam and the complete severing of his relationship with Weller thereafter. Just as he refused to participate in the documentary *Highlights & Hang-Ups*, he also turned down the opportunity to talk openly in his book. Weller, on his part, has shown no touches of kindness towards the two men who played their part in The Jam's success to the best of their abilities. They contributed in no small way to the energy and passion of the band at the height of their powers, but Weller has maintained a cold-shouldered aloofness that is perplexing given his growing ease with The Jam's legacy in the wake of his own solo success. Perhaps his determination to leave behind the first phase of his career as he ventured out with The Style Council and The Paul Weller Movement is too ingrained in his own mind. The loose, collective policy of The Style Council and the freedom he now enjoys in his solo work may actually throw the restraints of The Jam's format into even harsher relief. He's certainly in no mood to return to the role of band frontman. 'I'm really only responsible for myself,' he said recently. 'I really like working on my own and I kind of get into my own routine of working and writing. So I think it would be quite hard for me to get back into a band.'

As Weller enters a new phase of his career with a fresh collection of songs written in 1996, one thing is sure. The nervy, rodent-faced youth of early Jam and the clean-living cosmopolitan Councillor have been peeled away to reveal something of the real man inside. 'I don't think it's until now that people know the proper Paul Weller,' declares Nigel Sweeney. 'In The Jam it was almost like he was swept up by this thing. The whole thing was going very fast.

In The Style Council he tried to slow it down to an extent that it meandered, but I think he's got it about right now.'

The complex, passionate, soulful, self-doubting, cocky flux of musical influences and emotions in the music of his recent solo career show that Weller is impossible to pin down. He's listless, energetic, contradictory, modern and constantly in motion – there's no full stop.

Discography

THE JAM

SINGLES
(Highest chart position in brackets)

April 1977 In The City/Takin' My Love (40)
July 1977 All Around The World/Carnaby Street (13)
October 1977 The Modern World/Sweet Soul Music/Back In My
  Arms Again/Bricks And Mortar (36)
February 1978 News Of The World/Aunties & Uncles/Innocent
  Man (27)
August 1978 David Watts/'A' Bomb In Wardour Street (25)
October 1978 Down In The Tube Station At Midnight/So Sad
  About Us/The Night (15)
March 1979 Strange Town/The Butterfly Collector (15)
August 1979 When You're Young/Smithers-Jones (17)
October 1979 Eton Rifles/See-Saw (3)
March 1980 Going Underground/The Dreams Of Children (double
  A side) (1)
August 1980 Start/Liza Radley (1)
February 1981 That's Entertainment/Down In The Tube Station At
  Midnight (German import) (21)
May 1981 Funeral Pyre/Disguises (4)
October 1981 Absolute Beginners/Tales From the Riverbank (4)
January 1982 Town Called Malice/Precious (double A side) (1)
January 1982 Town Called Malice (special 12")
June 1982 Just Who Is The 5 O'Clock Hero?/The Great Depression
  (German import) (8)

September 1982 The Bitterest Pill (I Ever Had To Swallow)/Pity Poor Alfie/Swallow (2)
November 1982 Record 1: Beat Surrender/Shopping (1)
Record 2: Move On Up/Stoned Out Of My Mind/War/Beat Surrender/Shopping

ALBUMS

May 1977 *In the City* (20)
Art School/I've Changed My Address/Slow Down/I Got By In Time/Away From The Numbers/Batman Theme/In The City/Sounds From The Street/Non-Stop Dancing/Time For Truth/Takin' My Love/Bricks & Mortar

November 1977 *This is the Modern World* (22)
The Modern World/London Traffic/Standards/Life From A Window/The Combine/Don't Tell Them You're Sane/In The Street Today/London Girl/I Need You (For Someone)/Here Comes The Weekend/Tonight At Noon/In The Midnight Hour

November 1978 *All Mod Cons* (6)
All Mod Cons/To Be Someone (Didn't We Have A Nice Time)/Mr Clean/David Watts/English Rose/In The Crowd/Billy Hunt/It's Too Bad/Fly/The Place I Love/'A' Bomb In Wardour Street/Down In The Tube Station At Midnight

November 1979 *Setting Sons* (4)
Girl On The Phone/Thick As Thieves/Private Hell/Little Boy Soldiers/Wasteland/Burning Sky/Smithers-Jones/Saturday's Kids/The Eton Rifles/Heatwave

November 1980 *Sound Affects* (2)
Pretty Green/Monday/But I'm Different Now/Set The House Ablaze/Start!/That's Entertainment/Dream Time/Man In The Corner Shop/Music For The Last Couple/Boy About Town/Scrape Away

March 1982 *The Gift* (1)
Happy Together/Ghosts/Precious/Just Who Is The Five O'Clock Hero?/'Trans-Global Express'/Running On The Spot/Circus/The Planner's Dream Goes Wrong/Carnation/Town Called Malice/The Gift

235

Paul Weller

December 1982 *Dig the New Breed* (live album) (2)

In The City/All Mod Cons/To Be Someone/It's Too Bad/Start!/Big Bird/Set The House Ablaze/Ghosts/Standards/In The Crowd/ Going Underground/The Dreams Of Children/That's Entertainment/Private Hell

COMPILATION ALBUMS

October 1983 *Snap!* (2)

In The City/Away From The Numbers/All Around The World/The Modern World/News Of The World/Billy Hunt/English Rose/Mr Clean/David Watts/'A' Bomb In Wardour Street/Down In The Tube Station At Midnight/Strange Town/The Butterfly Collector/When You're Young/Smithers-Jones/Thick As Thieves/The Eton Rifles/Going Underground/The Dreams Of Children/That's Entertainment (demo)/Start!/Man In The Corner Shop/Funeral Pyre (remix)/Absolute Beginners/Tales From The Riverbank/ Town Called Malice/Precious/The Bitterest Pill (I Ever Had To Swallow)/Beat Surrender initially came with Live EP recorded at Wembley Arena, December 1982: Move On Up/Get Yourself Together/The Great Depression/But I'm Different Now

April 1992 *Extras* (15)

The Dreams Of Children/Tales From The Riverbank/Liza Radley/ Move On Up/Shopping/Smithers-Jones/Pop Art Poem/Boy About Town/A Solid Bond In Your Heart/No One In The World/And Your Bird Can Sing/Burning Sky/Thick As Thieves/Disguises/Get Yourself Together/The Butterfly Collector/The Great Depression/ Stoned Out Of My Mind/Pity Poor Alfie-Fever/But I'm Different Now/I Got You (I Feel Good)/Hey Mister/Saturday's Kids/We've Only Started/So Sad About Us/The Eton Rifles

June 1991 *Greatest Hits* (2)

In The City/All Around The World/The Modern World/News Of The World/David Watts/Down In The Tube Station At Midnight/Strange Town/When You're Young/The Eton Rifles/Going Underground/Start!/That's Entertainment/Funeral Pyre/Absolute Beginners/Town Called Malice/Precious/Just Who Is The Five O'Clock Hero?/The Bitterest Pill (I Ever Had To Swallow)/ Beat Surrender

October 1993 *Live Jam* (28)

The Modern World/Billy Hunt/Thick As Thieves/Burning Sky/Mr Clean/Smithers-Jones/The Eton Rifles/Away From The Numbers/Down In The Tube Station At Midnight/Strange Town/When You're Young/'A' Bomb In Wardour Street/Pretty Green/Boy About Town/Man In The Corner Shop/David Watts/Funeral Pyre/Move On Up/Carnation/The Butterfly Collector/Precious/Town Called Malice/Heatwave

July 1996 *The Jam Collection* (58)

Away From The Numbers/I Got By In Time/I Need You (For Someone)/To Be Someone (Didn't We Have A Nice Time)/Mr Clean/English Rose/In The Crowd/It's Too Bad/The Butterfly Collector/Thick As Thieves/Private Hell/Wasteland/Burning Sky/Saturday's Kids/Liza Radley/Pretty Green/Monday/Man In The Corner Shop/Boy About Town/Tales From The Riverbank/Ghosts/Just Who Is The Five O'Clock Hero?/The Great Depression/Shopping

VIDEOS

June 1982 *Trans Global Unity Express*

November 1983 *Video Snap!*

July 1991 *Greatest Hits*

THE STYLE COUNCIL

SINGLES

March 1983 Speak Like A Child/Party Chambers (4)

May 1983 Money-Go-Round/Headstart For Happiness/Mick's Up (11)

August 1983 A Paris EP: Long Hot Summer/Party Chambers/The Paris Match/Le Depart A Paris (3)

November 1983 A Solid Bond In Your Heart/It Just Came To Pieces In My Hands (11)

February 1984 My Ever Changing Moods/Mick's Company/Spring, Summer, Autumn (5)

Paul Weller

May 1984 Groovin' EP: You're The Best Thing/The Big Boss Groove (5)

October 1984 Shout To The Tops/Ghosts Of Dachau (7)

May 1985 Walls Come Tumbling Down!/The Whole Point II/Blood Sports/Spin' Drifting (6)

June 1985 Come To Milton Keynes/(When You) Call Me/Our Favourite Shop/The Lodgers (23)

September 1985 The Lodgers/You're The Best Thing (live)/The Big Boss Groove (live)/Move On Up (live)/Money-Go-Round-Soul Deep-Strength Of Your Nature Medley (13)

March 1986 Have You Ever Had It Blue/Mr Cool's Dream/With Everything To Lose (14)

January 1987 It Didn't Matter/All Year Round (9)

March 1987 Waiting/Francoise (52)

October 1987 Wanted/The Cost/The Cost Of Loving (20)

May 1988 Life At A Top People's Health Farm/Sweet Living Ways (28)

July 1988 1-2-3-4-A Summer Quartet EP: How She Threw It All Away/Love The First Time/Long Hot Summer/I Do Like To Be B-Side The A-Side (41)

February 1989 Promised Land (Juan Atkins Mix)/Can You Still Love Me? (27)

May 1989 Long Hot Summer 89 Mix/Everybody's On The Run (48)

The Council Collective – December 1984 Soul Deep/A Miner's Point (interview) (24)

SEVEN-INCH EPS: December 1987

Cafe Bleu: Headstart For Happiness/Here's One That Got Away/Bleu Cafe/Strength Of Your Nature

The Birds And The Bs: Piccadilly Trail/It Just Came To Pieces In My Hands/Spin' Drifting/Spring, Summer, Autumn

Mick Talbot Is Agent 1988: Mick's Up/Party Chambers/Mick's Blessing/Mick's Company

ALBUMS

March 1984 *Cafe Bleu* (2)
Mick's Blessing/The Whole Point Of No Return/Me Ship Came
    In!/Blue Cafe/The Paris Match/My Ever Changing Moods/Drop-
    ping Bombs On The Whitehouse/A Gospel/Strength Of Your
    Nature/You're The Best Thing/Here's One That Got Away/
    Headstart For Happiness/Council Meetin'

June 1985 *Our Favourite Shop* (1)
Homebreakers/All Gone Away/Come To Milton Keynes/Interna-
    tionalists/A Stones Throw Away/The Stand Up Comic's
    Instructions/Boy Who Cried Wolf/A Man Of Great Promise/
    Down In The Seine/The Lodgers (or She Was Only A Shop-
    keeper's Daughter)/Luck/With Everything To Lose/Our Favour-
    ite Shop/Walls Come Tumbling Down!

May 1986 *Home & Abroad* (live) (8)
My Ever Changing Moods/The Lodgers/Headstart For Happiness/
    (When You) Call Me/The Whole Point Of No Return/With
    Everything To Lose/Homebreakers/Shout To The Top/Walls
    Come Tumbling Down!/Internationalists

February 1987 *The Cost of Loving* (2)
It Didn't Matter/Right To Go/Heavens Above/Fairy Tales/Angel/
    Walking The Night/Waiting/The Cost Of Loving/A Woman's Song

June 1988 *Confessions of a Pop Group* (15)
The Piano Paintings: It's A Very Deep Sea/The Story Of Someone's
    Shoe/Changing Of The Guard/The Little Boy In A Castle/The
    Gardener Of Eden (A Three Piece Suite)/Confessions Of A Pop
    Group/Life At A Top Peoples Health Farm/Why I Went Miss-
    ing/How She Threw It All Away/Iwasadoledadstoyboy/Confes-
    sions 1, 2 & 3/Confessions Of A Pop Group

COMPILATION ALBUMS

March 1989 *Singular Adventures of the Style Council* (3)
You're The Best Thing/Have You Ever Had It Blue/Money-Go-
    Round/My Ever Changing Moods/Long Hot Summer/The
    Lodgers/Walls Come Tumbling Down!/Shout To The Top/

Wanted/It Didn't Matter/Speak Like A Child/A Solid Bond In Your Heart/Life At A Top People's Health Farm/Promised Land

June 1993 *Here's Some That Got Away* (39)
Love Pains/Party Chambers/The Whole Point II/The Ghosts Of Dachau/Sweet Loving Ways/A Casual Affair/A Woman's Song/ Mick's Up/Waiting On A Connection/Night After Night/The Piccadilly Trail/(When You) Call Me/My Very Good Friend/ April's Fool/In Love For The First Time/Big Boss Groove/ Mick's Company/Blood Sports/Who Will Buy/I Ain't Goin' Under/I Am Leaving/A Stone's Throw Away

March 1996 *The Style Council Collection* (60)
Speak Like A Child/Headstart For Happiness/Long Hot Summer/ The Paris Match/It Just Came To Pieces In My Hands/My Ever Changing Moods/The Whole Point Of No Return/Ghosts of Dachau/You're The Best Thing/The Big Boss Groove/Man Of Great Promise/Homebreakers/Down In The Seine/A Stones Throw Away/With Everything To Lose/Boy Who Cried Wolf/ The Cost Of Loving/Changing Of The Guard/Why I Went Missing/It's A Very Deep Sea

October 1996 *The Style Council in Concert*
Meetin' (Over) Up Yonder/Up For Grabs/Long Hot Summer/One Nation Under A Groove/Le Depart/Spring, Summer, Autumn/ Hangin' On To A Memory/It Just Came To Pieces In My Hands/ Here's One That Got Away/My Ever Changing Moods/Man Of Great Promise/Boy Who Cried Wolf/A Stones Throw Away/ Speak Like A Child/Mick's Up/You're The Best Thing/Move On Up/Down In The Seine/It's A Very Deep Sea/Heavens Above

VIDEOS

November 1983 *What We Did On Our Holidays – The Video Singles Part 1*

August 1984 *Far East & Far Out – Council Meeting In Japan*

December 1985 *What We Did the Following Year – The Video Singles Part 2*

May 1986 *Showbiz! – The Style Council Live!*

February 1987 *Jer USAlem*

October 1988 *Confessions of a Pop Group*

March 1989 *The Video Adventures of the Style Council (Greatest Hits Vol. 1)*

THE PAUL WELLER MOVEMENT

SINGLES

May 1991 Into Tomorrow/Here's A New Thing/That Spiritual Feeling (36)

PAUL WELLER

SINGLES

August 1992 Uh Huh Oh Yeh/Fly On The Wall/Arrival Time/ Always There To Fool You (18)

October 1992 Above The Clouds/Everything Has A Price To Pay/All Year Round (47)

July 1993 Sunflower/Kosmos SX Dub 2000/Bull Rush-Magic Bus (live)/That Spiritual Feeling (16)

August 1993 Wild Wood/Ends Of The Earth (14)

October 1993 The Weaver EP: The Weaver/This Is No Time/ Another New Day/Ohio (live) (18)

March 1994 Hung Up/Foot Of The Mountain (live)/The Loved/ Kosmos (Lynch Mob Bonus Beats) (11)

October 1994 Out Of The Sinking/Sexy Sadie/Sunflower (Lynch Mob Dub) (20)

April 1995 The Changing Man/I'd Rather Go Blind/It's A New Day, Baby/I Didn't Mean To Hurt You (live) (7)

July 1995 You Do Something To Me/My Whole World Is Falling Down (radio session)/A Year Late/Woodcutter's Son (radio session) (9)

Paul Weller

September 1995 Broken Stones/Steam (20)

February 1996 (for one week only) Out Of The Sinking (album version)/I Shall be Released/Broken Stones (radio session)/Porcelain Gods (radio session)

August 1996 Peacock Suit/Up In Suzie's Room (95)

ALBUMS

August 1992 *Paul Weller* (8)
Uh Huh Oh Yeh/I Didn't Mean To Hurt You/Bull-Rush/Round And Round/Remember How We Started/Above The Clouds/ Clues/Into Tomorrow/Amongst Butterflies/The Strange Museum/Bitterness Rising/Kosmos

September 1993 *Wild Wood* (2)
Sunflower/Can You Heal Us (Holy Man)/Wild Wood/Instrumental One (Part 1)/All The Pictures On The Wall/Has My Fire Really Gone Out?/County/Instrumental Two/5th Season/The Weaver/ Instrumental One (Part 2)/Foot Of The Mountain/Shadow Of The Sun/Holy Man (reprise)/Moon On Your Pyjamas/Hung Up* added to second edition of the CD.

September 1994 *Live Wood* (13)
Bullrush . . . Magic Bus/This Is No Time/All The Pictures On The Wall/Remember How We Started . . . Domino/Above The Clouds/Wild Wood/Shadow Of The Sun/Can You Heal Us Holy Man? . . . War/Fifth Season/Into Tomorrow/Foot Of The Mountain/Sunflower/Has My Fire Really Gone Out?

May 1995 *Stanley Road* (1)
The Changing Man/Porcelain Gods/I Walk On Gilded Splinters/ You Do Something To Me/Woodcutters Son/Time Passes . . ./ Stanley Road/Broken Stones/Out Of The Sinking/Pink On White Walls/Whirlpool's End/Wings Of Speed

VIDEOS

July 1991 *The Paul Weller Movement Live*

September 1994 *Live Wood*

November 1994 *Highlights & Hang Ups*

242

Bibliography and Sources

A Beat Concerto: The Authorised Biography by Paolo Hewitt,
   Boxtree
Paul Weller: Days Lose Their Names and Time Slips Away 1992–95
   by Paolo Hewitt & Lawrence Watson, Boxtree/Go Discs!
Something Beginning With 'O' by Kevin Pearce, Heavenly
Internationalists, Andrea Olcese & Sergio Gazzo, Riot Stories
England's Dreaming by Jon Savage, Faber & Faber
Mods! by Richard Barnes, Eel Pie
Keeping the Flame by Steve Brookes, Sterling
My Ever Changing Moods by John Reed, Omnibus
The Modern World By Numbers by Paul Honeyford, Eel Pie
As Tears Go By by David Wedgbury & John Tracy, Pavilion

Much of the material comes from interviews with Dennis Munday,
Chas de Whalley, Sara Silver, Gary Blackburn, Tony Fletcher,
David Munns, Lisa Verrico, Gilles Peterson, Eugene Manzi, James
Anthony, Sonja Phillips, Steve Brookes, Norman Jay, Terry Rawl-
ings, Pennie Smith, Gary Crowley, Richard Ogden, Nigel Sweeney,
Kim Tonneli, David Fricke, John Pearson, Peter Blake, Andy
Macdonald, Mike Heneghan, Phil Jupitus, Maz Weller and Johnny
Black.

Research material taken from articles written by: Dylan Jones,
Lucy O'Brien, Allan Jones, Michael Odell, Vie Marshall, Alan
McLaughlin, Jenny Tucker, Paul Mathur, Jóhn Mulvey, Andy
Coulson, Miranda Sawyer, Ted Kessler, Steve Clarke, Chas de
Whalley, Danny Baker, John Harris, John Reed, John Hamblett,
Lisa Verrico, Sarah-Jane Selvon, Adam Sweeting, Charles Shaar

Paul Weller

Murray, Paolo Hewitt, Lindsay Baker, Jim White, Caroline Sullivan, Lloyd Bradley, Julie Burchill, Phil Sutcliffe, William Leith, Jim Irvin, Tim Rostron, Neil Spencer, Sam Taylor, David Cavanagh, John Gill, John Aizlewood, Lee Leschasin, Danny Kelly, Deanne Pearson, Len Brown, Bev Perry, Mark Cunningham, Adrian Thrills, Danny Eccleston, Keith Cameron, Richard Lowe, Sean O'Hagan, David Lodge, Ashley Heath, Tom Hibbert, Paul Du Noyer, Max Bell, David Quantick, Paul Morley, Dave Hill, X Moore, Tony Parsons, Lynden Barber, Mike Stand, Ben Thompson, David Owens, Paul Moody, Mat Snow, Dave Marsh, Ken Emerson, Dave McCullough, Mike Gardner, Tim Hulse, Scott Isler, Gary Bushell, Robbi Millar, David Fricke, Declan Lynch, Vaughn Toulouse, Richard Grabel, Jon Wilde, David Stubbs, Gill Charlton, Roger St Pierre, Johnny Black, Jackie Brambles, Lucy Armitage, Simon Reynolds, Helen Howard.

Articles published in: *Q, NME, Melody Maker, Vox, Mojo, Select, Rolling Stone, Smash Hits, No 1 Magazine, 19, Sounds, Sun, Daily Mirror, Guardian, Australian Smash Hits, Loaded, Just 17, ID, Sky, Telegraph, Independent, New Hi-Fi Sound, Time Out, Barbed Wire, Oxford Mail, The Times, Total Guitar, Observer, Sunday Times, The Face, The Wire, Record Collector, Boys About Town, Jazid, Evening Standard, Daily Mail, Record Mirror, The Internet, Mail On Sunday, Blitz, City Limits, ZigZag, Look Now, Blues & Soul, Warrington Guardian, Manchester Evening News, The Voice, Jamming!*

Index

out with Nikki 181–2; and fans 49–50, 66, 99, 123–5, 129, 225; and fashion 11, 20, 24, 29, 32, 33, 37–9, 89, 107, 114, 121–2, 148, 209; and films 133–4, 160–1; and flying 126; and food 182; and friendships 13, 109–10, 202; and gay rumours 123; and Gill Price 53, 56, 58, 60, 62, 73, 79–80, 88–9, 96–7, 99, 135–7, 143; and girls 13, 15–16, 135–6; on guitar playing 138–9; homes 7–8, 33, 56, 62, 79, 176, 207, 215; and humour 3, 7, 74, 100, 107, 110, 120, 128–9, 161, 174; illnesses 93–4, 100; and interviews 73–4, 120–1, 140; and literature 82, 91–2, 138; and media 70, 73, 121–2; as Mod 19, 29–32; and money 43, 61–2, 76, 126; and mysticism 82, 192; and nineties scene 218–23; plays first gig 14; and poetry 76–7, 122; and politics 8, 21, 26, 44–6, 55–6, 73–4, 94, 115, 116, 122, 131–3, 139, 140, 144–51, 154–5, 160, 170, 174, 178, 192, 198; preference for vinyl 114, 156; President of International Youth Year (1985) 135; as producer 160; qualifications 26; and religion 8, 198; on requests for Jam songs 186; singing style 25, 36; and the sixties 9–10, 18–19, 27–8, 75–6, 178–9;

solo albums, 2, 186–7, 191–3, 195–6, 197–9, 200, 203, 207, 208–9, 210–15, 217; solo gigs 180–1, 186, 188, 190–1, 216; solo singles 184–6, 196–7, 199, 200, 203, 208, 210, 215–16, 217, 225; solo tours 194–5, 203, 208; as songwriter for The Jam 48, 56–7, 58, 59, 60, 63–5, 68–9, 71, 72–3, 75, 77, 81, 83, 84, 91–2, 93, 97, 105; as songwriter for Style Council 111, 133, 139, 155, 162, 173; songwriting in 90s 176, 177–8, 198, 213, 220, 225–6, 232; star sign 10; after Style Council 176–88; and War Child album 221; working class identity 30–1, 45, 132, 144, 154, 207; *see also* Jam, The; Style Council, The
Wembley Arena 102, 143
Wener, Louise 102
Whalley, Chas de 40, 48, 50, 51, 74, 193–4
Wham! 117, 163
Wheeler, Caron 100
Wheeler, Kenny 52, 79, 80, 118, 125, 130, 136, 142, 153, 158, 181, 182, 199–200, 230
'When You're Young' 68–9
'Whirlpool's End' 214
White, Jim 189
White, Steve 125, 134, 135, 138, 139, 141, 142–3, 153, 155, 159–60, 161; background & influences 115–16; leaves Style Council twice 159, 163; other projects 152, 159–60,